'This explosive new book . . . has already made its courageous lady author a hated figure in the corridors of Brussels and Westminster' *'This England'*

'We dare not desist from presenting the challenge of Europe to the British people.' *Lord Tonypandy, formerly Speaker of the House of Commons*

'If only this book could be read by the many thousands who still don't understand what the European issue is really about . . .' *Sir Richard Body M.P.*

A persuasive case that 'United Europe always was a political wolf disguised in economic clothing.' *Lord Harris of High Cross*

'Reveals in dispassionate and easy language the treachery of successive politicians . . . the appalling evidence is literally breathtaking . . .' *Vice Admiral Sir Louis Le Bailly K.B.E., C.B.E.*

'A case worth hearing.' *Sir David Cooksey*

'Writes with authority, clarity and analytical precision of the delusion which still grips the policy elites in Washington and London to this day.' *Dr Martin Holmes, Co-chairman the Bruges Group*

'A fascinating account of the behind-the-scenes formation and development of the European Union.' *'Freedom Today'*

BRITAIN HELD HOSTAGE
The Coming Euro-Dictatorship

The Author

Lindsay Jenkins has an honours degree in mediaeval and modern history from Bedford College, London University and an MBA from Cranfield School of Management. She spent nearly ten years as a senior civil servant in the Ministry of Defence and another ten years in the City of London working for both British and American investment banks. She is well known in the world markets as a leading forecaster.

In 1993 she contributed to the extra-parliamentary team briefing both the House of Commons and the House of Lords during the Second Reading of the Maastricht Bill. She is a former editor of *eurofacts*.

The Bruges Group

An expanded extract from this book, with a foreword by Sir Richard Body M.P., was first published by the Bruges Group, Suite 216, The Linen Hall, 162-168 Regent Street, London W1R 5TB in September 1996 entitled 'Godfather of the European Union, Altiero Spinelli'.

For my father
Maurice Hayes
who fifty years ago
understood the motives behind European union

and for

Anthony Martin
without whom this book would not have been published

For Charles Upton .

BRITAIN HELD HOSTAGE

The Coming Euro-Dictatorship

LINDSAY JENKINS

Illustrated by Alice Leach

With best wishes

Lindsay Jenkins

October 2004

Orange State Press
Washington D.C.

First published in 1997
Second edition 1998

by Orange State Press
a division of Orange State Communications
Suite 401, 1200 19th Street NW
Washington DC 20036
USA

UK Distributor

JUNE PRESS LTD
PO BOX 119, TOTNES
DEVON TQ9 7WA
Teleph   **TEL: 01548 - 821402**   )6
FAX: 01548 - 821574
web:www.junepress.com
Copyri̖   )7

ISBN 0–9657812–1–6

Library of Congress Catalog Card Number 97–76489

Phototypeset in $10^1/_2$ on $13^1/_2$pt Linotron Sabon
by Intype London Ltd

Printed in Great Britain by Biddles Ltd., Guildford

CONTENTS

ACKNOWLEDGEMENTS

I have received valued help from many people and it is invidious to begin a list for fear of having left someone out. There is also a much wider group of people who have been enthusiastic in their support of this project which has greatly encouraged me in what has otherwise been a lonely task: they are so many that I hope they will accept a general and heartfelt thank you.

I would specifically like to thank:

John Ashworth, Don Baker, Richard Batten, Sir Richard Body M.P., Keith and Alice Carson of *eurofacts*, William Cash M.P., Jonathan Collett of the Bruges Group, the late Lord Gladwyn, Mrs Maria Goldberger, Lord Harris of High Cross, Sir Anthony Kershaw, Colin Leach, Rodney Leach, Mrs Christopher Lewers, Ole Lippmann, Cdr. Trevor Lockwood R.N. (retd.), David Mathews, Ian Milne of *eurofacts*, John Murray, Sue Nelson, Loretto O'Callaghan, Henrik and Sharon Overgaard-Nielsen, Lady Pickthorn, David Pollard, Jane de Rome, Lee Rotherham, Michael Shrimpton, Dr. Helen Szamuely, Sir Teddy Taylor M.P., Lord Tebbit PC, Nick Turrell, and to the outstanding and understanding staff of the London Library.

Several federalists – supporters of a European superstate – have also helped but it would be undiplomatic to name them.

I would especially like to thank my much loved cousin, Klaus Hirsch, for his understanding. As I believe he knows, I am not anti-German but against specific policies which have been pursued to the detriment of my country.

FOREWORD
by
Frederick Forsyth

The year was 1863. The place a small town in Pennsylvania. The occasion the dedication of a cemetery.

The Secretary for War spoke for three hours and not a syllable that he used is recalled today. After him, a tall gaunt man with a hollowed face and a fringe of beard, his stovepipe hat held beside him in the November wind, spoke for three minutes and eighteen seconds.

What he said was later recognised as one of the noblest passages ever uttered, in spoken or written form, in the English language. It still comes to us today down the decades like a burning flame, a flame the lords of the European Union seek to extinguish in Western Europe forever.

In his peroration Abraham Lincoln gave a definition of parliamentary democracy that has never been bettered. The men beneath the headstones in front of him, he said, had died in an attempt to ensure that 'government of the people, by the people and for the people shall not perish from the earth.'

The more you look at the phrase the more the sheer craftsmanship impresses. Lincoln could have used the phrase 'the people' once; but he chose to use it three times, so that it could be preceded by the words 'of', 'by' and 'for'. In a superb irony this son of America was evoking the same intentions at the heart of the British constitutional upheaval known as the Glorious Revolution of 1688.

Then, the British people, through parliament, ousted the last absolute monarch at a time when the whole world was ruled by dictator-kings. In doing so the British went on to establish two precedents: the world's first constitutional monarchy in tandem with the world's first supreme and sovereign elected parliament.

Since then, almost every country on the planet, seeking to move from tyranny to democracy, has sought one way or another to emulate what became known as the 'Mother of Parliaments'. In Britain the franchise was steadily widened from landowners and merchants to householders, then working men and then women until that franchise became truly universal adult suffrage.

But the principle remained; that the people through the ballot box in secret choice should elect their members of parliament, one per constituency; and that this parliament should constitute the supreme governing authority under the crown for all matters concerning the governance of the British nation. Strange therefore that an American, speaking 175 years later, should re-define the three essential bases of parliamentary democracy.

'Government of the people'; meaning that power belongs to the people and all the people. At each general election, the people *lend* (not give) that power to a team of delegates charged by them to govern the land for five years. At the end of that time the incumbent government has the duty to return that power to the people and seek re-election. It does *not* have the authority to trade, parlay, negotiate or give away the sovereign power of the nation without specific single-issue permission freely given by the people to do so.

'Government by the people'; meaning that the people in a democracy rule themselves via their elected tribunes. No other body, not judiciary not bureaucracy, has the right to create new law to govern the people and require their obedience.

'Government for the people'; meaning that the only aim of democratic government is the maximisation of the security, prosperity, freedom and contentment of the people. It is not government for the advancement and benefit of civil servants, politicians, industrialists, bankers, tycoons, academics financiers and journalists.

Over the past two decades, since accession was granted by the British people in a trumpery referendum on a completely different question, the European Union has shown beyond any reasonable peradventure that it is dedicated to the creation of a single federal European superstate to be governed by radically different principles, procedures and structures.

Successive British governments have systematically traded away the parliamentary sovereignty with which they were entrusted; empowered by a series of ill-understood 'enabling acts' the Brussels Commission of unelected civil servants now enacts more new law in a year than the House of Commons in a decade; the costs to the British people have so far amounted to some three hundred thousand million pounds while the true and only beneficiaries have been among the eight professions listed above.

Through extensive employment of its habitual hand-maidens – stealth, guile, misnomer, euphemism, secrecy, obscurity and deception – the controlling forces of the European Union have concentrated more, more and ever more governmental power into fewer and fewer hands.

Power, said Lord Acton, tends to corrupt and absolute power tends to corrupt absolutely. What we British have silently witnessed these past two decades and continue to do so at an accelerating rate, is a bizarre phenomenon when set against the words of Lincoln.

Despite all the official verbiage about commercial prosperity or the prevention of some national future war, the sole end-game of the EU is power. We are witnessing the greatest single transfer of power since the dissolution of the monasteries and the Glorious Revolution. In the first, enormous power passed from the Church to the Monarch; in the second it passed from the Monarch to the People. Now it passes from the People to the Functionary. Already the power, patronage, profligacy and corruption of the institutions of the EU have become breath-taking.

On May 1st, 1997, the British elected a new government. Within a hundred days the new regime revealed its own long-term game plan. No process of logic whatsoever can avoid the conclusion, based on the measures already taken and the others in hand, that this intention is the transformation of the unitary kingdom into a federal republic prior to its subsumation into the Federal republic of Europe.

Mrs Jenkins' book may serve as a timely reminder to British readers how far things have gone, how they have been achieved and the prognosis for all our future. Whatever that may be, the three traditional pillars of constitutional monarchy, national sovereignty and parliamentary democracy are not going to be among them.

Hertford 1997

INTRODUCTION

Britain Loses Its Independence – By Stealth

The European Union (EU) is holding Britain hostage until all British sovereignty is signed over to Brussels. The result will be a dictatorship of Europe.

It is the thesis of this book that 'European union' has been sold to the British public based on campaigns of deceit and falsehoods and that political union, not free trade, has always been the ultimate goal of 'eurocrats'. Moreover, that goal of 'European union' includes the gradual, surreptitious and thus total loss to the British people of political sovereignty and independence.

Brussel's proposals are rarely presented intelligibly. Revolutionary proposals are cleverly buried within apparently innocuous clauses; consolidated treaties are not published; new treaties amend previous treaties and make little sense. In contrast, the Brussels' propaganda budget now stands at £200 million a year with an extra £45 million to popularise the 'euro'.

For years, unnoticed, very real authority has steadily been handed over to a new foreign state – the European Union. Meanwhile Britain's Ministers and civil servants have been buried in negotiations with Brussels over the minutiae of government. The horse trading and the short term successes of 'derogations' and 'time windows' to carry out change obscure what has really been going on.

Today, after two generations, a United States of Europe is close to success. Within ten years it may be complete. Today, Lord Howe, a former British Foreign Secretary, can admit for the first time that 'the fledgling Treaty of Rome launched the world's first experiment in democratic, supranational governance in January 1958.'[1]

EMU – The Last Hurdle

One major hurdle remains. Once European Monetary Union is established; once the ECU has replaced national currencies; once national reserves are controlled by the European Central Bank in Frankfurt, then it is a comparatively short and easy passage to the United States of Europe – one country.

The groundwork has already been laid for one police force, one judiciary, one legal system, one tax regime, and one army under one command. In none of these new arrangements will the British have any serious influence – the models are German and French just as they have been at every stage of creating the new state. The British systems will be abolished. An Anglo-Saxon model has never been welcomed.

European Monetary Union (EMU) is now a certainty unless a major economic crisis overwhelms it before it starts, just as the oil shocks and recession of the 1970s stopped the previous attempt at monetary union. It will begin for a majority of the EU's fifteen countries on 1st January 1999. Britain and Denmark have opt-outs.

The reason for EMU is political: all economic considerations have been dismissed and most of the criteria in the Maastricht Treaty have been fudged. EMU has little to do with the much publicised level playing field for businesses – that is merely the propaganda.

Labour Committed To The EU

For the first time since Edward Heath (1970 to 1974) Britain has a Prime Minister, Tony Blair, who favours Britain as a region in a United States of Europe, or the 'People's Europe' as he describes it.[2] There has, however, been no mandate from the British electors to abandon sovereignty.

One indication of Tony Blair's commitment to the European Union came in 1994 when he first became leader of the Labour Party. Roy Jenkins of the rival Liberal Democrats immediately lauded him in a 'Times' article and has supported Blair ever since. Jenkins, a former president of the European Commission, is a champion of the European superstate.

Deliberately keeping to the surreptitious approach, the Labour Party has made few policy pronouncements on Europe either before or after the 1997 General Election. That Tony Blair and his closest associates in the Labour Government believe in ending British sovereignty in favour of a socialist superstate has never been openly stated or even intimated. The diplomatic language of a more positive approach to Europe gave no hint of the revolutionary events of the first three months of the Labour Government. For public consumption Blair talks of flexible labour markets and reducing red tape.

Already the United Kingdom is being broken up. 'The constitution needs updating' was the facile excuse. First, on a wave of euphoria after the election landslide, referenda for a Scottish Parliament and a Welsh Assembly were rushed through.

Second, legislation will set up nine regional Development Agencies to start in April 1999. The agencies, apparently economic in purpose, are a blueprint for devolution.

Third, assemblies for the regions are planned to follow, probably by 2002, replacing the old County Councils and creating unitary authorities. Already British County Councils have established links with other regions in EU countries. Most have representation in Brussels and British Government Offices for the Regions already exist.

Thus Britain will fit into the EU pattern of regions. All regions will come under the EU Committee of the Regions. Westminster will be neatly by-passed and the nation state carved up.[3]

The British monarchy is now openly attacked – it is being 'downsized' and 'streamlined'. Indeed there is no role for the monarchy in the United States of Europe, of which the Queen is merely a citizen, though as a sop to residual national attachments it may be allowed to continue in low key cere-monies.

Britain's first-past-the-post voting system is likely to end. Proportional representation is already slated for the Euro-pean Parliament elections and the Welsh Assembly. In the Scottish Parliament over half the members will be elected as at present; the rest will be chosen from political party lists by a variant of proportional representation – the German system promoted by Chancellor Kohl.

The Labour Government quickly accepted the Social Chapter, which will wipe out the achievements of the pre-vious two decades to make Britain globally competitive. The Bank of England was given control over interest rates and its supervisory powers over the financial markets removed. Both are prerequisites of joining EMU, but the Government did not give EMU as the reason.

The End Of Sterling

Will Britain join EMU and abandon sterling? If so when? The answer is almost certainly 'yes' and 'as soon as possible'.

Publicly Blair has not committed himself to EMU – he is continuing John Major's 'wait and see' policy. The British electorate has been promised a referendum and the Chan-cellor of the Exchequer claims that Britain will not join EMU in the lifetime of the present parliament. But Blair has not explicitly ruled out a referendum on EMU before the next election in 2002.

If Blair calculates he can join first and still win the next election then Britain will lose its financial independence sooner rather than later. And under a Blair Government join it will.

Britain's primary trading partners from which it makes money, the US, Australia and Canada – and the Far East in better times – will be ignored. In recent years Britain has lost money in the EU – it is the only area with which Britain is in the red.

Ignored too will be the dominant high technology and service sectors of the British economy, sectors which are small in France and Germany. Those businesses are mainly denominated in US dollars which sterling roughly tracks. When sterling is forced into the strait-jacket of the single currency, inevitably tailored to the needs of France and Germany, those businesses will be severely disadvantaged world-wide.

Already the British fishing industry has been devastated and is scheduled for destruction in 2002; the British art market, the only one in Europe and with annual direct sales of £2 billion, is now moving to New York because of EU taxes;[4] and the beef industry has been decimated.

The constitution forming the new state, the Treaty of Rome, says it is irrevocable. Once Britain's money has been handed over to Frankfurt it will indeed be difficult to break-away.

One Law, One Police, One Tax, One Army

A document still under wraps called the Corpus Juris[5] spells the end of the British legal system. This law of 35 articles was unveiled to a select few in April 1997 with no press present and no publicity. British officials deny its existence until the questioner says he has seen it. Then vague, reassuring statements are made. Under the new legal system Habeas Corpus of 1679, preventing arbitrary arrest and detention, and trial by jury of the Magna Carta of 1215 will be no more.

Instead there will be a European Public Prosecutor with delegates in each country (note that the Labour Government has already opted for British regional public prosecutors supposedly in the style of the US) and a Judge of Freedoms. The Public Prosecutor will have the right to authorise arrests anywhere in the EU, imprison for months while awaiting trial wherever in the EU the crime took place and without any prior scrutiny of the prima facie evidence by a magistrate.

The present co-operation between all national police forces is a pre-cursor to one police force throughout Europe. The European citizen will be arrested, prosecuted and tried only by paid officials of the state.

With EMU will come one system of taxation. A uniform VAT was proposed by the Commission in 1996. Rates will probably be 18 per cent with a reduced rate of 5 per cent for some items as an inducement to co-operate. Britain's zero rate on food, children's clothes, books, newspapers, public transport, new houses, water and sewage services and pharmaceuticals will end soon after 2002. VAT administrators will have more powers and in preparation for this, Britain's Customs and Excise has been co-operating for three years on cross border investigations and audits.

Will the cry be heard again – no taxation without representation?

In the Amsterdam Treaty previously vague references to an EU defence policy and defence force are getting stronger. The WEU is to be integrated into the EU as its defence arm.

One armed force will be the last piece of the jig-saw to create the new country and NATO will have no place in it.

Eurosceptic Britain

'Ten years after Bruges, Euroscepticism is sufficiently powerful in Britain to curb the confidence of a new government with a large parliamentary majority, a clear electoral mandate and a heart firmly in the right place on European issues' wrote Lord Howe.[6]

Indeed until the Labour Government of 1997, Britain had fought back more than any other country in Europe. Britain objected to the growing powers of the European Court of Justice, to more regulation and social costs for business, to European control of British frontiers and immigration, to a European police force with wide powers, to pressure to break up the United Kingdom, and to more citizens' rights which could lead to duties such as military service or taxation.

Usually Britain appeared to be alone, but may other EU countries watched and noted Britain's fight. Despite their public rhetoric of contempt they have silently applauded Britain's actions which as small counties they are unable to do themselves. There have been notable exceptions – Greenland withdrew from the Community altogether and Denmark said a definitive 'no' to EMU and has yet to ratify the Maastricht Treaty. Changing their own inconvenient rules, the other member states have swept on to 'ever closer union' without that ratification.[7]

Small countries find it difficult to fight the strength of France and Germany combined with Italy, a willing accomplice – the Italian people privately regarding themselves as without a government.

Trojan Horses

No British Government since that of Anthony Eden has faced up to the reality of the EU and its forerunners, the Economic Community (EC) and the European Economic Community (EEC). In every battle to avoid a disliked European policy Britain has ultimately been outmanoeuvred. One previous Prime Minister, Edward Heath, fully understood 'Europe' and winningly embraced it signing away Britain's sovereignty. His Government colleagues were hoodwinked.

Within each Cabinet a minority group has actively worked for more 'Europe'. Roy Jenkins led the pro-Europeans in earlier Labour Governments; in recent Tory Governments Kenneth Clarke, Michael Heseltine, Geoffrey Howe and Douglas Hurd have forced Government policies favouring the EU.

When Margaret Thatcher realised what 'Europe' was about she was forced out of office. John Major's Government was held hostage by Clarke and Heseltine. They may join in Blair's 'patriotic front' to campaign for a 'yes' vote in the EMU referendum, just as Conservatives and Labour MPs united for a 'yes' vote in the 1975 referendum.

... And Tory Weakness

The Conservative Party, in government for eighteen years, was certainly hindered by the pro-Europeans in the Cabinet. Yet British pragmatism has hindered it even more. The EU is an ideology. As a result Britain under the Conservatives has helped the EU to run more efficiently – for example by insisting on a greater budgetary discipline or fines for Member States who fail to carry out European Court of Justice rulings – but inevitably Britain only won a few battles. It is losing the war of independence.

Some Conservative MPs, now in Opposition, still believe 'Europe' is about free trade to the benefit of Britain. Free trade was never on the federalists' agenda. While free trade is a concept close to the heart of Anglo-Saxons, none of the other key members of the EU shares that heritage.

Michael Howard, when Home Secretary in the last Conservative Government, displayed the typical misunderstanding of the Tory leadership: 'A Europe of nation states working together has brought substantial benefits to Britain's commerce and industry . . . we need to focus on how to enhance Europe's strength as an outward-looking, free trading community which brings its nation states together to co-operate . . . If others in Europe opt for a federal state, Britain, under a Conservative government, will not be part of it.'[8]

In every Government publication the language and the illusion has been the same: the European nation states are merely co-operating while the threat of federalism is low on the horizon. In a pamphlet[9] published before the parliamentary debates on the Maastricht Bill the Conservative Government described the EC as a 'unique international partnership', 'close neighbours work(ing) together' to bring about 'peace, stability, investment, jobs and prosperity'.

The Conservative leader, William Hague, still only feels politically strong enough – or probably does not understand 'Europe' – to rule out a single currency for the next ten years. A negative is not much of a rallying cry to galvanise the country and the five million Conservative voters who either stayed at home at the 1997 General Election or voted for the Referendum Party. It does not bear comparison with Winston Churchill's principled stand against the appeasers in the Conservative Party before the Second World War. It does nothing to rebuild the Conservative Party to withstand the final onslaught from Brussels.

The Democratic Deficit

Until the British know and understand the history of the EU, who made it happen and why, they are likely to continue to fall into every trap which Brussels lays for them until finally, they are unable to disentangle themselves other than by physical force.

Three great driving forces combined to create one super-state, a United States of Europe: socialist ideology, Germany's lust for supremacy, and the mixed motives of some American governments.

The result is a democracy in name only. What 'Europeans' call 'the democratic deficit' is vast.

The *de facto* government of the EU is a group of bureaucrats, non-elected Commissioners, nominated by Member Governments headed by the *de facto* President of Europe. They and their staff promise only to act in the interests of the EU, not in their national interests.

The European Parliament is a talking shop with minimal powers. It cannot start legislation, it does not sit in the same building or even the same town as the Commission. In its own interest it strengthens centralism and increases its own authority and that of its closest ally, the Commission. It is no friend of the nation state. The European constituencies are so large that not surprisingly voters take little interest in European elections. The 340 million electorate speaks twelve main languages with as many cultures and traditions.

Most European countries do not have a long history of independence or democracy. After the Second World War France, Germany and Italy had new constitutions – a regular occurrence for all of them. Then in France governments rose and fell in short order as they had since 1870,[10] usually lasting months only. In 1949 Germany, after twelve years of dictatorship, reverted to a democracy which it had only ever experienced for fourteen years from 1919 under the Weimar Republic. Italy had been without democracy for twenty-two years under Mussolini. It has only existed as a country for just over a hundred years and Belgium for little longer.

Sovereignty Three Quarters Gone?

Britain, without the agreement or knowledge of the British people, is steadily abandoning Parliamentary democracy forged over many centuries and admired, copied and adapted in many parts of the world. While routinely reviewing the workings of the Houses of Parliament in 1993 the Hansard Society was startled to find that about sixty per cent of Bills before the House of Commons originated in Brussels and were merely rubber stamped in London.

No-one knows what percentage of British legislation now comes from Brussels; no-one knows how close it is to one hundred per cent. It is certain that the sixty per cent has been substantially increased by the Single European Act and the Maastricht Treaty. Soon the Amsterdam Treaty will be ratified.

The Hansard Society reported: 'Any attempts by any government to try to mould Community legislation to its own wishes are doomed to failure, following the extension of policy areas now subject to majority voting, thus almost eliminating the use of the veto. Member States can now be more readily out-voted, inevitably weakening their ability to change the direction of Community legislation. If that government's individual Minister in the Council of Ministers is out-voted, parliamentary control of legislation is irredeemably weakened . . .

'. . . (the UK) Parliament has little, if any impact upon the process of European law making. Where successful changes are introduced from the UK, these are usually done by various interested sectors and bodies . . . In our opinion, this must have serious implications for the traditional view of Parliament as a legislative body.'[11]

EU legislation so overwhelmed the last Conservative government that it could not admit to having given away so much for fear of the repercussions in the ballot box. The Government was scarcely governing.

The many crises included the banning of British beef exports by the European Commission – a right it has held since 1975; the British servicewomen, dismissed as a result of becoming pregnant, who had to be compensated regardless of the terms of their original contract; the forty-eight hour working week which was introduced following a ruling from the European Court of Justice despite Britain's opt-out from the Social Chapter; and VAT on heating fuel compulsorily introduced to conform with an EC agreement.

It is not clear what would happen if the British Parliament refused to rubber stamp the EU directives.

All national institutions are steadily being weakened and becoming agencies of Brussels from parliament to the civil service to the law courts and the police. It is the deliberate result of centralising power in Brussels.

If the present pattern continues within a few years Britain will be a region in a Europe controlled by its main paymaster Germany. German territorial ambitions which were defeated at great cost to the Allies in two world wars, will at last have achieved their aim. Millions will have died in vain.

Why Surrender?

Why has Britain involved itself in something so opposed to its own traditions and interests and for which the British have never been enthusiastic? How is it possible to persuade a nation state, with over a thousand years of independence to hand over its government to another power in return for one voice at the table?

The numbers at that table have increased from six in 1957, to nine in 1973, ten in 1981, twelve in 1986 and fifteen in 1995. Applications are outstanding from eleven more states which will further reduce the influence of each individual state. Negotiations are underway with six of them. More countries including Russia itself, formerly behind the Iron Curtain, are now members of the Council of Europe, a significant staging post to European integration.

The crux of Britain's problem was summed up by Anthony Nutting, at the British Foreign Office between 1951 and 1956, latterly as Minister of State – fear. Nutting wrote, 'We must somehow find a way to make terms with Europe now, before we are weakened by the inevitable discriminations against us which will follow when the Common Market is in full operation'.[12] Fear of being shut out, bullied and alone was overwhelming.

Defeatism has characterised every step of Britain's path in Europe since Suez. With Margaret Thatcher as Prime Minister from 1979, Britain regained some of its self-belief, but fear, not an analytical assessment of Britain's place in the world, still dominates.

Lady Thatcher was persuaded that the Single European Act was necessary to create the Single Market in the interests of free trade. Too late she realised she had been badly misled. She said she would never have signed the Maastricht Treaty. Why did her successor, John Major, sign it?

The answer is extraordinary. Major was persuaded by the British Foreign Office that the Franco-German axis was weakening. The French were no longer so in tune with the German leadership. Britain could take over from France with a British-German alliance at the centre of the Community. From there Britain could lead the whole continent and have an influence on the world far beyond her size. That is a different interpretation of John Major's much quoted 'I want Britain to be at the very heart of Europe'.

The argument went further: the US is past its peak, the Russian Empire has broken up. Therefore a United Europe with Britain at its heart could be a leading force in the world.

The Franco-German Agenda

That argument misjudged the strength of the Franco-German axis – the foundation of the EU. It misjudged the German desire to reduce Britain from the world class economy it is today to a weak regional competitor. It ignored Britian's global trade.

During the Second World War the French Government was the only government in Europe to co-operate fully with the German invader.[13] After the war the French hoped they could control Germany and lead Europe. Within ten years it was obvious they could not. Now France is collaborating with Germany again, while still hoping that is a partnership of equals.

Newspaper articles in the US regularly comment negatively on the EU. Americans are acutely aware that the EU is a protectionist bloc which can act against them. Doing business in the EU is expensive because of the complex regulations. The only reason US firms invest there is from fear of being shut out of a large market. They fear the world-wide economic impact of a protectionist Europe with high unemployment and locked into one currency.

If the Americans can see the dangers of the EU from the other side of the Atlantic, why are the British so short sighted that they cannot see across the English Channel?

The British 'debate' has only been about uniting with Europe. There has been no debate at all about the fate of

Britain's business with its top trading partners, the US, Australia and Canada. If closer alliances are to be sought they should be with those countries upon which Britain's financial survival depends. It is from the rest of the world that Britain earns the money to subsidise the EU to which it is the second largest contributor.

With the process of creating 'Europe' carried on behind a smoke screen of propaganda and disinformation which passes for debate, the federalists' – and the Germans' – dream comes closer to reality and their goal is increasingly difficult to hide. What kind of confrontation does the future hold?

This book documents the history of European 'union' and seeks to place that convoluted and disjunctive history in a logical and proper context. At the end the reader may agree that the time to cast off the chains of a united Europe is now.

"Get out of my way"

CHAPTER 1: A GERMAN EUROPE

The Third Reich was the first modern experiment in running the whole continent of Europe. As Dean Acheson commented, Adolf Hitler 'organised Europe as had not been done even by Napoleon. (His) will reigned from Eastern Poland and Bessarabia to the Pyrenees and the Atlantic.'[1] The Third Reich was a powerful example of a united Europe which was not lost on some Germans and on non-German federalists. It was a beacon.

Charlemagne The Butcher

Hitler built Nazi Germany upon a dream of a United States of Europe: both Hitler and the European Union looked to Charlemagne as the ideal. While Himmler called Charlemagne 'the butcher of the Saxons', Hitler praised him. That should give the European Union pause for thought: 'Killing all those Saxons was not a historical crime, as Himmler thinks. Charlemagne did a good thing in subjugating Widu-kind and killing the Saxons out of hand. He thereby made possible the Empire of the Franks and the entry of Western culture into what is now Germany.'

Hitler was right. Charlemagne, like others before and since, had built his empire by cruel and brutal wars.[3] The king of the Franks from 768 to 814 doubled his inheritance through savage wars, massacres, and family struggles in which his two nephews, possible claimants to his throne, conveniently disappeared. As a result his lands stretched from the present day Netherlands to north-east Spain, from France through Germany to Austria, Hungary and Northern Italy – very close to the land area of the six founder members of the European Union. Thirty-four years of raids, campaigns of terror and mass deportations eventually cowed Saxony into defeat. It was forced to accept Christianity. Charlemagne's barbarity was total: he built his Christian Empire defeating not only the Saxons but also the Bavarians and the Avars in bitter campaigns.

Just after the Second World War Charlemagne's former capital Aachen, formerly Aix-la-Chapelle, instituted the Charlemagne prize for individuals who have contributed much to European federalism. Charlemagne's octagonal chapel still stands in Aachen Cathedral where today the European Union quite deliberately holds its services of celebration. Those who choose to see only the rebirth of architecture, painting and literature in a Christian state have badly misread the Carolingian Empire.

Prussia Paves The Way

Charlemagne's Empire is held as an idealistic forerunner of the European Union; Prussia showed how one Europe could be created, largely without force. Germany was the only country[4] in which economic unity came first and was deliberately used as a backdoor way of taking over unwary neighbouring states. In the nineteenth century Europe's tariff barriers were disappearing as roads improved and railways were built, but they were doing so in politically united countries.

Napoleon led the way: in 1797 to make Germany easier to administer he reduced the 1,800 German customs frontiers to 39 and abolished 195 principalities. Then just after the Napoleonic wars two ambitious Prussian civil servants, Maassen and von Bulow, carried on the process and created one tariff for the whole of Prussia. They replaced the sixty-seven local tariffs to make Prussia into one economic unit and decided to charge very high transit duties. That immediately aroused the wrath of the Union of Merchants which operated throughout Germany and in particular their secretary, Friedrich List. He began a campaign to scrap internal customs duties and raise a large protectionist wall round Germany – a Zollverein or a customs union. List's vision of a protectionist bloc included central production and central planning. He expected that protectionism would unite Germany and then protect its industry in the early stages of its development.

List went even further. He proposed a united Germany with great industries, a large mercantile fleet (at the time Germany had none – most of its exports were carried in British ships), a powerful navy and a great colonial empire. He wanted to unify currencies, weights and measures, banking, transport, education, patent laws and consular representation abroad. Only the merchants listened to List. He spent four months in Vienna trying to win over Prince Metternich but Metternich could see that under List's system princes would fall.

The far seeing Prussian civil servants could see only benefits.[5] List had created the means for Prussia to take over the whole of Germany. Prussia started negotiations with a tiny state within Prussian territory. In 1819 they reached an agreement on a customs union. Buoyed by that small success Prussia then took over all the little enclaves within Prussia and created one customs system.

It took ten years. Sometimes the negotiations were lengthy and required tact of the highest order. The Prussian civil servants knew what they were doing but their prey did not realise the full significance of these treaties until it was too late.

In 1828 Bavaria and Wurttemberg retaliated against Prussia's high transit duties by forming their own customs union in Southern Germany. Now there were two protectionist blocs, one Prussian led.

The Prussian Finance Minister, von Motz, explained to his King, Frederick Wilhelm III, that the economic union of Germany would lead to its political union 'under the protection of Prussia'.

Prussia raised the stakes. The news of a Prussian deal with Hesse Darmstadt, an independent state squashed between the two protectionist blocs, heightened the tension: 'At all the courts the first vague intelligence from Berlin was received with indescribable alarm, the news falling into the diplomatic world like a bombshell.'[6]

No-one knew that Prussia had signed two treaties with Hesse Darmstadt, an open one and a secret one. What appeared to be a bad financial deal for Prussia actually gave it wide powers over Hesse Darmstadt, including foreign policy. Hesse Darmstadt may have gained financially, but it had to introduce Prussian weights and measures which would harm its own trade.

In fear and alarm eight states joined together to create the Middle German Commercial Union. One Prussian called it 'a malicious and unnatural conspiracy against the Fatherland.'[7]

Within three years Prussia had encircled it with treaties and defeated it.

In 1833 Prussia took over the members of the South German Union. Prussia gave opt-outs from some of the conditions. They were not worth the paper they were written on. The Prussian Deutscher Zollverein now controlled 18 states of 23 million people with common tariffs in a protectionist bloc. It was regulated by a general conference which met at least every two years. Everything was agreed by unanimous voting.

The Austrian delegate to the old Frankfurt Diet said that 'the Zollverein is one of the chief nails in the coffin of the German Federation . . . Prussia is now taking over the actual leadership of Germany's policy, Austria's leadership being merely formal.'[8]

Rather than be isolated, the great Austria tried to join the Zollverein but Prussia deliberately kept it out. Prussia intended to break Austria's power over central Europe. Steadily the Prussian-led union became stronger until it dominated Austria.

Despite their Austrian sympathies, the smaller Southern German states were in no financial position to leave the Prussian dominated union. Out in the cold and unable to join it, Austria then tried to break the union but, even without firing a shot, Prussia was defeating Austria. It was economic blackmail.

Building the Zollverein over four decades created a highly professional Prussian civil service which was to serve the German Empire well. Prussian statesmen learnt how to cajole the smaller states, letting them think they were keeping their sovereign rights. Twice the Zollverein nearly collapsed and forceful persuasion was needed.

A customs union was of course only the beginning. After common tariffs came common systems of tax, weights and measures (the 1868 metric system[9]), currency (the Prussian Thaler naturally), railway tariffs, codes of commercial and maritime law, and uniform legislation on the regulation of industry and workers. Everything was based on Prussian practice to benefit Prussia.

Meanwhile Prussia had its eye on complete union and over many years promoted one culture by sponsoring shooting festivals, gymnastic events and educational associations. The idea of one state was fostered by the Nationalverein, a discussion forum.

By the 1860s the Zollverein, which had given the Prussians a German Empire, had also made it so strong and wealthy that it was able to fight to extend its interests even more. Otto von Bismarck, Prussia's leading Minister from 1862,[10] fought three highly calculated military campaigns.

First, in 1864 Austro-Prussian forces attacked Denmark and forced it to disgorge its territories of Schleswig and Holstein which had been ruled by the King of Denmark for four hundred years. Denmark lost a quarter of its fertile land which had long coastlines along both the Baltic and the North Sea. Prussia also acquired the superb Danish port of Kiel and immediately began to build its first naval base, which was used to such effect in both world wars.

Bismarck then defeated Austria and the Hapsburg Empire in one day: the great Hapsburg Empire had suffered a mortal blow. Prussia either annexed the six German states which had sided with Austria or forced them secretly to agree to hand over their defence to Prussia and exacted heavy indemnities. The King of Hanover lost his throne. Those States which had been enticed to join the Prussian Zollverein with special benefits and opt-outs lost them.

The pretence of a German Federation, maintained for so many years, ended. All the states north of the river Main now became the North German Federation under Prussia. It was both a political and economic union. The vice of the Zollverein was closing shut.

Prussia organised a new Zollverein for the whole of Germany. The old Zollverein Conference was replaced by the Federal Customs Council and the Parliament. In the old days of the General Conference unanimity was required. Now it was majority voting. Prussia was dominant with control of foreign policy for the whole of Germany. Her tariffs and weights and measures were standard throughout. Her trade alone profited.

Bismarck next hectored and bullied France until a chance came to depose it as the strongest power in continental Europe. France gloried in having the best army in the world, though it had not been tested for a long time. After only one month's fighting on 1st September 1870, the ailing French Emperor capitulated. France was forced to become a republic.

For the next four months General von Moltke encircled and bombarded Paris, forcing the Parisians to near starvation. On 28th January 1871 Paris fell. The Prussians exacted a war indemnity of five billion marks and left.

For the next twenty-five years Germany controlled the continental balance of power.[11] Britain stayed detached.

Germany Hijacks A Dream

The Pan Europa movement, which began in 1923, is scarcely known today, yet it influenced a whole generation of European politicians. From it a customs union between Germany and France nearly emerged.

If the courteous and erudite Count Richard Coudenhove-Kalergi, whose ancestry spanned nearly all the countries of Europe and went back to Charlemagne, had been born in another era he might have done no more than bury himself in his library and write on his abiding passion, philosophy. In his impressionable late teens and early twenties Coudenhove-Kalergi lived through a total upheaval of the civilised world as what he called 'unbridled German racism' tore through Europe. With the Treaty of Versailles the Austro-Hungarian Empire of his youth was dismembered and with it went the protection for the many minority races of Central Europe. At the same time a revolution was taking place in Russia which most people falsely thought would be short lived.

Out of the nightmare of an Empire in its death throes, Coudenhove-Kalergi cast about for some hope for future peace: 'What I was seeking but failed to find was some special brand of socialism which played down the materialistic aspects of Marxism.'[12]

Sitting in his library at Castle Ronsperg in Bohemia, Coudenhove-Kalergi literally spun his globe and spotted a possible division of the world into five huge regions: Pan America, the new USSR, the British Empire, and the new link between Japan and China, which left Pan Europa with as he said 'a common civilisation, common history and common traditions.'[13]

Dr Alfred Fried had recently published a book on how the states of South and Central America had made great strides towards 'PanAmerika'[14] over a hundred years. Dr Fried said the movement had lessons for Europe. In Castle Ronsperg it fell on impressionable soil.

Pan Europa was highly idealistic. What Coudenhove-Kalergi thought he could see from his globe was unreal. The unity of South America was an illusion though its problems could not be seen clearly from the distance of central Europe. The union between China and Japan was stillborn, which left the totalitarianism of the USSR, on the one hand, and the trading-based British Empire on the other.

Coudenhove-Kalergi promoted a united continent in which

all states would give up sovereignty to a central authority, with central institutions working closely with Britain and its world empire which 'would not want to tie herself into such a venture, nor would she want a united continent from which she herself was excluded.'[15] He thought nationalism, especially unbridled nationalism, was the root of the European evil.

Winston Churchill wrote of Coudenhove-Kalergi's proposals, ' . . . when the idea of the United States of Europe drifted off upon the wind and came in contact with the immense accumulation of muddle, waste, particularism and prejudice which had long lain piled up in the European garden, it became quite evident that a new series of events had opened . . . The form of his theme may be crude, erroneous and impracticable but the impulse and the inspiration are true.'

Even the few sympathetic British thought he had no understanding of the institutions that would be needed – his 'Europe' was based on the complexities of the old Austro-Hungarian Empire. His parallels with the US and Switzerland were dismissed – both were centralist and had little in common with the scale of the multi-lingual, multi-cultural Continent of Europe.

In 1923 Coudenhove-Kalergi published his first book himself, 'Pan Europa', with great success: in the first month alone 1,000 people sent back the membership application card inside each book. In 1924 'Pan Europa' was translated into many languages and Coudenhove-Kalergi started a monthly periodical. For the rest of his long life Coudenhove-Kalergi spent all his energy writing, speaking and entreating for European union. Beginning with family contacts at the highest levels, he used his diplomatic talents to persuade politicians of the benefits of his ideas.

Within months he had set up an Austrian committee

chaired by the then Chancellor; a Czech Committee was chaired by the Foreign Minister and there were more groups in Belgium, Hungary, Poland, Spain, Bulgaria, Romania, Yugoslavia, Estonia, Latvia and Lithuania, even New York.

In 1926 Coudenhove-Kalergi organised the first Congress of Europe in Vienna with 2,000 delegates from more than twenty-four countries who agreed to set up a European political and economic union. Behind the rostrum hung portraits of what Coudenhove-Kalergi called the famous ancestors of Pan Europa: Charlemagne, Sully, the Abbe de St Pierre, Kant, Napoleon, Victor Hugo, Mazzini and Nietzche. Over all was the new flag of the United States of Europe, a golden sun with a red cross superimposed on a background of sky blue.

As the movement reached its zenith in 1929, French and German politicians took it over for their own ends. The linchpin for European union, as it is today, was the axis between France and Germany. Their interests overshadowed those of every other nation.

France was dominated by its fear of an aggressive Germany and had a strong interest in a United States of Europe as a protection. Germany had invaded France three times in a hundred years, millions had died. Winston Churchill observed, 'All their lives they had dwelt in fear of the German Empire . . . The Kaiser's "mailed fist" and "shining armour" might be received with ridicule in England and America: they sounded a knell of horrible reality in the hearts of the French.'[16]

In contrast Germany's interests were not overtly political. In German newspapers the main themes were contempt for the French Government and the injustice of the Versailles Treaty, especially the high level of reparations.

Germans wanted a European customs union, an extension of the 1926 steel cartel between Germany, France, Belgium,

Luxembourg and the Saar (the International Raw Steel Community). The cartel's creator and a principal beneficiary was the steel baron, Fritz Thyssen. It was exactly the same idea as the Zollverein, which Prussia had used to take over the states and principalities of Germany.

Germany had a second reason to want a European customs union: its food production was no longer enough to feed its industrialised population and it needed ever increasing exports to buy food. Because Germany was protectionist, its neighbours blocked its exports. It was a potentially dangerous spiral.

Aristide Briand, the great French orator temporarily out of political office yet at the height of his authority in France, was president of the entire Pan Europa Union. His chief adviser, especially on economics, Louis Loucheur was also president of the French Pan Europa committee.

To talk to their German equivalents, Loucheur brought together the heads of the steel, aluminium, coal, electricity, ship building, chemicals, silk and wool industries. Loucheur suggested industrial cartels between France and Germany to protect French industry, and then to work towards removing tariffs. Steel was top of the list.

But Hitler was just beginning his rise to power: within a few months, three bankers from the German committee, E. G. von Strauss, Herbert Gutmann, and Carl Melchior became Hitler's main financial supporters for their own self-interest.

In the summer of 1929, Briand announced to the press that he was putting European union at the top of the League of Nations' agenda, building on the triumph of the Briand-Kellogg pact and the reassurance of the Young Plan on Germany's reparations. The press gave him enormous coverage and there was wide European support but not in Britain : the British Prime Minister, Ramsay Macdonald, diplomatically replied that such an initiative was premature.

Having prepared the international ground well, Briand made a now famous speech to the French Parliament, which had just elected him Prime Minister for the eleventh time. He declared his conviction that European unity was the only way for Europe to live in peace. He repeated his message at the League of Nations meeting in Geneva on 5th September 1929.

For true federalists it was both a welcome beginning and a bitter disappointment: Briand proposed only co-operation between governments. Sir Arthur Salter of the League of Nations wrote later that all the European nations wanted was 'on the plane of absolute sovereignty and of entire political independence.'[17]

Four days after Briand's speech the German Chancellor, Gustav Streseman, replied but his oratory descended to the merely practical. Germany would, he said, co-operate on reducing customs barriers – the Zollverein again. The British said they favoured a European organisation within the League of Nations which they knew would have no influence.

On 9th September 1929 Briand told representatives of twenty-seven European countries, mainly Foreign Ministers, at a lunch at the Hotel des Bergues in Geneva that he would work out concrete proposals to put to the next General Assembly the following year.

Then Briand's initiative came to a halt. Suddenly Streseman died. Three weeks later Wall Street crashed. The Crash unleashed an international banking crisis and worse. American loans to Germany, used to buy raw materials and food, dried up. Production fell, millions were out of work.

Total turmoil helped to propel Hitler to power in Germany. Although Coudenhove-Kalergi continued with his Congresses until the outbreak of war, all hope for Pan Europa faded. The only organisation to emanate from his diplomacy was a European Commission. It operated within the framework of the League of Nations without any influence, just as the British had advocated.

Winston Churchill was clear about Britain's position when he wrote in the 'Saturday Evening Post' of 15th February 1930: 'Every step that tends to make Europe more prosperous and more peaceful is conducive to British interests . . . The prosperity of others makes for our own prosperity; their peace is our tranquillity; their progress smoothes our path . . . We rejoice at every diminution of the internal tariffs and martial armaments of Europe . . . But we have our own dream and our own task. We are with Europe, but not of it. We are linked but not comprised. We are interested and associated but not absorbed . . .

'The conception of a United States of Europe is right. Every step to that end which appeases the obsolete hatred and vanished oppressions which makes easier the traffic and reciprocal devices of Europe which encourages its nations to lay aside their precautionary panoply, is good in itself – is good for them and good for all.'

At the second Pan European Congress in Berlin in May 1930, Colonel Leo Amery, the British delegate, praised Briand's vision, but added that 'Our hearts are not in Europe; we could never share the truly European point of view nor become real patriots of Europe . . . The character of the British people makes it impossible for us to take part seriously in any pan European system . . . we in Great Britain . . . give our warmest sympathy and support to a movement which can make such a significant contribution to the building up of a genuine and lasting peace.'[18]

In 1932 Goering, the economic dictator of the Third Reich, interviewed by a Swedish newspaper on his views on a united Europe, said pointedly, 'I am all in favour of Pan Europe, but not the Pan Europe of Coudenhove-Kalergi.' The movement was proscribed in Germany.

By 1938 there was only one possible leader of a European movement left and that was Britain. On 2nd June 1938 Coudenhove-Kalergi talked at Chatham House in London of the Sudeten crisis and his fears for Europe. At the time 'The Times' newspaper was publishing editorials backing the views of the appeasing Prime Minister, Neville Chamberlain. In broken English Coudenhove-Kalergi exhorted his audience to unite along the lines of Switzerland, with Britain in the lead. If Britain did not lead, he said 'I do not think that either France or Italy could ever be strong enough to control the European continent . . . these Germans who are strong not only by their courage and by their power of organisation will certainly become masters and rulers of Europe.'

He predicted that eleven to twelve states would be the battle field between Germany and the USSR for the control of Mitteleuropa. If Mitteleuropa became one economic unit, he said Germany would play the same role as Prussia played, first with the Zollverein and later in Bismarck's federation. Coudenhove-Kalergi's warnings about Germany and Central Europe may be as relevant to succeeding generations as they were to his own.

As ever Coudenhove-Kalergi received only polite sympathy from his British audience.

Hitler's Mentors

Today popular attention is focused on the Nazi ideology of racial purity and the Holocaust. Yet what Hitler long planned to do as he wrote in 1925 and 1926 in 'Mein Kampf', was in descent from the policies of Kaiser Wilhelm's Weltmacht (or world power to wrest leadership from Britain), Bismarck's military domination of Continental Europe, and Prussia's Zollverein to take over Germany.

Like the EU today, Hitler resurrected the idea of the Holy

Roman Empire of a thousand years ago. German school children studied a Nazi primer of mediaeval Europe and then saw those maps realised: Nazi-occupied France of 1940 had the same boundaries as those of 900 AD; the Nazi creation of Croatia in May 1941 had almost the same borders as the Kingdom of Croatia of about 1000 AD.

Hitler's ideas had socialist pedigrees. He developed the Lebensraum concept – free space – from an Englishman, Sir Halford Mackinder.[19] He first proposed it in a 1904 lecture to the Royal Geographical Society, 'The Geographical Pivot of History.'[20] It went unnoticed and in 1919 he tried again in 'Democracy and Reality' to show just how close Germany had come to controlling the 'Heartland' of the world in the Great War. The only people to take Mackinder seriously were General Haushofer in 'Geopolitik' and his pupil Hitler in 'Mein Kampf'.

Mackinder, who moved in the intellectual socialist circles of the Webbs in London, had a two dimensional view of world history: he spread out a world map on a table and that one page gave him all the answers, just as a spinning globe gave Count Coudenhove-Kalergi his.

Mackinder deduced that the sea-based civilisations of the ancient world were doomed to be overthrown from the great 'Heartland' of the main 'World Island': all the land from the River Elbe to Vladivostock. Great sea powers, like the British Empire, had no future because in the long term huge resources would be needed to service them.

Hitler's conquests seemed to prove Mackinder's thesis. The post-war edition of his book was taken seriously by the US State Department, newly aware of the Communist threat and the need for Mackinder's idea of an effective barrier of independent nations between Germany and the USSR. Mackinder's ideas were behind the American State Department's post war planning towards the USSR. Today they have reappeared yet again in Russia's call for a united Europe from the Atlantic to Vladivostock – Russian controlled of course.

Hitler's European economy was largely run according to the ideas of the socialist, Walter Rathenau, whose 1914 plan 'Mittel Europa' had saved Germany's faltering economy. Rathenau's mentor was Fredrich List, who had devised the Zollverein to unify Germany in a protectionist bloc. Today, the economy of the European Union is being run along those same lines devised by List, developed first by Rathenau and then by the Nazis.

Rathenau was a brilliant, cultured and versatile Jew. He was too versatile to be fully trusted so he was never given any secure Government post. Yet after his triumph in 1914 of remedying the serious shortage of raw materials which would have crippled Germany's war effort, he successfully introduced State socialism and what he called the classless society. After the war in 1921 and 1922 he was rewarded with the job no-one else wanted, Minister for Reconstruction. Briefly he was Foreign Minister of the Weimar Republic but was shot dead in the street on 24th June 1922 by extreme right wing assassins.

Rathenau agreed with the popular view of him: 'a dilettante in sixteen fields of activity and a company director in his spare time.' From a wealthy family – his father had founded the successful German electrical engineering company, AEG – he was one of many over the years to have maintained a lavish lifestyle while espousing socialism.

After the First World War Rathenau's writings became popular. One biographer wrote that he was 'the most widely read and the most passionately discussed German author'.[21] 'Von kommenden Dingen' ('In Days to Come') sold 60,000 and in one year alone 30,000 copies of 'Die neue Wirtschaft' ('The New Economy') sold.

The secret of Rathenau's success in ending the dire wartime shortage of raw materials was to put them all under State control. He confiscated stocks from other countries as they were over-run and bought for a central stockpile from neutral counties. He replaced overseas sources by home production: that policy of self-sufficiency features strongly, and expensively, in the Common Agricultural Policy of the EU. He introduced 'War-Corporations' jointly owned by the Government and the owners of the raw materials. The War-Corporations 'for the first time united a whole economic system for joint action'.[22]

Rathenau had moved control of the economy from the individual to the government, or society as he called it. He raised income taxes to fifty per cent, imposed high import taxes on luxuries, introduced a purchase tax to cut buying of non-essentials and imposed heavy death duties to remove what he called the 'drones' from society. The harsh tax regime plus equal opportunity in education was designed to bring about the classless society.

Another of Rathenau's socialist ideas to resurface later were the Works Councils, first introduced to Germany during the Weimar Government, revived after the Second World War and then adopted by the European Union.

An expert on the German economy wrote, 'All subsequent efforts of Weimar Germany and . . . of the Third Reich to develop the State economy on non-bureaucratic lines and to create intermediary institutions between private and public business management are to be traced back to Rathenau's organising genius.'[23]

The Europaische Wirtschaftsgemeinschaft Or EEC 1933 to 1945

Once in power the Nazis took only seven years to control the whole of Continental Europe. They aimed to control the world. All that Hitler did in his first four years, and largely ignored by the British and French Governments, was to prepare for that greater Germany. While Hitler carried out phase one of his strategy – to consolidate power at home, return Germany to work after the Depression, and build alliances to end Germany's isolation – his economic planners in Berlin prepared for one European (or common) market with four year plans.

Using the blueprints of List and Rathenau, Nazi scholars, such as Werner Daitz[24] and Anton Retinger (of the great I G Farben steel works) began work as early as 1934. The countries to the east of Germany were designated agricultural with an open market for staple goods. Germany provided technical assistance to increase production.

In the second four year plan from September 1936 the Nazis used Rathenau's ideas to make Germany self-sufficient to survive a blockade. They were anticipating stage three of the master plan when Hitler was finally to go to war with France. To achieve that and to take over eastern Europe, they needed South East Europe's foods and raw materials, especially oil.

The plan worked: the Nazis advanced south-eastwards. First, the Anschluss with Austria in 1938, then they seized the Sudetenland, and, with the craven support of the British, French and Italians, and the Americans merely watching, Czechoslovakia was dismembered. That opened the door to central and eastern Europe. Economic "agreements" with Slovakia, Bulgaria and Romania quickly followed. Raw material supplies were assured.

But when Reichsmarschall Hermann Goering was made the Plenipotentiary of the Four Year Plan bureaucracy, red tape and executive agencies took over. Goering had no more knowledge of business than Hitler did.[25] Dr Walther Funk, the Minister of Economics, ruefully commented 'official communications now make up more than one half of a German manufacturer's entire correspondence' and 'Germany's export trade involves 40,000 separate transactions daily; yet for a single transaction as many as forty different forms must be filled out.'[26]

Despite the bureaucracy, the use of Rathenau's plan was again successful. Imports were reduced to a bare minimum, severe price and wage controls introduced, dividends restricted to six per cent, great factories set up to make synthetic rubber, textiles, fuel ... and a giant Hermann Goering Works established to make steel out of the local low-grade ore.'[27]

Hitler did not rely upon Goering's business sense. In 1936 an organisation was set up under the brilliant General Georg Thomas which included economists, engineers, and trusted businessmen. Using the experience of the previous war and more of Rathenau's ideas, this team was ready to impose a war economy in conquered countries with ruthless efficiency and speed. They were only hours behind the front line troops and moved at high speed into each country as it was defeated, taking over key supplies, commanding industry and railways, and re-routing state and private money plus valuables to Berlin. All foreign trade negotiations were then conducted through Berlin.[28]

British Industry Sells Out

Before unleashing full scale war, Hitler needed the British Empire to supply raw materials for his own increasing

Empire. As General Thomas pointed out to him even before the invasion of Poland in 1939, economically Germany could not sustain a world war which the Polish invasion was to unleash – even with a United States of Europe. Hitler had to reach agreement with the British, in his eyes a fellow Teutonic race.

Agreement seemed likely. Hitler had already been given far more than he had demanded from the British Prime Minister, Neville Chamberlain, at Munich two years before – carte blanche to occupy Czechoslovakia. The British establishment was steeped in appeasement. Some thought that if Hitler had waited two or three years after taking Czechoslovakia to let the British get used to the idea, he might even have got away with conquering Poland.[29] Given the attitude of British industry leaders, he might have done.

In March 1939 at Dusseldorf, the Federation of British Industries[30] (the predecessor of the Confederation of British Industry, the CBI) negotiated an agreement with their opposite numbers, the Reichsgruppe Industrie. That agreement was never published, which is not surprising given that the intent was to eliminate 'unwholesome competition' and to promote 'international trade on a solid, progressive and profitable basis.'[31]

Germany's plan, completely missed by the Federation of British Industries, was to secure industry by industry agreements with Britain and then to 'integrate' British industry with Germany's, forcing Britain to adopt the German system. The F.B.I. was actually prepared to sell out British industry.

According to reports in 'The Times' newspaper the British delegation, led by the F.B.I.'s President Peter Bennett, made several industry agreements and were beginning negotiations for a further nine industry groups. For the Germans it was a similar exercise to one they had tried with the French in 1929 and an extension of the Prussian Zollverein.

'The Times' reported that 'Agreements between England and Germany on prices or other factors represent only one, although a highly important step towards a better organised system of world trade ... (and would) render co-operation between the branches of both countries as complete as possible'.[32]

Things were going so well that the British invited the Germans to come to England in June 1939.

At the time of the British visit to Germany and even while they were being wined and dined by Reichsmarschall Goering in Berlin, the Germans were marching into Moravia and Bohemia, ordering Romania to switch to an agricultural economy exporting only to Germany and compelling the Lithuanians to teach their children only in German. All of that was also reported in 'The Times', along with more reports on British rearmament. The F.B.I. chose to ignore what everyone could read at their breakfast tables.[33]

When less than six months later Britain did not do what Germany wanted it to do and then declared war, Nazi propaganda resurrected the idea of a 'perfidious Albion' always perpetuating the disunity of Europe – a familiar position today.

One Europe – Under Hitler

Hitler had to start stage three of his plan without British supplies. He intended to invade Poland and then dispatch France, Germany's 'bitterest enemy'. He said that he wanted 'a final active reckoning with France ... only then will we be able to end the eternal and essentially so fruitless struggle between ourselves and France'.[34]

Hitler intended to dismember France into its mediaeval parts of Burgundy, Normandy, Brittany and perhaps even Basque, Catalan, and Provence regions. The same principle of breaking the nation states into regions, divide and rule, is being used today by the EU employing the Regional Fund and the Committee of the Regions.

Despite the fact that most Germans were hostile to the USSR (Bolshevism was a version of the hated Judaic materialism) Hitler followed Bismarck's example by signing a treaty with the USSR, the Molotov-Ribbentrop Pact. A minority of Germans believed in a close affinity between the two countries, and certainly a greater affinity than with the supposedly Teutonic Britain.

At last, in April 1940 Hitler began his attack on Western Europe, rapidly over-running Denmark and Norway. By mid-June Western Europe had fallen. Germany was then free to expand to the East to seek new lands for the Teutonic race.

Seen from Berlin, Germany looked unstoppable: it was to be the Reich to last for a Thousand Years. While England had not become the ally Hitler had hoped, German tanks already faced it across the Channel and conquest looked as though it was only a matter of weeks away.

A German owned and run Europe was close to reality. Professor Allan Nevins, an American on a six month visit to Britain, wrote in early 1941 about Hitler's United States of Europe as he described it. Food, Nevins wrote, was already being sent to the Reich from the mainly agricultural outer Europe. All European production was to be regulated in detail from Berlin and all trade controlled by a multilateral clearing system, which Germany had already set in operation among eleven or twelve states – another Rathenau idea. The problem, Nevins reported, was that the United States of Europe was still fragile and not all subjugated.[35]

The new European economy was based on four principles: a closed economy, price stability, wage stability and control over investments. Based on the socialism of List and

Rathenau it was a protectionist bloc and the antithesis of free trade.

Before the Nazis took over, cartels were endemic in Germany and although the Nazi programme included anti-trust law, cartels were far too entrenched for the laws to be enforced. Interlocking directorates were ultimately connected with big, powerful German industrial interests. After the war the Allied High Commission fought a successful battle against cartels, which was quickly reversed under Chancellor Adenauer.

The closed economy had an unexpected bonus: as markets were lost overseas, 'they were replaced to the extent of at least 80 per cent by increasing trade within Europe'.[36] That was of course in war time. The protected economy of the EEC was to produce a similar bonus for its members as trade barriers first came down, but that was only a one-off, it has not continued.

In July 1940 Dr Funk, the Nazi Economics Minister, chaired a conference of Chancery departmental heads to talk through ideas for the final economic unification of the Europe economy in stages as the opposition was quelled, a unification underway since 1934.

The new Central Economic Union (a development of the Zollverein) was to include the Netherlands and Denmark to the West and Slovakia, Romania, Bulgaria and Hungary to the East. Belgium, Norway and Sweden were on the 'B' list to be part of the European Economic Area. Special arrangements were to be made in peace treaties with both France – just conquered – and Britain – about to be conquered.

Dr Funk told the conference that 'The large scale economic unification of Europe can be achieved in various ways. States which economically complement Germany or resemble it in economic structure can largely be unified with it. This is especially true of the Scandinavian countries and the Netherlands, Belgium and Luxemburg. With other states the ties will be less close.'[37]

The countries to the West (Denmark, the Netherlands, Belgium, Norway and France) were to be fifty-fifty agricultural and industrial. So Denmark had to reorient itself away from its overseas markets. Czechoslovakia too had major problems.

The Netherlands, with a similar economy to Germany, fitted the new pattern well. It merely switched its exports from Britain to Germany. Dutch agriculture was organised to benefit all Nazi occupied Europe and production considerably increased. After the war the starving Dutch population needed the revival of the German economy, but that tied their own economy and their politics into those of Germany. They then had little choice but to make the best of German enthusiasm for a united Europe.

Political take-over was planned in stages. Some countries remained fictionally independent only. Denmark, for example, was formally occupied as late as 1943. Bulgaria, Slovakia and Romania had "economic agreements" with Germany, and Hungary was Germany's "ally". By an edict of 1941 Germany created the state of Croatia (or NDH) including the whole of Bosnia and Hercegovinia. Occupied in two zones by both Italy and Germany, the Croats welcomed their new 'independence' and freedom from Belgrade, however it was created or governed.

Luxembourg, Alsace and Lorraine were just annexed. Luxembourg had been part of Germany's Zollverein until the end of the First World War, but was the only state not to be part of the German Empire. Both Alsace and Lorraine had been annexed by Germany in the war of 1870 and held until 1919.

The 'B' list countries of the European Economic Area were

likely to be incorporated later. Neutral Sweden, with a pre-
ponderance of German barons among its ruling elite, was
seen as a natural leader of a Scandinavian federation. The
King of Sweden, a 'staunch friend of Germany'[38] in the First
World War, sympathised with Nazi Germany as did some
leading Swedes. For many, Germany was their cultural centre.

Norway, ruled by Quisling from October 1940, was
intended to have a 'voluntary union' with Germany. The
truth was obvious. Satellite Finland was given worthless
reassurances of independence.

Conquered Belgium was to be divided into two, with the
Flemings becoming part of the Reich and Wallonia semi-
independent rather like Slovakia. Today, ironically, some
Belgians are pressing for a similar division.

The issue of France was debated hotly. Hitler said France
would be annexed but other Germans believed France was
key to an integrated Europe. That, naturally, was echoed
by the Vichy Government. Of all the countries conquered by
Germany, only France took over Nazi doctrine, and it did so
completely. Pétain's first message in 'New France' on 10th
July 1940 was a literal copy of the National Socialist Programme of 1920. The Vichy Government in 1940 and 1941
went on to pass a series of acts reproducing all the main
Nazi laws from those on the economy to the elimination of
the Jews, which they then stringently enforced.

The Hitler-Pétain axis was to be repeated by post-war
French and German governments. Today that same axis is
Europe's heart.

Hitler was prepared to give Italy a leading position in the
Mediterranean scheme, identical to the twelfth century when
the Kingdom of Italy was a dependency of the Kingdom of
Germany. Meanwhile Mussolini did not think of a united
Europe so much as of two spheres of influence, the German
and the Italian.

Only Poland was missing from the countries in Hitler's Central European Union and European Economic Area. Poland was the empty space, the Lebensraum, free for German settlement. In a secret protocol to the Molotov-Ribbentrop pact, not known until after the war, Poland and the rest of Eastern Europe were divided between the USSR and Germany.

Poland was administered ruthlessly: many leaders and educated people were killed, all lost their rights and two million Poles were deported to other parts of Poland. Soviet troops occupied the Eastern provinces and employed similar methods to the Nazis: 1.7 million Poles were deported, mainly to Asian Russia. In Lublin province alone (including most of Warsaw, Crakow and Vielce) 12 million people became slaves of the Reich.

Hitler's EMU

Dr Funk's July 1940 conference agreed that the Central Economic Union countries, the inner group, were to have fixed exchange rates tied of course to the Reichsmark. That was exactly the same system as the European Monetary Union (EMU) of the Maastricht Treaty.[39] By 1940 independent currencies in Nazi Europe were fictional and monetary union was nearly complete. As Thomas Reveille wrote soon afterwards, 'All eleven countries balance their exchanges multilaterally, all transactions being calculated in Reichsmarks. No foreign exchange is needed. And by price control violent market fluctuations have so far been prevented.'[40]

The Reich Economics Ministry was against a single European currency on the grounds that politically it 'would damage the self-esteem of member states'. The newly subjugated peoples could not of course be guaranteed to comply. The head of the Reichs-Kredit-Gesellshaft AG's economics department, Dr Bernhard Benning, wrote in 1943 'There is no argument about the position of the Reichsmark as Europe's leading currency. Berlin will take over a similar position – albeit significantly stronger to that occupied formerly by London within the sterling area.'

Meanwhile local currencies were deliberately over-valued which automatically adjusted the conquered countries' prices and wages up to German levels, which were much higher and uncompetitive. The same thing is happening today in preparation for EMU.

Just as in the Prussian Zollverein, customs barriers were to be abolished, quotas, prices and sales in particular economic groups were to be fixed. Agriculture was to be protected in the same way. Funk's conference concluded that 'such a central European union would give a powerful impetus to the European economy' and a central European bloc ... would comprise a much larger population than the United States' 130 million.'[41] The same argument was used to create the EEC and the EU.

Plans for a Bank of European Settlements, or the Europabank, in Vienna were detailed by the Economics Ministry. The share capital would come from member countries according to their pre-war financial obligations. All payments between countries would be made through the new bank. It would have the power to set the level of minimum reserves and control the money supply. In design, it was the forerunner of today's European Central Bank in Frankfurt.

Centralisation In The Dying Days

On 22nd June 1941 Germany opened a second front and attacked the USSR. After the war, German planners in Madrid gave the reason for taking that high risk policy, 'Hitler's policy had run into a blind alley, and the hard decision had to be made to ensure by means of the sword access to the gigantic resources of raw materials in the East, which Russia would never have delivered voluntarily, and without which we never could expect to force a show-down against the Anglo-American bloc.' Failure to reach an agreement with Britain had exacted a high price.[42]

Fear of Bolshevik Russia was used to rally the whole of Europe. Himmler and the SS recruited substantial troops from France, Denmark and Italy. Goebbels, the Minister for Public Enlightenment and Propaganda declared, 'Either Berlin or Moscow'.

Hitler was reported to have justified the invasion: 'The task of bringing together the European family had to begin now. With modern military technology small nations could no longer exist independently. In a time when 600 km could be covered by an airplane in an hour, a great territorial integration of nations was necessary. In this sense the construction of a tremendous bulwark toward the east was the first requirement for the security of Europe. Since time immemorial Russia had pushed toward the west. Not only under Bolshevism, but as long as history had existed the east had threatened the west, no matter what regime had ruled in Russia.'[43]

In the early 1980s a European federalist, Professor Michael Salewski, wrote, 'The Nazis at that time had only to stretch out a hand to the Europeans, and a decisive step would have been taken on the road to unification of the continent. Instead, they wasted their own initiative by a blatant display of egoism, cruelly disappointing the soldiers of the 'Germanic' legions recruited by Himmler, and crushing the hopes of the western parts of the Soviet Union who had been freed from Bolshevism'.[44] That a leading federalist should write in those terms of the Nazi Empire over forty years later may have unpleasant ramifications for the situation today.

War on two fronts intensified the need to unify the European economies to supply the German war machine. Albert Speer, in charge of Armament and War Production, extended Rathenau's production plan throughout occupied Europe. He visited Bichelonne, the French Minister of Production and collaborator in September 1943. The two agreed that French workers should remain in French factories, not be shipped to Germany at the rate of 50,000 a month.[45] Speer set up a Pan-European production planning council with non-Germans as "equal" partners and extended the scheme to Belgium, the Netherlands and Italy.

Speer justified his central planning after the war, 'I was even prepared to prevent what Hitler had in mind in the way of carving up France, all the more so since in a Europe integrated economically it did not matter where the frontiers ran.'[46]

In 1943 the Association of Berlin Business People reviewed the success of the Reich's European Economic Community.[47] The President, Professor Dr Heinrich Hunke, wrote 'At the turn of the year 1939-40, the main part of Europe was still under the spell of the English concept of economic organisation ... But in the course of recent years, this concept has been swept out of the Continental European countries in political, military and economic terms ... The transformation ... must be placed alongside the greatest economic revolutions in history ... signifying fundamentally a turning-back by European economies to the time prior to the formation of the English overseas Europe.'

Hunke ended, 'Europe is much more than a geographical term ... the only possible aim of economic co-operation must be the establishment of the European Economic Community.'

Dr Benning, director of the Reichs-Kredit-Gessellschaft AG, gave the Reich's views on harmonising European rates of exchange. Dr Funk, the Economics Minister and President of the Reichsbank, elaborated how member states would work together directed by Germany. Dr Emil Woermann of the University of Halle wrote on the European Agricultural order and how to increase European food production. Dr Anton Retinger of I. G. Farben reviewed ways to restore Europe's lost domination of world industry, state planning and direction of European industry by Germany. Gustave Koenigs, a State Secretary, devoted his paper to European Traffic Questions, shipping, internal marine and motorways (today's Trans European Networks).

European unity evoked a chorus of official approval in the occupied countries. Marshall Pétain told Goering, 'naturally Germany would play the leading part in this new Europe because of the basic power that emanated from a mass of over 100 million Germans who excelled in organisational talent, courage, and intelligence and were entirely unified as a nation through National Socialism. Europe was to take on a new appearance, that of a master, for it was clear that Europe with its ancient culture deserved a master's role in the world.'[48]

Pierre Laval broadcast to France, 'A new Europe will inevitably arise from this war . . . To build this Europe Germany has agreed to make huge sacrifices . . . I welcome the German victory because without it Bolshevism would be established everywhere tomorrow.'[49]

Anton Adriaan Mussert, leader of the Dutch National Socialists (NSB) and fellow traveller wrote, ' . . . there must first be a union of all who are of the same blood, the community of Germanic peoples expressed in a political form.' The East, the Lebensraum, should belong to the Germanic peoples and 'they offer great opportunities. We must go to work there in the sweat of our brow, just as we Dutch did for centuries in the Indies. What can be achieved there may be seen by looking at what the Dutch people did in Java and Sumatra, the model colonies of the world'.[50]

Quisling wrote 'in due course the Germanic union will be a fact, and then Norway will take its free and honourable place in the new Europe.'[51]

Yet the tide had already turned against Germany. The Axis lost at El Alamein on 24th October 1942. By Christmas the Germans were retreating from Stalingrad. By May 1943 the Axis armies in North Africa had capitulated. By the middle of 1943 survival began to dominate Nazi thinking.

A German Europe Lives On

In 1944, when defeat was certain, German teams in the safety of Madrid began to plan for Germany's renaissance as a world power after the war. A united Europe was part of that plan.

After the war, though the Nazi regime was widely abhorred, the ideas it had developed and practised remained. The policies of List, of Rathenau and of the Nazi planners, Hunke, Funk, Daitz, Woermann and the rest continued. The knowledge that Europe could be united, albeit by force of arms, was an inspiration to many on both sides of the Atlantic. Nazi Germany acted as a perverse model.

While National Socialism was ostracised (and continues to be so) most Germans who put the United States of Europe into practice remained in senior positions. Only the highest ranking Nazis were removed. Former Nazis were slowly integrated into post war life, especially after 1950. Attempts at denazification were an impossibility, so large was the scale of the problem.[52]

Most who served in the war-time Reichsbank quickly returned to its successor, the Bundesbank. 'Until 1969 ... there were never fewer than four ex-Reichsbank men on the eight or nine-man directorate' of the Bundesbank.[53] Dr Benning, for example, was interned for five years by the Russians and returned in March 1950 to take charge of banking and credit. Dr Woermann, like others in the University group, continued with a distinguished academic life, in 1955 becoming Rektor of the University of Halle.

In the 1951 German Foreign Office, 134 out of 383 officials and employees were former Nazi Party members and 138 had served in Ribbentrop's team. An investigating committee of the German Federal Parliament said some 'diplomats had such a black record that they were absolutely inadmissible to any position in the diplomatic service'.[54] A year later the Associated Press reported the views of a German radio commentator: that eighty-five per cent of the Foreign Office were former Nazis. So it was in most other walks of life. All danced to the new tune, but the ideas practised by the Nazis did not die.

Professor Adam Zoltowski, formerly of Poznan, Poland, writing in enforced exile in London in 1942, had warned 'that if Germany were placed in the framework of a federation on an equal footing with other nations, that equality might very soon give place to Germany's unchallenged domination, secured ... by all those methods of penetration, subversion, espionage, subtle propaganda, conspiracy and disruption in which Germany has proved a past master.

' ... The attempt to extend Russian supremacy as far as the Eastern frontiers of Germany would be doomed to failure and would only be paving the way for a renewed political, economic and military bid on the part of the Reich to gain mastery over these lands and eventually over Russia herself.'[55] His words were prophetic.

The Nazi United States of Europe failed but others took up the baton.

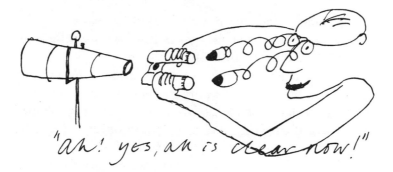

"ah! yes, ah is clear now!"

CHAPTER 2: TOWARDS A SOCIALIST VISION

British Federalism

Today the British idea of federalism is based on the practical experience of the British Empire and Commonwealth. Federalism to the British means co-operative arrangements and not centrally controlled superstates. In the nineteenth century British federalism was an answer to the threat of German expansion. Once underway it developed its own momentum which led to the British Commonwealth.

The first ever Colonial Conference was held in 1887, led by the Imperial Federation League, formed three years earlier. The Prime Ministers of all the self-governing colonies came to London for Queen Victoria's Jubilee – fifty years on the throne.

The Jubilee was only the excuse: the Prime Ministers feared rising German nationalism and the threat to the British Empire. The German Chancellor, Bismarck, had started to win colonies for Germany. By then the Prussian-led customs union or Zollverein had been operating for sixty years, had been enlarged by military conquest, and German industry, protected by a tariff barrier, was beginning to challenge

Britain's trade. Germany's population was increasing rapidly and doubled in just over fifty years reaching 56 million by the turn of the century, overtaking Britain.

Germany's deliberate shift of the European balance of power was a threat to the status quo not just in Europe but round the world. That had galvanised the rush for colonies regardless of their worth. German protectionism led to talk of the world dividing into regional trading blocs.

The leaders of the British Empire were alarmed by the speed with which all the colonial powers, France, Portugal, the Netherlands and Britain, were vying with each other to win more colonies. The opening of the Suez canal fifteen years before had encouraged a last push for unexploited lands, the Scramble for Africa.

Lord Salisbury, the British Prime Minister, told the delegates to the Imperial Conference that the immediate necessity was 'to form neither a general union nor a Zollverein but a Kriegsverein – a combination for purposes of self defence.' 'The combination' debated was a federation.

The Conference had the example of the Canadian Provinces which twenty years before, faced with an ever more powerful and threatening United States across the border, had joined together in a federation. The role of government was limited, absorbing perhaps a tenth of national income, and federation was a relatively simple affair.

Nothing came of the Jubilee initiative.

Germany wanted to displace Britain from its 'place in the sun', with its Empire apparently all too easily and cheaply built up partly, as it saw it, by using Germany as a pawn against France.[1]

Admiral Georg von Muller, Chief of the Kaiser's Naval Cabinet wrote in 1896 that 'world history is now dominated by the economic struggle, (that) Central Europe is getting too small and (that) the free expansion of the peoples who live here is restricted ... by the world domination of England.' An early war with England was out of the question because Germany did not have the sea power, but von Muller added the 'two Germanic world empires would ... with absolute inevitability have to go to war to determine which of the two should dominate.'[2]

In 1897 Kaiser Wilhelm II led an Imperial school favouring Weltmacht or world power. Weltmacht dominated German politics, the press and the armed forces.

Into this dangerous and escalating situation stepped the British Colonial Secretary Joseph Chamberlain. A radical by nature, in his youth he had advocated turning Britain into a republic and ending the monarchy. He made an early fortune manufacturing screws enabling him to concentrate on politics.

He was appointed Colonial Secretary in 1895, which coincided with an increased importance for the colonies in foreign affairs: rather than confront Britain directly Germany's first attack was in the colonies by backing the Boers. Nonetheless, twice Chamberlain sought an alliance with Germany until in 1901 Lord Salisbury, the Foreign Secretary, pointed out the futility and damage an alliance with Germany could cause.

Germany believed Britain was being weakened by its colonial problems such as the war in South Africa and was bound to seek Germany's friendship. It thought the price it could exact for that alliance was bound to rise. It was only a question of time.

For several years Germany failed to realise the game was up. It was only after the British signed an Entente with France in 1904 and then with Russia in 1906 that the Germans finally recognised that Britain was allying with its previous enemies.

While Britain had had alliances with Prussia in the past –

notably at Waterloo – Chamberlain's plan had ignored the reversal of power which had taken place on the Continent. Prussian-led Germany was now the most powerful country on the Continent of Europe. Never before had Britain aligned herself with the strongest European power: that could only mean taking German orders on Continental matters where Britain's naval writ could not run.

If Germany and Britain were on the same side, no other country could withstand the force of German leadership. Germany would dominate Europe and that would end balance of power politics which had served Britain so well for several hundred years. The balance of power was to be replaced after the First World War by the fashionable belief in the League of Nations, a belief which was seen to fail absolutely in 1939. Balance of power is again decried by the European federalists, who have failed to learn the lesson of German power.

Chamberlain's next big issue was to promote protectionism and Imperial Preference, a form of customs union. He linked this to a belief in Imperial Federation for which he had already battled for years to no avail. Chamberlain fervently, almost religiously, espoused the cause of uniting the British Empire in one federation. As he had told an applauding audience in Toronto in 1887, 'It may yet be that the federation of Canada may be the lamp lighting our path to the federation of the British empire . . . Let us do all in our power to promote it and enlarge the relations and goodwill which ought to exist between the sons of England throughout the world and the old folks at home.'[3]

From 1900 for the next six years Chamberlain's pursuit of Imperial Preference dominated and split the Unionist Government. Chamberlain made Imperial Preference versus Free Trade the single issue of British politics. It was divisive and a disaster for the Unionist Government most of whom believed in free trade. Arthur Balfour, the Prime Minister, cared little for the issues, though Chamberlain thought he did. Balfour only relished the fight to hang on to power as his party split.[4]

The impact of German expansion reached Australia and in 1900 the six already self-governing Australian colonies federated.[5] Germany in Papua and, to a lesser degree, France in Tahiti, sent shivers of apprehension down Australian spines. There was an Asiatic threat too. The wilds and vastness of the Northern Territories were an expensive administrative challenge, which would be better met by one government to prevent white Australia facing a Japanese invasion and settlement.

The six Australian colonies occupied a huge continent which was impractical to manage as one unit despite having one language, one culture and the same law and institutions. So it was logical to maintain the individual states yet have a federal government with limited powers, especially for defence.

Chamberlain pushed hard to federate the Empire at the 1902 Fourth Colonial Conference in London, attended by Canada, Australia, New Zealand, Newfoundland, Cape Colony and Natal. The colonial premiers were not interested. Their experience of the Boer War had increased their sense of nationhood. Only on the issue of trade did the colonial premiers show signs of wanting unity. They voted for Imperial Preference. They hoped the home country would adopt it. The British Government, long committed to free trade, disagreed.

That winter Chamberlain visited South Africa to arrange a customs union between the four colonies. New Zealand and Australia quickly followed suit. When Chamberlain came home his popularity was higher than ever.

He called for tax barriers to retaliate against foreign tariffs.

But that raised the fear of a food tax all over again. The 1840s, or 'Hungry Forties', were then as painfully remembered as the Depression of the 1930s is for some today. Then Cobden had won the argument for free trade, ending the protection against cheaper foreign corn – the repeal of the Corn Laws was followed by decades of increasing prosperity.

Soon Chamberlain resigned to promote Imperial Preference from the back-benches. From his early position for preference for Empire goods, Chamberlain subtly shifted ground until he was calling for protection for British food and manufactures backed by businessmen like himself.

Behind it all was a fear of Germany, heightened by the Boer War. At last the impact of Germany's Zollverein or customs union was putting pressure on the British Empire to answer in kind. As George Meredith, one of the leaders in creating the Commonwealth, said there was a need to draw closer together because of increasing attacks notably from Germany, upon the Empire and 'to keep British trade in British hands'. Leo Amery commended Bismarck's protectionist policies based on Friedrich List's ideas.[6]

Americans Influence The British Empire

One of the Imperial Preference campaigners, Fred Oliver, wrote in the Pall Mall Gazette under the pseudonym 'John Draper' (he was a partner in Debenhams, a department store) and criticised what he called the rigid free trade attitude. Amery suggested he study Alexander Hamilton, the father of American federalism. Unexpectedly he became so absorbed that in 1906 he published the story of Hamilton's life. Oliver's book landed on unexpectedly fertile soil – that of Milner's Kindergarten in South Africa.

The dismissively named Kindergarten was a band of young

men gathered together by Sir Alfred (later Lord) Milner, the High Commissioner in South Africa, from his old University, Oxford – and mainly New College and from Toynbee Hall in the East End of London – to help his programme of reorganisation and social reform and to rebuild South Africa after the bitterness of the Boer war.

While at Oxford himself, Milner had been strongly influenced by a contemporary, Arnold Toynbee, and his discussion group, 'noctes Oxonienses'. Toynbee Hall in the East End of London was named after him and was intended as a genteel way of 'bring(ing) the classes into relation' and 'enabl(ing) University men to live with the poor'.[7]

After Milner left South Africa in April 1905, his Kindergarten continued under Lionel Curtis, his secretary for the past five years. Curtis 'rediscovered' the idea of federal self-government for the colonies. He was a highly academic man but always wanted action. Throughout his long life, he set up organisations, drove them forcefully and his sheer energy attracted others. He was likened to T.E. Lawrence.[8]

Of the half dozen or so in the Kindergarten, all young men in their twenties, Lionel Curtis and Philip Kerr (later Lord Lothian) were the most active. Kerr had gone out to South Africa in 1904 to work in the Transvaal and transferred to Milner's group. One of the others was Geoffrey Dawson, later the appeasing editor of 'The Times' in the 1930s.

Years afterwards, Curtis explained[9] that he first admired federalism when trying to find an answer to the breakdown which led to the Boer War. He read Oliver's biography of Alexander Hamilton and that led the Kindergarten group to study the Federalist series of pamphlets of 1787 by Hamilton, Madison and Jay.

The pamphlets demonstrated conclusively to the Kindergarten that agreements between sovereign states, such as the thirteen American colonies or indeed the four South African governments, could never be kept and constant civil wars were bound to follow.

The American pamphleteers had suggested the only option was a centralised state, a federal government which would draw its authority directly from the people and not from the constituent states. One confederal state, with good policing, could end civil wars.

The Kindergarten did not realise that this was just one side of a public relations battle. The pamphlets were propaganda for the constitution drawn up at the 1787 Philadelphia Congress which had secretly decided to create a centralised state and feared it might be unpopular.

So Hamilton had argued emotively that as a young soldier in the American War of Independence he was appalled by the confusion caused by thirteen states: their soldiers were paid erratically, if at all, and yet they had to fight the might of Britain. He proposed one 'great Federal Republic'. He demanded complete sovereignty of the new federal state over its citizens, but, as a compromise to win the day for his policy, he said he would only centralise the limited functions of foreign policy, finance and trade regulation. Internal affairs would still be the responsibility of the thirteen states.

The issue of sovereignty was fudged to appease both groups, the federalists and the supporters of the individual states. Naturally the individual states said the new constitution was centralist. The federalists talked glibly of sharing sovereignty, but in private said that was an absurd idea.

Hamilton and his friends were trying to reverse the situation of a few years earlier when the thirteen states had resisted British attempts to control them from London in the American War of Independence. They did not want to be part of a British superstate. Once free of London they were thirteen individual states with no national identity, no American flag, no national anthem.

When Hamilton and the others pushed through a new constitution they also created a new meaning for the word federal. Until then confederal and federal had meant the same thing. Now federal meant a centralised government by-passing the thirteen states. Far from creating peace, the centralist constitution eventually led to the American Civil War, which was less about slavery and more about the futile attempt of the South to secede.

The sovereignty issue has remained fudged ever since. Sovereignty is divided and the division supervised by the Supreme Court. The US Constitution, a remarkably short document of some 7,500 words, did not specify a formal system of power sharing between the Federal Government and the States. Unlike a specific and lengthy constitution, it was easy to amend.

The precarious balance between the states and Washington held good – bar the Civil War – until 1913 and President Woodrow Wilson. An income tax amendment to the US constitution abolished the restrictions on the central government's ability to tax directly by revising the US Supreme Courts' decision in the 'income tax' case of 1895. The door was opening to more and more power for the Federal Government.[10]

Curtis And The Round Table

Inspired by the American revolutionaries, the Kindergarten group worked on ways to create a political union of the four South African colonies, already a customs union. To promote it Lord Lothian edited a monthly review, 'The State', and the rest of the group wrote for it. In 1907 Lionel Curtis submitted a memorandum to all the South African Governments suggesting a South African federation. Then he took the unusual step of resigning as a civil servant to advance it. Meanwhile at the 1907 fifth Imperial Conference an attempt to create a defence union within the British Empire failed but the idea of Imperial Preference was steadily gaining ground.

After the Union of South Africa was successfully formed in 1909, Curtis returned to Britain, and with Lothian, decided to take the same idea to the Empire. The timing seemed right. Increasing German militarism, which had first spurred federalism in the British Empire, was encouraging talk of further ways to federate.

Curtis and Lothian organised a week-end reunion of some of the Kindergarten joined by other Imperial Preference men such as Leo Amery, Lord Lovat, Ned Grigg (Lord Altrincham) and Arthur Maitland. The group agreed to start a quarterly political review the 'Round Table', which still exists today, to promote the concept of the Commonwealth with a wide range of Empire contributors.

Within the Round Table group there were different opinions about the future of the Empire. Curtis was the most single minded and radical of them all with Lord Lothian the most sympathetic to his point of view. Curtis wanted a federation of all white peoples of the Empire. Those views went far beyond what the Kindergarten, the Round Table, and the British and Empire governments wanted.

Most hoped that some kind of constitutional union might be possible. But any union would have to be based on co-operation, and not go nearly as far as Curtis' separate executive and parliamentary system. That majority view was shared around the Empire, and led to the British Commonwealth – a free association of countries. It was strongly supported by the 'Round Table'. Imperial, later Commonwealth, Preference was another long lasting success.

As Leo Amery was to put it later, 'where ... the instinct and, still more, the conscious desire for a full national life are strong, as they are in the young nations of the Commonwealth, it (federation) offers no solution to the problem of maintaining unity. The approach there can only be along the lines of that free co-operation, which Hamilton and Washington rightly condemned as inadequate in the American case, but which is yet capable of much fuller and more effective development than was realised in their day.'[11]

Curtis remained at the cutting edge of the debate: he was the first to say that non-Western people had the same right to self-government. The Round Table group grew, its overseas branches driven by Curtis' enthusiasm and total commitment for federal constitutions as each country of the Empire reached self-government.

In 1921, Lloyd George made Curtis adviser on the Irish Treaty and he helped to frame the Irish constitution. He wanted self-government for Ireland as a member of the British Commonwealth. He played an important role in the federation of India and travelled its length and breadth to sell his idea of stage-by-stage self-government to the Indian Civil Service.

Curtis' views developed into a crusade to unite the British Empire under one federal government, as a step to world government and so to end all wars. Because of his religious zeal for politics and his strongly Protestant faith, he was known as the 'Prophet'. With Lord Lothian he proposed that a federal empire should start with a union of Britain, Australia and New Zealand.

Curtis wrote prolifically and his largest work, 'Civitas Dei', a world history, took ten years to complete and five to publish. Curtis' thesis was how the present has come out of the past, and he started with the Stone Age.

Curtis' single minded determination ignored his friend Fred Oliver's advice in his introduction to the life of Alexander Hamilton, 'Our eternal warning should be the Chinese tailor who copies a coat even to its patches.'[12] Older federations with common geography, culture, and history, created when government was simple, have been the most successful – the United Kingdom, the US, Canada and Australia and South Africa. The two World Wars have so expanded the role of the state that new federations with substantially devolved powers are probably impossible to sustain.

Leo Amery commented of the twentieth century federations, which Lionel Curtis almost single handedly created, that they all have one thing in common: they 'spring from the delusion that it is the constitutional machinery that creates unity, forgetting that the machinery itself can only come into being where the sense of unity is already dominant. Where the existing national life is deeply rooted and highly complex, even the strongest desire and need for unity may have to find other ways of achieving that end than the formal surrender of sovereign powers to a new central authority'.[13]

Most recent federations have failed because of religious, social or cultural stress. The 1935 Indian federation, for which Curtis worked so hard, placed Moslems under a Hindu majority and led to bloodshed, Partition and the creation of Pakistan. Attempts to federate the Caribbean and Central and Eastern Africa have all failed. The successes have been Nigeria (not forgetting the Biafran War) and Malaysia.[14]

A Transatlantic Alliance

Lionel Curtis may have been almost alone in his wish to unite the British Empire as a step to world government but when Lord Robert Cecil appointed him to the League of Nations section of the British delegation to the Paris peace talks, which opened on 18th January 1919, he found new allies and a new direction. His old friend, Lord Lothian, was there as private secretary to the Prime Minister.

The League of Nations became the fashionable idea and

for nearly twenty years it was a focal point of international politics which by its very existence, with a headquarters building in Geneva and permanent staff, promoted the ideal of a world organisation to preserve the peace. As President Woodrow Wilson had remarked, 'the balance of power cannot work, there has to be a better way.'

The early years of the League were full of hope and new ideas. Many idealistic liberals were attracted to the Mecca of Geneva, including from Britain, Alfred Zimmern, Sir Arthur Salter[15] and Sir Walter Layton (later Lord Layton)[16] all of whom were later to promote a United States of Europe.

It became an article of faith to say that war had been eradicated by the League: it was unacceptable to voice doubts. Naturally those who worked there and realised its inadequacies wanted a stronger League. Especially in the 1930s, many articles and books were published bemoaning the ineffectiveness of the League.

In practice, the League of Nations was doomed from the start because the American Congress would not back it. No leading politician would accept the top job. When Sir Maurice Hankey, the British Cabinet Secretary, refused it, the title was downgraded and passed to a British diplomat, Sir Eric Drummond. His deputy was Jean Monnet, then aged only 30, who had failed his medical for the French army and spent the war as the French representative on the Allied Executive Committees for the re-allocation of common resources.

Lionel Curtis wanted even more than the League of Nations. He was so taken with the opportunities of the Paris Peace talks, where over a thousand leaders and civil servants from more than thirty Allied States were assembled, that just as most delegates were returning to their peace time lives, Curtis invited some British and Americans to meet on 30th May 1919 in the British delegation's headquarters. He suggested they form an Anglo-American society to 'keep members in touch with the international situation and enable them to study the relations between national policies and the interests of society as a whole.'[17] Like his 'Round Table' group, he intended that branches closely linked to London were to be set up in the Dominions.

As a British Prime Minster, Edward Heath, recalled 'Later this body was divided into two institutions, the Council on Foreign Relations (CFR) established on 29th July 1921 in New York and the British (later Royal) Institute of International Affairs, better known as Chatham House.'[18]

Apart from Curtis and Lothian the British leaders of the new Institute were Arnold Toynbee, the economist, John Maynard Keynes and Alfred Zimmern. Zimmern's father had brought his family to Britain from the free City of Frankfurt afraid of the likely results of its take-over by Prussia. Although the young Zimmern grew up in Britain he had a Continental view of the world and Toynbee, admiringly, thought him cosmopolitan.[19]

Zimmern and Toynbee were close friends from Oxford University; Zimmern had lectured Toynbee on ancient history at New College. The two had then worked together in the Political Intelligence Department (PID) of the Foreign Office. During the war Zimmern had introduced Toynbee to both Lord Lothian and Lionel Curtis.

On the American side, the enthusiasts of Woodrow Wilson's internationalism were led by his alter ego, Colonel House, and included Christian Herter, Tasker Bliss and the two Dulles brothers, Allen and John Foster. Other Americans of this group who were to be influential, such as the journalist Walter Lippmann and the future President F.D. Roosevelt had already left for home.

The first formal meeting of the British group was held at

the Royal Society of Arts on 5th July 1920[20] with Lord Robert Cecil in the chair.

From that time members attended regular meetings, a quarterly journal was published and the first annual International Survey was written by Toynbee in 1924. John D. Rockefeller made a substantial contribution.

Robert Schuman and Paul Warburg provided the main impetus for the American organisation, the Council on Foreign Relations (CFR),and it was partly financed by the Rockefeller Foundation and the Carnegie Endowment for International Peace. Chatham House noted with some envy that the CFR had a 'select membership roll' of less than two hundred because they were able to charge much higher subscription rates.[21] The CFR journal, 'Foreign Affairs' and the British, 'International Affairs' had a similar format and both rapidly became prestigious publications with a wide spectrum of contributors from around the world.

For most members attending meetings and reading the journals, Chatham House and the CFR were exactly what they said they were, unattributable briefing forums of a high standard which by their very existence would foster understanding and help to prevent future wars. Yet from the first, a few of those at the centre of both organisations sought to influence the direction of British and American foreign policy in an underhand way.

The Dulles Brothers

The link between Chatham House and the CFR remained especially strong because of the friendship between John Foster Dulles and Toynbee who regularly exchanged visits. Their friendship was to prove to be critical for the future of European union. They had in common a dogmatic belief that the nation state should die, though their politics were poles apart. Toynbee's views were an evolution of Marxism, while Dulles was a Republican who saw the end of Europe's nation states as the answer to end the wars to which America had perforce risked troops.

John Foster was very close to his brother Allen, five years his junior. The two had commanding personalities. Their father was a Presbyterian Minister who drilled discipline into them though John Foster seems to have inherited more from his severe father than did Allen. Both were given a good start in their careers by their uncle, the Secretary of State, Robert Lansing.

People regarded John Foster with a mixture of veneration and hatred. He had an overbearing manner and embraced ideas with a religious fervour. He never understood the meaning of the word compromise. So when he became American Secretary of State in 1953 he approached diplomacy as though it were the practice of law. On top of that he could be both devious and tortuous.

His first foreign visit was to Paris for the 1919 Peace Conference: he liked France and he disliked Britain, a dislike which bordered on hatred.[22]

Allen Dulles had a much more practical and engaging personality than his doctrinaire brother. The astute Joseph Retinger, who was General Sikorski's right hand man in London during the Second World War, recalled meeting both brothers.

John Foster 'was almost entirely concerned with ethics. He believed more in morality than in God . . . being fanatically minded . . . the end sanctified the means . . . What a difference between them! John Foster looked like a clergyman, or rather a Catholic prelate, vivid and somewhat nervous. Allen gave the impression of being what he was, namely a very successful lawyer; quiet, relaxed, but at the same time hard working. They were both extremely intelligent . . . I thought

Allen relied on his brains, and John Foster on his faith . . . I formed the impression that John Foster conceived an idea and had it carried out by his experts, while Allen worked on an idea given to him by others . . . I think Allen was loved by the men who worked with him, while John Foster was respected.'[23]

After the Paris Peace talks ended John Foster returned to practise law with the firm of Sullivan and Cromwell in the US. He became Secretary of State under Eisenhower.

Allen, after a spell with the State Department, joined the same firm in 1926, the year in which John Foster became senior partner at the young age of 38. Sullivan and Cromwell was a leading New York firm with an international business. The Second World War changed Allen's career – he joined the Office of Strategic Services (OSS) the first American intelligence agency, and later the newly formed CIA, of which he became Director.

Both brothers were involved in politics for the whole of their adult lives. They were leading members of the Council on Foreign Relations (CFR) for half a century,[24] and Allen became its president. Like Woodrow Wilson, both believed in a world federal system. Wilson's socialist ideas were debated in private conferences, meetings and papers throughout the 1920s and 1930s against the background of pervasive internationalism and an admiration for the Soviet Union, whose black record was not then widely appreciated in the West. As Henry Kissinger later wrote, the CFR was the school for Wilsonianism.[25]

Toynbee At Chatham House

Arnold Toynbee was the central figure at Chatham House for thirty years from 1925 until his retirement in 1955. With his high intellect and total commitment, he became pivotal in the campaign for world federation. Toynbee was the Chatham House Director of Studies, which he combined with a Professorship at the London School of Economics. His written output was prodigious: apart from books and the Chatham House Survey, he was a regular newspaper contributor, including a weekly column in the 'Economist'.[26]

Through his academic career in Byzantine and Greek language and literature, the quiet and charming Toynbee developed an exotic theory of civilisations which he published in twelve volumes, 'A Study of History', between 1931 and 1961. It was to bring him international fame: he became a cult figure in the US after the Second World War. His ideas on the cyclical rise and fall of nations has caused sharp debate and he has many profound critics among respected historians.

Toynbee had a very different approach to federation from his friend Lionel Curtis, the Chatham House Secretary. Toynbee wanted to destroy the nation states and replace them with larger blocs, which might one day, though probably not in his life time, lead to a world government. He was prepared to seize any opportunity as later events were to show. Toynbee said Curtis, the supporter of Empire federation with its sovereign states, was suffering from 'monomania'.

Toynbee ran a series of international study conferences which he used to promote internationalism: for example, in 1935 he chose the subject of 'Collective Security' and in 1936 'Peaceful Change'. From backstage in the relative shadows, his influence was considerable.

Perhaps his most outspoken and revealing talk was at Copenhagen[27] in 1932 when he set out his views on the nation state. If allowed to continue unchecked he thought nation states would deal knock out blows to each other until in the end only one empire would be left. That view was based on his visits in the 1920s to Turkey, then at war with

Greece, and to China: some fellow members of Chatham House were cynical about Toynbee's understanding of foreign affairs.

Toynbee pursued his argument that even if politically and economically Europe lost out to other parts of the world like China or South Africa, yet, 'the new international society, if it comes to maturity, will be an outgrowth of Western civilisation, a tree whose branches overshadow the whole earth but whose stem springs from European roots.'

He praised the shift from nationalism towards internationalism while skating over the long list of failures of the League of Nations, like the American Senate's refusal to ratify its covenant.

He broadcast his disloyalty to the nation state: 'If we are frank with ourselves, we shall admit that we are engaged on a deliberate and sustained and concentrated effort to impose limitations upon the sovereignty and the independence of the fifty or sixty local sovereign independent States . . . The surest sign . . . that this fetish of local national sovereignty is our intended victim is the emphasis with which all our statesmen and our publicists protest with one accord . . . at every step forward which we take . . . that the sacred principle of local sovereignty is (not) really being encroached upon and its sphere of action reduced and its power for evil restricted. It is just because we are really attacking the principle of local sovereignty that we keep on protesting our loyalty to it so loudly.'

How should it be done? Toynbee said 'I will merely repeat that we are at present working discreetly but with all our might, to wrest this mysterious political force called sovereignty out of the clutches of the local national states of our world. And all the time we are denying with our lips what we are doing with our hands, because to impugn the sovereignty of the local national states of the world is still a heresy for which a statesman or a publicist can be . . . ostracised and discredited.

'I believe that the monster is doomed to perish by our sword. The fifty or sixty local states of the world will no doubt survive as administrative conveniences. But sooner or later sovereignty will depart from them. Sovereignty will cease in fact if not in name to be a local affair.'

He forecast that if the nation states 'surrendered their sovereignty in good time, they can look forward to preserving their existence as non-sovereign institutions for an indefinite time to come'.[28]

A Shadowy Network

Toynbee's friends and acquaintances included nearly all the pioneers of the EU. Some of those friendships began at Oxford University. A Wykehamist and outstanding scholar, Toynbee was invited to study at Balliol College. It was an exceptional opportunity: at the turn of the century the elite Balliol was the launching pad for members of the Liberal establishment. Toynbee ignored that chance and never became part of the mainstream of Balliol life.

His uncle, also called Arnold, had had a short but influential academic life at Balliol which influenced his nephew strongly. The uncle died aged only 31 but he left behind an analysis of the industrial revolution, published posthumously.[29] His work had led to his support for the friendly societies, the co-operative movement and trade unionism and had deeply affected contemporaries like Lord Milner. He had reached an influential audience, lecturing to those going out to administer India. His name was commemorated in the social settlement movement in Whitechapel in the East End of London. Some of Lord Milner's Kindergarten had worked there. Today Toynbee Hall might be called 'social engineering'.

The younger Toynbee developed his uncle's scholarship into new avenues. His network of friends and acquaintances shared his left wing political views: many were members of the Fabian Society. Toynbee was not himself a member but sometimes spoke at their meetings.[30] He wrote that he wanted the state to be 'transformed into an instrument of social justice.' He thought William Beveridge's administration of the National Insurance Commission in 1905 was only the beginning of the road to socialism. When writing at the end of his life, in the late 1960s, he considered there was still a long way to go.[31]

Toynbee met a fellow spirit at Oxford, who inspired him. Alexander Lindsay, then a young Scot and classics tutor, bluntly despised what he saw as toadying to the rich and well born who dominated Balliol life. Lindsay, a leading member of the socialist Fabian Society, went on to be Master of Balliol and then Vice Chancellor of Oxford University.

When Toynbee was fired by his first employer, King's College London, another Oxford friend came to the rescue, the historian Professor Harry (R.H.) Tawney; he offered Toynbee the Professorship of International History at the London School of Economics (LSE) which he combined with his job at Chatham House. Tawney introduced Toynbee to a school friend, William Temple, later Archbishop of Canterbury. The outspoken Tawney and Temple, kindred spirits and life long friends, were widely known as Bolsheviks.[32]

Tawney's brother-in-law was the LSE's Director, William Beveridge. During the Second World War Beveridge fathered the revolutionary Fabian blueprint for the British welfare state, the Beveridge Plan, which deliberately extended the role of government to unprecedented proportions.

The LSE, founded by the Fabians in 1895, was then a

centre for socialist education. Beveridge was a protégé of Sidney and Beatrice Webb who for half a century were the intellectual heart and guiding lights of the Fabian Society.[33]

G. D. H. Cole, a leading Fabian and outstanding historian and economist, wrote that they wanted a 'British Socialism in the British tradition, rather than Russian Socialism.'[34] The Fabians did not recite dogma and Marxist ideas, or believe in violent revolution. They believed in the right to criticise, in the approach of penetration and what they called 'permeation'. Fabians were free to join any political party. Not exclusively Marxist, they studied other revolutionary writers too, especially the intellectual inspirer of the 1871 Paris Commune, Jean Pierre Proud'hon.

The Fabian influence was a subtle one. Cole's wife, Margaret, wrote: 'Fabians appeared in so many desirable liberal (and cultural) connections that they could scarcely be believed to be subversive of private property or of liberty.'[35] With a maximum of 3,000 members before the First World War, they began a quiet revolution in Britain.

Or as Prince Metternich had put it, revolutions were never the work of the great masses of people but of small groups of ambitious men including 'paid state officials, men of letters, lawyers, and individuals charged with public education.'[36]

Despite periods of partial eclipse, the Fabian Society was then, and remains today, at the cutting edge of socialism in Britain, and of the drive to create a superstate.

It has had a world-wide impact. Many who are, or have been, members of the Fabian Society may be surprised at the influence of a few of their number on European union. Its deliberately academic, intellectual and low key nature can obscure its practical effects. Fabian policy, as Margaret Cole explained, has been to operate circles within circles, encourage divergent views, so the waters are deliberately muddied. For long periods a small core of Fabians has had an considerable influence on both national and international affairs.

The most useful colleagues for Fabians have been idealistic liberals, preferably members of the Liberal Party through which they worked for many years. For example, Lord Lothian, a leader of the Liberal Party, was cultivated by the Webbs, who used both him and his party to further their own causes. Lord Layton was another who from 1952 to 1955 was deputy leader of the Liberal Party in the House of Lords. He was to be particularly influential as editor of the 'Economist' from 1922 to 1938, later becoming its chairman. While he supported a United States of Europe, he was only converted to Britain's membership late in the day.

Federal Union Lays Foundations

In 1939 the Fabian Society quietly set up Federal Union, to promote their answer to war, a federal Europe. Federal Union, an apparently well meaning organisation with a wide membership, was a classic example of Fabian 'permeation'.

If present European Union plans come to fruition, what was mapped out by Federal Union in 1939 and 1940 should be reality around the millennium. As one Fabian wrote then, 'Hitler is already creating a "New Order" in Europe . . . None of the nations of Europe, which was free in the days before Hitler, will be free again in this "New Order". Europe will be organised for the benefit of Germany . . . The British and the Allies must have an alternative to offer . . .'[37]

Fabians dominated the Federal Union Council and its Research Institute,[38] with only three Liberals (Curtis, Lothian and Lionel Robbins) and one Conservative. The advisory panel had thirty-five prestigious names including Lionel Curtis, Lord Lothian, Toynbee and his friends the Archbishop of York, William Temple, and the Bishop of Chichester,

George Bell. The advisers asked their friends for support. Toynbee brought in the appeasing 'Cliveden Set' led by Lord Astor.[39]

Federal Union held its first public rally in May 1939 with Professor Joad speaking. As Germany became more threatening so the group's numbers snowballed. Local branches spread, within a year the membership had reached 3,000 and by 1940, over 10,000.[40]

From the time of Munich in September 1938 to the fall of France in June 1940 Federal Union members wrote an avalanche of pamphlets they called 'Federal Tracts', plus books and articles. All had the same theme: national sovereignty causes war, therefore there should be no sovereign states, only federations or superstates. The headmaster of the progressive Dartington Hall School in South Devon, W. B. Curry,[41] supported the movement both by writing 'The Case for Federal Union', a Penguin Special which sold over 100,000 copies, and holding a summer school. The Fabian Society had been holding a central part of its education programme at Dartington since 1938 – its important summer school which dated back to 1907.

To most people, the 100,000 who bought Curry's paperback and the 10,000 who joined Federal Union, even to some close to its heart, it must have seemed like a spontaneous and hopeful response to another devastating war. How could the general public know just how organised this was?

The biggest sensation on both sides of the Atlantic was caused by Clarence K. Streit's 1939 'Union Now'. Streit was a Rhodes Scholar who had been on Woodrow Wilson's staff at the Paris Peace talks. He became the American correspondent of 'The New York Times' at the League of Nations in Geneva. Streit proposed a federation of Britain and America as the nucleus of fifteen democratic countries.

Even in the 1950s it was pushed by the Socialist International, especially by the Belgian Prime Minister, Paul-Henri Spaak.

Few knew that the idea of Anglo-American union was not Streit's, he merely promoted it. As an American in Britain he had more impact. The source was a member of the Fabian International Bureau,[42] R. W. G. Mackay, and it may well have emerged from wider discussions within the Bureau.

Toynbee brought the idea of Franco-Anglo Union to Federal Union. Its National Council meeting at the end of March 1940 debated a union of 'the Allies', Britain and France, and expected that in due course Germany would be added.

When the Federal Union Research Institute under Sir William Beveridge got into its stride from the autumn of 1939 onwards,[43] his writers proposed specific forms of federal government for the post-war world. They advocated France and Britain as the heart of a federal Europe.[44]

To produce such a flood of propaganda so quickly, the writers borrowed widely from the American 'Federalist' pamphlets or the Communist Sir Norman Angell's 'The Great Illusion' of 1909.[45] Another Communist H. N. Brailsford, heavily influenced by meeting Lenin in 1907, proposed that each state 'must surrender the primary prerogative of sovereignty, the right to make war . . . They must agree . . . to form a Federation.'[46]

The LSE economist, Professor Lionel Robbins, wrote 'Unless we destroy the sovereign states, the sovereign states will destroy us.'[47] He flirted with socialism, became a Liberal, and finally sat in the Lords on the Cross Benches. His two seminal works of 1937 and 1939, 'Economic Planning and International Order' and 'Economic Causes of War' have contributed substantially to the economic framework of the European Union.

In the summer of 1939 Lord Lothian, about to be Britain's Ambassador in Washington, advocated one European state

with its own police, defence, currency, and trade. He wrote:
' . . . anarchy cannot be ended by any system of co-operation
between sovereign nations but only by the . . . principle of
federal union . . . only by . . . pooling some part of national
sovereignty in a common organism which represents, not the
national units or the governments, but the people of all
the member nations . . .'⁴⁸ In Washington he was highly
regarded and died *en poste* in 1940.

At the beginning of the war, Federal Union organised three
conferences in Oxford on the proposed European constitution, its economy and the future of the colonies. The
powers they intended to be transferred immediately to the
central state were substantial.

As Sir William Beveridge put it 'this means, in the end,
that all the armed forces of all the federated nations will
become a single force, owing allegiance to the federal government and not to the national governments. There will be no
British Navy, no *German* army, no *French* air force, but
British, German, French, Swedish, Belgian and other contin-
gents of a federal navy, army and air force.'⁴⁹

The barrister R. W. G. Mackay, an Australian who had
settled in Britain, put together much of the constitutional
work.

Mackay's compilation of the Fabians' thinking differed
little from the substance of the Treaty of Rome, the Single
European Act, the 1993 Maastricht Treaty, the 1997
Amsterdam Treaty and subsequent proposals.

Some resistance leaders in occupied Europe took the
Fabians' ideas for European union as their own. They provided the base for all post-war planning for the United States
of Europe. Because Mackay produced a clause by clause
constitution, he had a particular influence, especially on the
Italian Spinelli who copied his 'practical' approach.

Mackay advocated a parliament, an executive responsible

to parliament based on the British model; a President to be elected by the Parliament for a three year term to replace the Crown; a Judiciary; one defence force under the command of the Federal defence; and one foreign policy. A customs union or Zollverein for Europe would have centrally run trade, commerce, a single currency, money supply and control of all banking.

The individual country foreign offices, defence departments and armed forces would disappear. Part of the Department of Trade, the Home Office and the role of Chancellor of the Exchequer would go from the British Government. Health, education, agriculture, transport and social security would remain.[50]

The economic case was put by Harold Wilson, then a Fellow of University College helping Beveridge with his research.[51] Later Wilson chaired the Fabians in 1954 and 1955, and was British Prime Minister for over nine years. 'A federal union should begin as unambitiously as possible in the economic sphere, to avoid severe dislocation, and to secure the acceptance of those who advocate collectivism . . . a closely knit economic unit is . . . a factor making for political unity.'[52]

The issue of the colonies was debated at great length just as it was to be when Britain applied to join the EEC. The overwhelming majority wanted supervision of member states' colonies by the federation, a transfer of sovereignty.

Lionel Curtis was still beating the drum for a federation of the British Empire and Commonwealth. He argued for one legislature and one executive for Britain and the Dominions to maintain security and raise revenues.[53]

Toynbee at Chatham House arranged the publication of Eight essays in 1940. Chatham House had a more public persona and the 'World Order Papers' had some variety of views though most were along Fabian lines. The playwright, novelist and Fabian, J. B. Priestley,[54] put the argument in an interesting way, curiously echoed in a 1993 speech by the British Prime Minister, John Major:

'If I thought federalism meant the cosmopolitan touch everywhere, I would certainly oppose it . . . It is good that Hardy's novels should come out of the Dorset soil, that Cezannes's landscapes should belong to Provence, that the symphonies and tone poems of Sibelius should give us the cold glitter of his Finnish lakes. But (that) . . . is not nationalism but regionalism, a very different thing, not political at all . . . the removal of national barriers, many of which are purely artificial, and the disappearance of cunningly stimulated national feeling, might increase the natural attachment of all sensitive persons to the region in which they live, an attachment that can be of great cultural value.'[55]

Toynbee's father-in-law, Professor Gilbert Murray, a Fabian sympathiser, wrote that he was not of Attlee's view that 'Europe must federate or perish'[56] (Attlee never developed this theme: it was probably no more than a striking political phrase). The strength of sovereignty led him to be cynical and to give only tepid support to a federation.

Only one writer opposed giving up sovereignty: Percy Horsfall, a managing director of Lazard Brothers in the City of London. His arguments have been used many times since. 'We who are opposed are concerned not only with abstract principles but with the answer to the questions whether it will work and how it will work'.

Horsfall said it was impossible to have a federal foreign policy and defence if the commercial policy, with all its possible variations from protectionism to free trade, remained in the hands of the individual states. What then would the central foreign policy be? Without a single citizenship and one state, there could be no central armed forces. Without a federal state, where would the army's loyalty lie?

Finally, there was no homogeneity of language and political tradition to create a tight organisation. 'When the members of the British Commonwealth, with a common language and the same political tradition, find that their unity is best served by a loose organisation, without defined obligations and with the greatest possible measure of freedom in the constituent parts, it is surely folly to expect organic union to flower overnight among the heterogeneous communities of Western Europe.'

Franco-Anglo Union

The turmoil of war created the chance for Toynbee and his friends to begin the destruction of the sovereign state. They seized it. Federalists today remember Franco-Anglo Union as the first step on the road to European union. By describing it as Winston Churchill's proposal, they think it has a greater legitimacy and authority. Yet Churchill was only a bystander.

The times were desperate. Within three weeks Germany over-ran Belgium, the Netherlands, Luxembourg and northern France. In a repeat of the First World War, the defeated French government fled from Paris to Bordeaux. An invasion of Britain looked as though it was only weeks away, with little to stop it.

On 13th June Jean Monnet, now widely called the founding father of 'Europe', wrote and promoted a draft declaration in London suggesting that 'only total union between France and Britain could safeguard the hope of final victory'.[57]

Monnet gave pride of place in his memoirs to the Franco-Anglo Union project and wrote that he had help with his declaration from his assistant René Pleven, Sir Robert Vansittart, the Permanent Under Secretary of the Foreign Office, Major Desmond Morton a close friend of Churchill and his colleague, Sir Arthur Salter. Monnet and Salter were members of the Anglo-French Committee to organise war supplies, jobs which they had held during the First World War but in reverse seniority.

Despite his conviction, the Franco-Anglo Union was not Monnet's idea at all but his substantial ego would never have allowed him to acknowledge that. It suited the purposes of others too: Monnet was being willingly and knowingly used as a front man.

The real story has so far gone unremarked. A year earlier, in the summer of 1939 and even before Britain declared war, Professor Toynbee had written a privately circulated Chatham House memorandum 'First Thoughts on a Peace Settlement'. He proposed a full political union between Britain and France. This idea was much discussed and written about in his circles for the rest of the year.[58]

Toynbee put his ideas to the Centre d'Etudes de Politique Etrangère in Paris and study groups were formed on both sides of the Channel. Toynbee asked his friend Alfred Zimmern, then Professor of International Relations at Oxford University, to draft for the Foreign Office an Act of Perpetual Association between France and the UK to become effective at the end of the war.[59] The project was remarkable in many ways, but not least for being conceived and driven from outside government. The revolutionary proposal included 'common citizenship, joint organs for defence, foreign, financial and economic policy'.[60]

On 1 March 1940 during the phoney war, the Prime Minister, Neville Chamberlain had approved the idea and so too had the Foreign Secretary, Lord Halifax. A key link in the chain between Toynbee and the Prime Minister was Lord Hankey who was in the War Cabinet as Minister Without Portfolio. When Churchill became Prime Minister, he ousted

Hankey from the Cabinet and two years later dismissed him – a hatchet job some said.

Monnet wrote in his memoirs that he had conversations with Neville Chamberlain about it that spring. Monnet's colleague, Sir Arthur Salter, probably introduced Monnet to the Franco-Anglo Union idea. Salter was committed to a United States of Europe; he had written a book with that title in 1933 in which he called for 'a Zollverein of Europe' leading to 'political rapprochement'.

The draft document was taken off the shelf sooner than expected, and used less than three months after it was written. It was a well chosen time of maximum confusion: France had fallen and a German invasion of Britain seemed almost certain. On top of that Britain had a new Prime Minister and Government.

The professed idea behind using the Franco-Anglo Union plan at that particular time was to create such a psychological shock for the shattered French Government that they would regroup and fight on from North Africa. The French army and navy would be encouraged to join with the British, and the important French naval fleet would not fall into the hands of the Germans.

Obviously that was also just the time when a revolutionary plan might have got through a new British government with its back to the wall and it nearly did.

When the plan was discussed with a tired de Gaulle in the evening of 15th June by Monnet and the French Ambassador Corbin, he thought its chances slim. He had just flown to London from the defeatist atmosphere of Bordeaux. Paris had fallen. Large numbers of Frenchmen were escaping on foot, on bicycle, by horse, by car, by any means from the advancing Germans. Most of the French Government, Members of the Chamber and the Senate were in a state of shock.

As Emmanuel Monick recorded 'Not knowing what to do they spent the whole day there (the Bordeaux house where the President of the Chamber was staying) standing or sitting on the steps. Asking each other questions, they passed on the most unlikely rumours, and smoked countless cigarettes. Everywhere one trod on cigarette ends.'[61]

Winston Churchill, made Prime Minister only a month earlier, was far from convinced. He wrote, 'I was not the prime mover. I first heard of a definite plan at a luncheon at the Carlton Club on 15th (June), at which was present Lord Halifax, M. Corbin (the French Ambassador) Sir Robert Vansittart and one or two others. On 4th (June) Vansittart and Desmond Morton had met M. Monnet and M. Pleven, and had been joined by General de Gaulle, who had flown over to make arrangements for shipping to carry the French Government and as many French troops as possible to Africa. (Their plan was to give) M. Reynaud some new fact of a stimulating nature with which to carry a majority of his Cabinet into the move to Africa and the continuance of the war. My first reaction was unfavourable. I asked a number of questions of a critical character, and was by no means convinced . . . (At Cabinet) I was somewhat surprised to see the staid, stolid, experienced politicians of all parties engage themselves so passionately in an immense design whose implications and consequences were not in anyway thought out. I did not resist but yielded easily to these generous surges.'[62]

Monnet wrote of de Gaulle and Churchill in his memoirs 'it was clear that both by their upbringing and their mystical belief in national sovereignty, (they) were deeply opposed to aspects of the plan which they regarded as inconceivable and impracticable'. Churchill and de Gaulle were proved right and Monnet wrong.

Monnet liked to think that Churchill thought him indispensable, but in Churchill's own account of the war in six volumes, Monnet only receives six brief mentions, four of them in connection with the ill-fated Franco-Anglo Union plan. Monnet was a small fish in a large pond.

The plan was sent and also read out by telephone to the French Prime Minister in Bordeaux. Paul Reynaud agreed to meet Churchill and some of his Government in Concarneau, in Southern Brittany. Churchill only got as far as the train to Portsmouth when the message came that the French cabinet had turned the plan down. He left the railway carriage 'with a heavy heart'.[63]

Meanwhile Monnet, Pleven and others flew to Bordeaux where they witnessed a scene of defeat. Reynaud had been forced to resign the premiership the night before in favour of the octogenarian Marshal Pétain, the hero of Verdun.

The French Council thought a union between France and Britain was far too radical. The issue of British citizenship alone revived a bitter history with the French. The plan badly misjudged the effect on men who had lost hope.

If the French had received what they were expecting from the British – a release from their obligations to Britain so that they could seek terms from the Germans – then there was just a chance that they might have sent their fleet to join the British, keeping it out of the clutches of the Germans.[64] Toynbee's scheme ended all hope of that. It played into the hands of those French seeking an armistice.

General Weygand led the defeatists, 'In three weeks England will have her neck rung like a chicken.' (Later Churchill replied, 'Some chicken – some neck!').[65] Jean Ybarnegaray exclaimed 'Better be a Nazi province. At least we know what that means'. Nothing Reynaud, or his stoutest ally Mandel, could say made any impact.

Some felt that the British had left France in the lurch at Dunkirk, others that Pétain's armistice with Hitler was a plot and he had been in touch with Germany since 1939. Others feared a Bolshevik uprising more than Nazi domination – 'plutôt Hitler que le Front populaire'.

'The Times' of London reported on 18th June that 'Marshal Pétain, the new French Prime Minister, announced yesterday morning that during Sunday night the French army had been ordered to stop fighting, and that he had been in touch with Hitler to conclude an honourable peace.'

Franco-Anglo Union had failed but it only encouraged those who had conceived it.

To Penetrate The Foreign Office

Balliol College, Oxford, where Professor Lindsay was the Master, became the centre for a noteworthy infiltration project. When the war started, Toynbee persuaded the Foreign Office to make Chatham House's research department the research group for the Foreign Office under his direction. He wanted to resurrect his old Foreign Office department of the First World War – the Political Intelligence Department – which provided intelligence for the decision makers.

At first Toynbee met resistance, but through the good offices of a former PID colleague still in the Foreign Office, Rex Leeper, most of his research department, by then moved to Balliol College, became part of the Foreign Office. It was known as the Foreign Research and Press Service (FRPS) – a quasi-government agency. By early 1943 Toynbee had 177 staff, some of them were from the University working part time.[66]

In 1942 the British War Office started 'Leave Groups' for 70 to 80 service men and women to spend a week hearing lectures at Balliol College. More than 3,000 people took part. The theme was how to prevent a third world war. It was quite an operation and a subtle form of propaganda.

Curtis published a compilation of their views in 1945 entitled 'World War; its Causes and Cure'. Not surprisingly, the answer to war was to merge countries and champion the United Nations.

CHAPTER 3: UNDERGROUND

An Italian Godfather

The influence of the Fabians' Federal Union was not limited
to Britain alone. In Italy it found a ready made disciple who
was to become one of the most influential builders of
'Europe' and inspirer of the Maastricht Treaty.

Altiero Spinelli was born in Rome two years after Lenin's
first and abortive coup in St. Petersburg. Growing up he was
attracted to the ideas of Lenin and Trotsky. In 1924, aged
only seventeen, he joined the Communists. His was not an
academic interest in political theory. The Communists were
in the thick of resisting Benito Mussolini and his blackshirted
Fascists who had taken power in October 1922. So Spinelli,
and others like him, were active in resistance years before
the outbreak of the Second World War and the existence
of the well known resistance movements throughout Nazi
occupied Europe.

Within four years of taking power Mussolini was absolute

dictator of Italy. The opposition, the Anti-Fasciti, was made up of several parties which formed and reformed. Those who resisted mainly had to do so from abroad, usually in France and to much less effect from North and South America. Those at home who were too vocal found themselves in front of Mussolini's dreaded Special Tribunal and spent years in prison. Resisting was a highly dangerous business and it proved so for Spinelli.

On 6th April 1928 in a series of crack-downs on the leaders of the Communists, the Partito Communista Italiano or PCI, Spinelli was arrested and took his turn in front of Mussolini's Special Tribunal. He was sentenced to jail and spent twelve years in different prisons until he was eventually sent to the prison island of Ventotene.[1]

With time to think, he broke with Stalinism in 1937. Yet he was never to move far from his Stalinist roots. Spinelli's certainty, drive and ambition, partially born of his Communist training, were later to be critical in creating the European Union.

Revolutionary Prison

The prison island of Ventotene became the enforced headquarters of the PCI underground with Communists outnumbering all the other groups. More arrived after the fall of Paris in June 1940, when many of those who had been refugees there, some for ten years or more, were shipped back to Mussolini and to prison. By that time there were about 1,000 prisoners on Ventotene. It was a revolutionary hothouse.

Spinelli strongly believed that the days of national sovereignty were dead. In Italy, federal ideas have a long pedigree dating back to the days of the Risorgimento and earlier to Guiseppe Mazzini[2] and Carlo Cattaneo. During the First

World War some Italian socialists advocated European federation. In 1916 the revolutionary socialist, Guiseppe Modigliani, wrote in the journal 'Avanti!' that a United States of Europe would be the inescapable result of economic progress breaking down national boundaries, and forcing the creation of new institutions which the socialists could take over.

On the prison island, Spinelli came under the influence of two men: his fellow prisoner Professor Ernesto Rossi,[3] the Giellisti leader sentenced to twenty years in prison, and, through his writings, Rossi's friend, Professor Luigi Einaudi.

Immediately after the First World War, Professor Luigi Einaudi, a liberal economist, argued in articles and letters to newspapers against national sovereignty. Using the pen name 'Junius' in the 'Corriere della Sera' he criticised the plan for the League of Nations because it left the sovereignty of states intact. He wanted a Europe based either on the US or on the English union with Scotland with the power to tax, one army, and control over customs, postal communications and the railways.[4] He inspired others who were also writing along similar lines, such as Giovanni Agnelli (of Fiat) and Attilio Cabiati.[5]

Between the wars European federation was part of the platform of the Giustizia e Liberta, a party formed in 1929 and inspired by the firebrand socialist Emilio Lussu and by Carlo Rosselli.[6] The 'Giellisti', a coalition of Socialists and Liberals, wanted agrarian reform, co-operatives, socialist public utilities and progressive income tax. Despite the personal dangers the 'Giellisti' attracted increasing numbers of supporters to oppose Mussolini. By 1933 the 'Giellisti' had 800 followers in Rome and around 3,000 in the central and southern provinces.

Ventotene, the 'confino' island, is in the Gulf of Gaeta off the Italian coast between Rome and Naples. When it was a revolutionary prison it was linked to the mainland by a supply boat which went back and forth twice a week enabling Professor Einaudi to send federalist reading material to his friend Rossi. Occasionally underground tracts could be smuggled out.

Among the strongest written influences on Spinelli, courtesy of Professor Einaudi and his British socialist, friends were the American eighteenth century revolutionaries Hamilton, Jay and Madison. Among the contemporary writers were members of Federal Union: Sir Walter Layton of 'The Economist', American Clarence Streit, Lord Beveridge and Barbara Wootton. All were advocates of European federation.

Years later, in a 1957 speech, Spinelli acknowledged the importance of the Anglo-American literature he had received on Ventotene. He said he had whiled away some of his time by translating Professor Lionel Robbins' 'The Economic Causes of War' into Italian. He commented that the British pre-war literature was first class and 'even superior to the average Continental literature . . . The Italian movement has absorbed much from the British.'[7]

Spinelli and Rossi, leaders of the federalist prisoners, joined with like minded others,[8] to write a crucial work, the 'Manifesto for a Free and United Europe'. Spinelli's hand was dominant. In July 1941 Rossi smuggled the tract to the mainland. Rossi's wife, Ada, took the final version, written on cigarette-papers and hidden in the false bottom of a tin box, back with her on the supply boat. For cigarette-papers, it was a lengthy document.

Later widely known as the Ventotene Manifesto it inspired those who drafted the policies of the post-war Italian parties and became the basic document of the European Federalist Movement.

In the Manifesto Spinelli argued that a Federal Union of

Europe had to be the top priority for post-war Italy. The workers of both capitalist and Communist countries had to be liberated. Not surprisingly given Spinelli's background, it reads like a Communist tract:

'A free and united Europe . . . will immediately revive in full the historical process of the struggle against social inequalities and privileges. All the old conservative structures which hindered this process will have collapsed or will be in a state of collapse . . . In order to respond to our needs, the European revolution must be socialist . . .'

Spinelli wanted to abolish private property but flexibly. He deplored Stalin's 'doctrinaire principle that the private ownership of the material means of production must, as a general rule, be abolished.' In Russia, he said, 'the . . . population was subject to a restricted cell of bureaucrats who ran the economy . . .'

Instead, 'private property must be abolished, limited, corrected or extended: instance by instance, not dogmatically according to principle.'

Like Lenin, Spinelli thought war would lead to a period of chaos when his revolution could take hold, when 'the fallen governments lie broken, during which the popular masses anxiously await a new message and are, meanwhile, like molten matter, burning, susceptible of being poured into new moulds, capable of welcoming the guidance of serious internationalists . . .'

Ending the nation states of Europe would have other benefits. For one, the German problem would be solved. 'The multiple problems which poison international life on the continent have proved to be insoluble: tracing boundaries through areas inhabited by mixed populations, defence of minorities, seaports for landlocked countries, the Balkan question, the Irish problem, and so on. All matters which should find easy solutions in the European federation.'

All the main functions of a state were to be centralised with just a little freedom left for the old nation states. The new Europe would 'have at its disposal a European armed service instead of national armies; . . . sufficient means to see that its deliberations for the maintenance of common order are executed in the single federal states, while each state will retain the autonomy it needs for a plastic articulation and development of political life according to the particular characteristics of its people.'[9]

In a second paper, 'The United States of Europe', Spinelli recommended 'set(ting) up a few simple federal institutions, which must be solid, irrevocable *(a word we have heard many times since)* and easily understood. It will not be necessary to trouble much with individual national problems. The federation would provide the necessary internal order to which progressive forces would naturally adjust and from which they would derive their future character.'[10]

A third paper emphasised the need for an educational system to train men of initiative and to choose the right men now.[11] That was more important than the new institutions. After the war the College of Bruges was founded to do just that.

Fellow prisoner, Professor Rossi, was afraid that if they waited until the war was over for Spinelli's 'European consciousness' to appear of its accord they would miss the boat. In the Risorgimento small elites had successfully unified Italy. So Rossi thought they should pressurise the victorious countries using the Risorgimento's methods to achieve a united Europe.[12]

In August 1942, Italian refugees organised a Pan-American Congress to endorse European Federation and tried to influence the American State Department to accept European federalism as the ultimate post-war goal. Their efforts failed because the State Department thought their views were not part of the Italian mainstream in Italy itself.

Spinelli too was sceptical of the refugees' vague and impractical aims. He forecast that the US would support European Federation and therefore that would be a key part of the post-war world. Spinelli proved to be right.[13]

Swiss Declaration

In August 1943, a month after Mussolini was overthrown, Spinelli and Rossi were released from prison. The ex-prisoners made no attempt to join up with the Allies advancing in the wake of their successful landings in Sicily, but quickly travelled north to Milan to link up with Professor Silvio Trentin, formerly a leading lawyer at the Venice School of Economics.

After the murder of a political colleague in 1925, Professor Trentin went into exile in Paris with the Italian Socialist party. When the Germans marched into Paris, he fled south to Toulouse. Using a book shop as cover, he became the focal point for Italian and Spanish Republican exiles. Again behind the facade of Trentin's new Milanese book shop, Spinelli and friends started to re-organise.

Within a few days of their arrival in Milan they secretly held the first meeting of what would become the influential Movimento Federalista Europeo (MFE). Between fifteen and twenty former prisoners from the island of Ventotene met in the home of Mario Rollier. Rossi and Spinelli were the joint secretaries of the new movement. They produced a six point declaration based on the Ventotene Manifesto.[14]

The MFE group expected there would be bloody revolution as the war ended, just like the First World War when the Russian revolution spread to parts of Germany. They hoped to take advantage of the upheaval to start a federal

Europe in which all European citizens would control the executive, the legislature, and the judiciary.

Milan became the federalists' publishing centre. Labouring under great difficulty, the MFE produced eight clandestine issues of its newspaper 'L'Unita Europea',[15] and stencilled copies circulated. Four issues included reprinted articles by Sir Walter Layton, Lord Beveridge and Barbara Wootton. They also reported on Allied policy for post-war planning, analysed Italian foreign policy and discussed federalism.

The MFE was deliberately a movement not a party. Guglielmo wrote in 'L'Unita Europea', 'It aims to create an organization of its own, capable of spreading the federalist idea and of acting resolutely in a revolutionary sense in the context of today's underground political life. Tomorrow when politics become legal again it intends to lose no opportunity of operating on the level of political parties.'

The influence of the MFE was to be astounding: all the post-war Italian parties, except the Communist PCI, included federalism in their programmes.

On 8th September 1943, the Germans seized the Po valley and life in the occupied North became more hazardous. Thousands of Italians fled across the border to Switzerland and joined the few already sheltering there. The true resistance stayed in Italy to fight against the Germans.

Unlike some of their colleagues, Spinelli and his friends[16] believed that working for a federal Europe was more important than remaining in Italy to fight the Nazis. Spinelli was briefly in touch with the chief Special Operations Executive representative in Switzerland, Jock McCaffery. But from the autumn of 1943 Spinelli concentrated not on defeating the Germans in which he had never had much interest but rather on creating a United States of Europe in the post-war world. He continued to do so until he died over forty years later.

From Switzerland the group sent back many articles to Colorni and his secret printer in Milan. Enrichetta Ritter braved the dangers of crossing the frontier into German-held Italy. Under the pen name, Thelos, Rossi wrote a pamphlet called 'L'Europe de demain', and Colorni managed to print a staggering 10,000 copies. In May 1944 they were smuggled into occupied France. The following year the pamphlet was reprinted by the Geneva Centre d'Action together with other federalist articles.

Geneva was not only safe but it was also possible for Spinelli to contact other national groups operating within resistance movements round Europe. They quickly identified them and worked hard to co-ordinate their activities and programmes.

Help came from an unexpected quarter, the Dutch Secretary-General of the World Council of Churches in Geneva, the Rev Dr Willem Visser 't Hooft.

The Italians needed a safe house from which to conduct their illegal activities. Within a few weeks of their arrival in Switzerland, 't Hooft was introduced to them by Jean-Marie Soutou, who had represented the French underground newspaper 'Témoignage Chrétien' in Geneva since the spring of 1943 and was an agent of the Mouvements Unis de Résistance.[17] With the constant problem of Swiss neutrality to be respected and the fear of the dire results if it was not, Spinelli's proposed meetings had to be held in secret. They were reported in the press in vague terms as international meetings 'somewhere in occupied Europe' of resistance leaders, which was stretching the truth somewhat – some were, some not.[18] Because travel in occupied Europe was hazardous the meetings took months to set up. Not all those invited could come.

Between March and June 1944 five meetings were held in 't Hooft's house. No full record of those attending was kept but there were about fifteen people. The Italians were represented by Spinelli, Rossi and Professor Egidio Reale of the Italian Republican Party. Representing France were Jean-Marie Soutou, Laloy, the official representative in Geneva of the French National Committee in Algiers, and François Bondy, born in Austro-Hungary later a Swiss national, who maintained contact with French socialist resistance groups. From Germany came Hanna Bertholet of the Militant Socialist International (ISK), linked with the German trade unions and in touch with German resistance groups, and Hilda Monte[19] also a member of the ISK from Germany with links to the remnants of German resistance. 't Hooft represented the Dutch resistance.[20]

There was some debate about whether to allow any Germans to be present, but a majority allowed Hilda Monte and Hanna Bertholet to slip into the room. Hilda Monte was later shot at the border when she illegally tried to cross back to Switzerland from Germany.

Nearly everyone wanted the internationalist concepts of the League of Nations to form the foundation for any federal Europe. The French and the Italians wanted to go much further than the rest and curtail national sovereignty. That was to be the forerunner of many later battles.

Edited by the Italians and based on the Ventotene Manifesto, the participants signed the International Federalists' Declaration. They wanted 'to go beyond the dogma of the absolute sovereignty of the state and unite in a single federal organisation. The lack of unity and cohesion that still exists between the different parts of the world will not allow us to achieve immediately an organisation that unites all civilisations under a single federal government. At the end of the war one will therefore have to be content with setting up a universal organisation of a less ambitious kind, but one able to develop in the direction of federal unity.'

The writers believed that the destruction of two world

wars was due to the existence of thirty sovereign states; 'this anarchy must be remedied by the creation of a Federal Union between the European peoples.' It was not of course the case that thirty states caused either World War: in both cases it was German ambitions.

'The Federal Union must not prejudice the right of each . . . member country to solve its own special problems according to its own ethnic and cultural characteristics. But . . . states must irrevocably surrender to the Federation those aspects of their sovereignty that deal with the defence, relations with states outside the Federal Union and international trade and communications.'

They called for a government responsible to the people, one army responsible to the supra-government excluding all other armies, and a supreme tribunal. Finally they wanted a permanent headquarters from which to build the Federal Union.[21]

Secretly, the Declaration was sent from Switzerland to all occupied countries in Europe and to Britain. Reaction was mixed.

In Britain where most of the ideas came from in the first place, the Socialist Vanguard Group[22] was enthusiastic. Sir Walter Layton, whose influence on the Italians had been so marked, told the audience at the annual conference of the Geographical Association in January 1945 that there should be a world organisation combined with regions. He endorsed Spinelli's declaration which had been sent to him from Switzerland for 'a central government for Europe responsible not to the various state governments but to the people.'[23]

Some French were positive: in Lyons in June 1944, the CFFE (Comité Français pour la Fédération europénne) newly created by some of the resistance movements, agreed a similar declaration. After the Germans retreated, it was circulated in pamphlet form and as wall posters in most Southern French towns.

Only four of the Dutch resistance groups replied and they were not interested. One said, 'this may seem surprising in Switzerland, but it is understandable to anyone who knows and experiences conditions here. The resistance groups are fully occupied with their own task, with day-to-day cares and the constant risk to their lives – executions of late have risen to over 500 a month – and cannot be expected to find time or opportunity to consider such international questions with the necessary calm and deliberation.'[24]

After the Allied landings in Normandy in June 1944, the resistance movements in all countries became totally absorbed with the last battles against the Nazi occupiers and with their own national positions post-war.

In the late summer of 1944 Spinelli left Switzerland to return to Italy, and immediately became a leader of the Action Party Secretariat for Upper Italy, which took over from the Giellisti. In December the Action Party proposed that the principle of the transfer of sovereign rights to a 'democratic European federation' should be embodied in the Constitution of the Italian Republic:

'the Italian State considers its own absolute sovereignty to be provisional and is prepared to transfer those sovereign functions which are of supranational concern to a future democratic federation of Europe in which Italians would enjoy all the rights and assume all the obligations of federal citizens.'[25]

In 1947 this supranational clause was made part of the new constitution of the Italian Republic. Most of those who voted for it did not understand what they were doing: in the under-stated words of one historian, it 'proved quite useful.'[26] It was an outstanding success for Spinelli who was to remain a leading campaigner for the United States of Europe for the next forty years.

Professor Ernesto Rossi worked for the MFE and for the Action Party and, until his death in Rome in 1967, wrote extensively and fought for the United States of Europe.

Professor Einaudi, declared soon after the war 'the next goal is the United States of Europe.'[27] From 1948 to 1955 his influence was paramount: he was President of the Italian Republic.

French Underground Federalists 1939 to 1945

The Italians resisters passed on their interpretation of the British federalists plans to the French resistance. The idea of a federal Europe was already well established among some leading politicians and academics before the war thanks to Count Coudenhove-Kalergi. While his dream of Pan Europa was partially supported by the then Prime Minister, Aristide Briand, who wanted co-operating nation states only, a later Prime Minister, Léon Blum, was to go much further.

In October 1939, just after France and Britain had declared war on Germany Blum proposed that ultimately Germany should be integrated into a 'federal and disarmed' Europe. He wrote: 'I hope, in a word, that a true German democracy can be integrated into a true international democracy.'[28]

Blum had been a socialist for over thirty years. If he had an over-riding philosophy, it was for justice: he had supported Alfred Dreyfus at his trial. When Briand was honorary President of the whole Pan Europa movement, Blum was on the French committee as leader of the French socialists. In 1936 he became Prime Minister leading the 'Front Populaire', and was the theorist of the French socialists. When war broke out, the French socialists split into two: those who followed Blum – by then in opposition – and were anti-Fascist, and those who preferred the anti-war position of the Party chairman, Paul Faure.

On 15th September 1940 after Germany had occupied part of France, the Vichy Government arrested Blum, and charged him with encouraging industrial unrest and failing to rearm while Prime Minister. That was true. The Germans stopped his trial, but he spent the war in prison, latterly in Buchenwald concentration camp.

While in a French prison, Bourassol near Riom, he wrote on peace in Europe. It was published at the end of the war as 'A L'échelle humaine' and translated into many languages. Federalists regarded it as a key work, on a par with Spinelli's Ventotene Manifesto and Geneva Declaration. Even from prison, Blum had a substantial influence on socialist members of the resistance movements.

He wrote ' . . . I have always been attracted by the ideas put forward by Rathenau after the collapse of Germany in 1918 . . . interstate anarchy must be replaced by a voluntarily recognised supreme authority'.

Blum wanted international socialism with the bourgeoisie stripped of economic and political power: 'There must be progressive legal expropriation, carried out by peaceful means, but none the less ruthless in its action. . . . France must be integrated in a human or universal order.'[29]

Perhaps more in France than in any other German occupied country, politics and resistance were intertwined. That was because the French Government had not chosen exile and resistance from North Africa, as it could so easily have done. With a collaborating government, nobody in France could ignore the subject of what kind of France they were fighting for – an independent sovereign France (de Gaulle) or a France united with Germany in a centralised Europe, either German run (Pétain), or federal (Blum).

Marshal Pétain and his Vichy Government were widely

supported and France was the only occupied country with a totally collaborationist government. Both Pétain and Laval, the Vichy Foreign Minister, sure that Germany would successfully conquer the whole of Europe, pushed for co-operation with the victor, and for a role for France second only to Germany in the New Order.

Admiral Darlan optimistically wrote to H Freeman Mathews, the First Secretary at the American Embassy to Vichy France: 'Even if Germany wins the present war, France will, given the strength and character of her people, and German weaknesses, eventually be the dominating continental force . . . A German victory is really better for France than a British victory.'

Few Frenchmen heard General de Gaulle's call to arms via the BBC in London on 18th June 1940, 'France is not alone! . . . No matter what may happen, the flame of French resistance must not, and will not, be extinguished.' Only in retrospect did the Free French think of it as the moment when resistance to the Germans began. De Gaulle, the most junior general officer in the French army, was at first battling virtually alone, and was hardly known outside his immediate army circle. Marshal Pétain sentenced him to death in absentia.

Among the relatively few Free French in London and their sympathisers in France not only was the Vichy Government anathema, but so were Léon Blum's proposals for a federal Europe.

De Gaulle believed that if France chose the route of a united Europe it would soon become a fortress dominated yet again by Germany. France should be allied with the world outside the continent of Europe and pushed for an association with the Anglo-Saxon world. He was to fight the idea of a federal Europe until he died.

With de Gaulle at their head, the Free French laid stress

on reawakening a belief in France and the French nation, and in persuading their allies that France had a future as a sovereign state. That sense of self-belief proved to be critical: the Americans, planning for the end of the war, thought that France should be administered by the Allies in the same way that the defeated Germany was to be governed. That this did not happen was due to the personal courage and authority of de Gaulle and the backing of Churchill.

The French resistance was slow to take off: in the occupied North of France it was a year or more before the ever increasing brutality of the German invaders persuaded more than a brave few to join the resistance. Inevitably most groups were local and limited.

At the urging of one resistance leader, Christian Pineau, de Gaulle made a declaration in June 1942 that 'once the enemy is driven from our land, all French men and women will elect a national Assembly which, in the full exercise of its sovereignty, will determine the country's future.' Nearly all the underground papers published his message and recognised him as their external leader: he would be no Pétain and democracy would return at the end of the war.

Yet there was a considerable gulf between de Gaulle and some of the larger groups. De Gaulle wanted a sovereign France and the socialists wanted a federal Europe. In July 1942 de Gaulle made André Philip, a top socialist sent by his party to London, his Commissioner of Home Affairs. After a disagreement, Philip said to de Gaulle, 'General, as soon as the war is won I shall part company with you. You are fighting to restore national greatness; I am fighting to build a socialist and democratic Europe.'[30]

Philip's hope for a future federal Europe was shared by the three major groups in the free zone of the South. The strongest and best organised, Combat, was open to all, but it had a socialist leaning, and was led by Capitaine Henri Frenay, a career army officer, who was sickened by the Vichy Government. For several months after the fall of France he had worked there as a staff officer. Before the war he studied in Germany, at Strasbourg, and from 'Mein Kampf' understood exactly what he was fighting. In the early days Frenay was one of the few: even his own mother travelled from her home in Ste Maxime-sur-mer to Lyons to tell him that unless he was loyal to Marshal Pétain she would denounce him to the police – she did not, of course.

Libération Sud, a much bigger group than Combat with about ninety per cent socialists and trade unionists, was led by a former naval officer, Emmanuel d'Astier de la Vigerie. They distributed a fortnightly newspaper, 'Libération Sud' with one of the highest circulation of any underground paper, by 1943 it was nearly 140,000. The third group was Franc-Tireur set up by the left wing socialist, Jean-Pierre Levy.

While Frenay supported de Gaulle, he also wanted a federal Europe. He remarked, 'I summed up my attitude on these lines. If Hitler were, as is claimed, the man destined to unite Europe, albeit by force, instead of a demon destroying its body and soul, then I as a French officer would offer my services to the German army. But as it is, we must embark on resistance with all our strength.'[31]

The most effective and largest of the left wing groups were the Communists. But in line with Moscow they were strongly anti-federal and opposed to the prospect of a new bloc on the USSR's western border.

Some of the most important theorists of a federal Europe were members of the Libérer et Fédérer resistance group whose main emphasis was their journal with a circulation of about 5,000. Based at the book shop in Toulouse set up by Spinelli's friend, Professor Silvio Trentin, the exiles were mainly French and Italian with some Spanish republicans.

Among the Toulouse group was the socialist Vincent

Auriol, one of Léon Blum's closest associates since 1919. In January 1947 Auriol was elected as the first post-war President of the new Fourth Republic.

Alexandre Marc was its leading theorist. Born in 1904 in Odessa, Russia, Marc had studied in Germany and emigrated to France as a young man.[32] He was a disciple of Proud'hon, the philosopher who had inspired the 1871 Paris Commune.

For post-war European union this mix of top academic and political Italian and French federalists was important. Together they had faced a common enemy, Fascism, in dreadful circumstances and the bond that forged was strong.

Unlike Blum, the members of Libérer and Fédérer wanted a 1789 style of revolution of the whole people, with France leading the way to a federal, but decentralised Europe.[33] It was a split which was to become a major battle after the war.

Trentin drafted constitutions for both France and for Italy with a similar first clause. The French clause read, 'France is a founder member of the United States of Europe. She is herself a Republic composed of twenty-five autonomous regions, each of which in its turn constitutes a federal order.'[34]

He wrote that 'the union of sixteen Socialist republics is there to prove that countries of different language, customs and traditions may form a structure no less solid than a centralised state, when their union is cemented by a common ideal.'[35]

As the war went on, the influence of the large federalist Left was strongly felt in the new French political organisations. In the spring of 1943 de Gaulle moved to Algiers from London, which became the Free French headquarters. In August de Gaulle was internationally recognised as head of the French Committee for National Liberation (CFLN), the fore-runner of the Provisional Government of France.

That November de Gaulle was strong enough to reorganise

the CFLN, but the eighteen Commissioners had a radical, socialist and federal bias. Among them were the resistance leaders, Frenay and d'Astier de la Vigerie, the former as Commissioner for Prisoners, Deportees and Refugees, and the latter as Commissioner for the Interior.

Acutely sensitive to his own future Jean Monnet arrived in Algiers from his war-time post in Washington to secure his credentials with the future Government of France. Monnet was soon the centre of a group of socialist friends with a common ideal. They included René Mayer, briefly to become Prime Minister in 1953; Robert Marjolin, an economist; Hervé Alphand a brilliant diplomat; and Etiénne Hirsch. All contributed to the thinking of de Gaulle's National Committee on its future European policy.

Monnet recalled that, 'Hervé Alphand had studied how to establish an economic union going well beyond a mere customs union. René Mayer had been thinking in terms of an industrial 'Lotharingia' – a single economic entity in the coal-and-steel producing areas spanning the French, German, and Belgian frontiers.'[36]

According to his memoirs, Monnet told the Committee of National Liberation, 'There will be no peace in Europe if states re-establish themselves on the basis of national sovereignty . . . The countries of Europe are too small to give their peoples the prosperity that is now attainable and therefore necessary. They need wider markets . . . To enjoy the prosperity and social progress that are essential, the States of Europe must form a federation or a 'European entity' which will make them a single economic unit. The British, the Americans and the Russians have worlds of their own into which they can temporarily withdraw. France is bound up in Europe. She cannot escape.'

With the Left strong in de Gaulle's Provisional Government and wide support among politicians and civil servants, though not united on the means, there could be little doubt about France's post-war attitude to the prospect of European unity if de Gaulle were not standing in the way.

Germans Talk, Not Fight, 1933 to 1944

Only a few Germans resisted Hitler and most of them wanted not a German led Europe, but a Europe based on International Socialism not National Socialism. With a German occupied Europe becoming a reality they did not need the British Fabian model of a united Europe.

From 1933, Hitler could only have been ousted by force and there was no serious opposition. Hitler had bought off large sections of the population. Apart from the farmers and industrialists, most Germans were relieved that the economy was recovering and the newly employed thanked him. The natural Teutonic respect for authority, die Obrikgeit, ensured a general obedience that might seem strange in many other countries.

The Generals backed a leader opposed to the iniquities and restrictions of Versailles, standing up for Germany and giving them the chance to rebuild the glories of the German army. Even when defeat looked certain, only a few Generals were prepared to plot against Hitler. Of the resisters even the most determined lacked that ultimate strength of purpose to ensure success. Most were from old families, whose forbears had served Germany or Prussia with distinction, with a total distaste for the jumped up Hitler and the rabble which surrounded him.

One of the few to oppose Hitler actively from as early as 1936, three years after Hitler became Chancellor, was the mayor of Leipzig, Carl Goerdeler. He was revolted by the Nazis' anti-Semitism and warmongering and put his heart and soul into opposition. For years, he was the *de facto* leader of a tiny group of conservatives who tried tirelessly and against all the odds, to warn the major powers of Hitler's intentions. They wrote of their dream of a United States of Europe, but a German-led Europe without Hitler. They were the only non-socialists among any resisters to the Nazis in Europe to promote a federal Europe.

They came mainly from an intellectual group, the Wednesday Club, which met weekly to discuss culture and included the Prussian Minister of Finance, Johannes Popitz, a scholar; a German ambassador, Ulrich von Hassell and a General, Ludwig Beck.

Popitz and von Hassell only woke up to the horror of the Nazis in 1938 and coincidentally that was when both were forced out of office. The apolitical Beck caused some to question but never to act. Von Hassell noted in his diary that 'the principal difficulty with Beck is that he is very theoretical. As Popitz says, a man of tactics, but little will power'.[37]

Beck, Chief of the General Staff, tried to resist Hitler's plans to invade the Rhineland and Czechoslovakia but when Hitler found out Beck quietly resigned, so quietly that unfortunately no-one in Paris or London learnt of it for another three months, well after Hitler had marched into the Sudetenland. Beck calculated that if Germany invaded the well-armed Czechoslovakia it would probably have to fight France as well. If it fought on two fronts, it would lose. This critical point was not appreciated in Britain or the US and Beck had no outside support.

Only Winston Churchill, then still in the 'wilderness', supported the plotters. He sent a crystal clear message that 'crossing of the frontiers of Czechoslovakia by German armies . . . will bring about renewal of the World War . . . Do not, I pray you, be misled upon this point.'

Once Czechoslovakia was conquered the top generals savoured the chance to prosecute a war, even against neutral countries. General Halder, only the year before a conspirator when it looked as though Germany would lose, now relished the prospect of leading the attack on Western Europe.[38]

In October 1940 Carl Goerdeler, the mayor of Leipzig, wrote, 'In view of our country's central position our country has the strongest possible interest in co-operation among civilised peoples of the white race, especially in Europe. Its mission today is to prepare on a larger scale what Prussia achieved in the Zollverein (customs union) a hundred years ago. Then it was a question of German unity, today a club of European states. Given modest and unobtrusive leadership the club will develop into European union of its own accord ... voluntary co-operation among the European states under German leadership is infinitely more important than acquiring territory we do not need, simply for the sake of power or prestige or the gratification of fantastic ideas.'[39]

Just after the German army had attacked Russia in 1941, Goerdeler suggested to the German generals that if Germany stopped the war then 'a European confederation under German leadership could be a reality in ten or twenty years.'

He forecast accurately, 'If we do everything to make our leadership invisible, going out of our way to defer to others in superficial matters, it will be child's play to guide the European states for our mutual benefit. Then, and only then, we shall ... unite the military forces of the European nation states ... The unification of Europe cannot be achieved by ruthlessly forcing nations to toe the line: it must be guided by the kind of wisdom that Bismarck showed over the unification of Germany. The European nation states must be free to conduct their internal affairs in accordance with their own characters and needs ...

'All that is needed to begin with is a system of co-operation so that the member states play the game by the same rules – harmonising their budgetary policies, stabilising their currencies, gradually reducing customs barriers and obstacles to travel... Given that degree of co-operation they could advance in a few years to customs unions, regional associations, currency regulation and so on, and in due course there would be a federal state with military agreements.'[40]

In August 1941, the Beck and Goerdeler group of conspirators tried once to kill Hitler. It was not until the spring of 1942 that the group formally adopted a leader, and because of his seniority and the respect in which he was held, it could only be General Beck, the former Chief of the General Staff.

By 1943 the realisation that Germany was certain to lose the war boosted the number of conspirators. They built sufficient military support to make at least six more attempts on Hitler's life but were frustrated by bad luck and Hitler's deliberate policy of last minute timetable changes.

After that there was virtually no-one left alive to plan any more attempts. Goerdeler and von Hassell were quickly arrested – and the Gestapo rounded up everyone on their list of suspects, which ran to over 7,000 names and the leaders executed. Goerdeler was left alive until 2nd February 1945, in the hope that he might lead the SS leader, Heinrich Himmler, to his contacts in Switzerland and Sweden.

The main civilian group was led by Count Helmuth von Moltke, a great-grandnephew of a famous Field Marshal who ensured Bismarck's military successes against the Austro-Hungarian Empire in 1866 and France in 1870. He formed a group of thinkers known as the Kreisau Circle after his family estate in Upper Silesia. Von Moltke brought together aristocrats, professional men, government officials, trade unionists and the church. His mentor was the diplomat, Ulrich von Hassell of the Beck group. The two groups met to have lively debates about Germany's future.

Von Moltke had found the Germany of the 1930s stifling, and read for the English Bar. As a result he had a network of English friends of similar political views to himself including Lord Lothian and Lionel Curtis.

The Kreisau Circle's philosophy was Christian Socialist. In contrast to Beck's group, all were relatively young. Some, like von Moltke, looked to the West for support. A few found it more natural, particularly from the geographical position of Upper Silesia (now in Poland), to look to Russia and the East for support.

Another leader of the group, Adam von Trott zu Solz, also had strong links abroad. A Rhodes Scholar at Oxford before the war, he went on to do research work in the Far East for the Rhodes Foundation. Then he joined the Foreign Ministry and found there a number of fellow spirits. Von Trott thought Hitler would be overthrown and the Germans would link up with the Russians in a brotherhood of the oppressed, which most of the others feared and the Russians would certainly not have wanted.[41]

In 1942 von Moltke managed to get a letter through to Lionel Curtis using the Rev Hans Schönfeld as a messenger to take it to Bishop Bell of Chichester, who was visiting Stockholm. Von Moltke gave a bleak picture of the tyranny inside Germany, but also talked positively of the spiritual reawakening and the full churches. 'Can you imagine what it means to work as a group when you cannot use the telephone, when you are unable to post letters, when you cannot tell the names of your closest friends for fear that one of them might be caught and might divulge the names under pressure?'

Von Moltke and his friends tried to contact other resistance groups and, like Altiero Spinelli in Italy and Henri Frenay in France, thought of themselves as part of a single European movement which should be co-ordinated. Von Trott received the six 'Political Propositions for Peace' of March 1943 from the American Federal Council of Churches of Christ in which John Foster Dulles played the leading role.

Visser 't Hooft, the General Secretary of the World Council of Churches in Geneva, acted as the post box and returned von Trott's reply eight months later. Von Trott agreed with Dulles on the need for an international organisation especially for Europe, but emphasised that it must not be done by force and must be achieved by the countries concerned. He added that outside support – presumably American – might be needed for the transition period.[42]

The Circle ran a series of conferences advocating nationalisation of heavy industry, banking and insurance. They wanted a European federation of states in which Germany as a sovereign state was abolished. Among the papers the group left behind was one written by von Moltke in April 1941. 'Initial Situation, Aims and Tasks' is ranked by federalists in importance with the Ventotene Manifesto and Léon Blum's 'A l'échelle humaine' and is similar in content.[43]

In common with Spinelli, most members of the Kreisau Circle had little or nothing to do with active resistance against Hitler and the Nazi regime. In the words of the American journalist, William Shirer, they were planning for 'the millennium'.

Von Moltke's American friend Dorothy Thompson appealed to him in a series of short wave broadcasts from New York in 1942. She called him guardedly, 'Hans', and reminded him of their last meeting drinking tea on a terrace by a lake. 'I said that one day you would have to demonstrate by deed, drastic deeds, where you stood ... and I remember that I asked you whether you and your friends would ever have the courage to act ...'[44]

With the single exception of Adam von Trott, who took part in the 20th July plot, they did not. That lack of action was the difference between the Kreisau Circle and the Beck group. The Kreisau group was sentenced to death by hanging, simply for thinking.

'God Moves In Mysterious Ways'

A few friends took over the Protestant Churches and put their authority behind a United States of Europe. The process can be dated to the 1920 Lambeth Conference of the Church of England[45] when one man moved the ecumenical movement from the purely spiritual to the political. William Temple, then Bishop of Manchester, towered over that meeting: he was one of the greatest preachers of his day; his sermons packed churches and he was widely known as a radical Bolshevik. Temple rapidly led the Protestant churches towards a much less spiritual role. They were looking increasingly like a political party, and a very left wing one.

The high point was July 1937 when Temple, by then Archbishop of York, aided and abetted by the then Dean of Canterbury, George Bell, later Bishop of Chichester, launched the World Council of Churches (WCC).

Thirty-five clergymen attended the 1937 meeting at Westfield College, London University and Temple hoodwinked most of them. Only two bishops voted against the motion to set up the WCC because they guessed its purpose was political, not spiritual. It was: Temple and Bell had deliberately manipulated the meeting.[46]

Since 1923 Bell had been an enthusiastic supporter of Chatham House: he had persuaded the Church of England to set up its own Council on Foreign Relations, named after the American group.

To create the WCC the two main ecumenical movements,[47] representing over a hundred Protestant and Orthodox Churches, were to be combined into one. Every Church had to approve it and, interrupted by the war, it was to take a long time. Meanwhile the chairman of the Provisional Council was William Temple, with the Dutchman Dr Willem Visser 't Hooft and a Presbyterian Minister, William Paton,[48] as joint general secretaries.

Naturally, the headquarters of the WCC was Geneva. When Visser 't Hooft first went to work there in 1924 with the World Committee of the YMCA, it was 'the Mecca of the new internationalism'. 't Hooft wrote, 'Many believed firmly that a fundamental change had taken place in international relations. The task of the churches and the international Christian organisations appeared therefore to be to create the new spirit of brotherhood and internationalism which would enable the League to live and to develop.'[49]

In the summer of 1939 with world war only two months away, fifteen theologians and fifteen laymen held a last minute meeting in Geneva to discuss 'the Churches and the International Crisis'. The lay group was dominated by international lawyers including Professor Alfred Zimmern from Britain, and John Foster Dulles from America.[50]

Dulles, an increasingly important figure in American politics, though without any official position other than his membership of the Council on Foreign Relations, was prepared to make considerable concessions to Nazi Germany. Slow to realise the enormity of the Nazi regime, he thought Hitler was a passing phenomenon. According to John McCloy, the late UN High Commissioner to West Germany, Dulles tried 'to rationalise this Hitler movement'. His cold intellectual mind did not help him to see all the angles of a problem.

Dulles shook his partners in his New York law firm. He was prepared to carry on dealing with Germany after 1935 when the Jews were deprived of their German citizenship. They forced him to change his mind. He was isolationist and strongly against American intervention in Europe. He wrote, 'The fundamental fact is that the national system of wholly independent sovereign states is completing its cycle of usefulness.'

The Geneva meeting set an agenda to be discussed during the war by groups in the US and Britain such as 'how far would the creation of federal organisations in each Continent be a useful step towards the organic organisation of the world in regional bodies?'[51]

William Paton had already set up a British organisation, the Peace Aims Group, in 1937 to discuss those very issues. When they went home after the Geneva meeting, Rosswell Barnes and J. F. Dulles launched its American counterpart, the Committee for a Just and Durable Peace.

William Temple chaired the British group based at Balliol College, Oxford. The others were the agnostic Professor Toynbee, Professor Sandy Lindsay, and Professor Sir Alfred Zimmern – all friends. The Peace Aims group was like a reincarnation of the Cataline Club they had formed as students which met every week for what they called an 'Unholy Lunch'.

The enthusiastic Toynbee organised yet another Peace Aims Group in his Foreign Research and Press Service (FRPS) which he had already manoeuvred within the British Foreign Office. It soon meshed with the first Peace Aims group.

The policies of the World Council of Churches, run by a group of radical socialists, fed into one of the central and most important British Government departments and reached equally influential circles in the US. The Council on Foreign Relations in the US – Dulles and friends – had a group called 'War and Peace Studies' which was annexed by the State Department along with its CFR staff.

Throughout the war the British and the Americans consulted on each step of their debate on the future of the world and of Europe. Both groups tried to use their powerful contacts in the American State Department and the British Foreign Office to influence British and American plans for the future. In Britain they were unsuccessful; in the US they were eventually to dominate American policy.

When war broke out, Visser 't Hooft in Geneva continued to push for a condemnation of Nazi Germany by the members of the World Council of Churches. Top priority for his small Swiss group was a post-war settlement, even though the war was only weeks old and the victor far from certain. His German colleague, Dr Schönfeld, suggested that the big four states of Britain, France, Germany and Italy should create a system of multilateral pacts to establish the new European order that would become a United States of Europe.

But it was difficult to get the leading churchmen even to condemn 'the violation of whole nations'; in early 1940 the majority wanted peace mediation between the main powers and the German Government. None of them wanted to criticise Germany which was successfully conquering Europe and, importantly for some of them, allied with their friend, Communist Russia.

That same year Germany tried and failed to replace the Ecumenical Council by an 'inter-church working group of Continental churches'. Germany wanted to control the Churches and the WCC, even in neutral Geneva, was forced to fight hard for its survival.

The pressure from the British and American federalists working together was unrelenting. In January 1941 William Temple organised what became a famous landmark conference for the Churches at Malvern. Dulles followed it a year later[41] with the Delaware conference in the States; their peace proposals took another year to be published.

At Malvern, Temple added five proposals to the spiritual

ones Pope Pius XII had carefully made in his Christmas 1939 address;[52] Temple's went far beyond the spiritual. He orchestrated the British Bishops to call for a monetary system to make all production available to everyone, support for the unemployed, equal status for labour and capital, material needs to be more important than the balance of trade, and last but not least 'the unification of Europe as a co-operative commonwealth, first in common effort for the satisfaction of general need and secondly in such political institutions as express the common purpose and facilitate its development.'[53]

In October 1941, the first delegation of American churchmen from Dulles' group[54] visited Toynbee and his friends at Balliol College, Oxford to discuss the issues. The Malvern Declaration took three months to reach Visser 't Hooft in Geneva by an underground route. He added more detail[55] and sent it back to Temple and Dulles. He thought that ' . . . some form of European federation will probably be acceptable to the large masses of Europeans who seek above all a real insurance against further wars and against economic ruin. And most countries will probably be willing to accept a considerable limitation of their sovereignty.'[56]

Like Hitler and some French and German socialist resisters, 't Hooft wanted to break the nation states up into smaller units like 'Prussia, Bavaria, Austria, Alsace-Lorraine, Northern France, Southern France . . .', divide and rule.

The British Peace Aims group (Temple, Toynbee, Zimmern, Paton and Lindsay) said they wanted European unity, because 'multitudinous national sovereignties' had led to Hitler's rise. Paton reported that since what he called the highly logical approach of Franco-Anglo Union had failed, some kind of British-American association based on human rights should be the new world order.

Toynbee had thought up the Franco-Anglo Union plan,

Zimmern had drafted it and they had used Jean Monnet to push it into the British Cabinet. Now that it had failed they were returning to another Fabian idea, published by Clarence Streit two years before in 'Union Now': Anglo-American union as the heart of a group of democracies. These powers should police the world.

Their German colleague in the WCC in Geneva, Hans Schönfeld, disagreed and reiterated the case for a European Commonwealth to include Germany, from which federation would slowly grow. That was the old Prussian approach also adopted by Carl Goerdeler, the German resister.

J. F. Dulles organised the Delaware conference, between 3rd and 5th March 1942 at Ohio Wesleyan University. Three hundred and seventy-seven delegates from Protestant churches from all over North America endorsed a peace settlement, the result of two years work by a Commission, also chaired by Dulles.

They wanted a world government with 'an international legislative body, an international court with adequate jurisdiction, international administrative bodies with necessary powers, and adequate international police forces and provision of world-wide economic sanctions.'[57]

Dulles brought the results of that conference to Oxford himself, and Toynbee acted as unofficial go-between with the Foreign Office. He met more members of the British Fabian Society including the journalists Barbara Ward, the assistant editor of the 'Economist', and the Communist assistant editor of 'The Times', Professor E. H. Carr.

Dulles was introduced to Sir Anthony Eden, the Foreign Secretary, and Sir Alexander Cadogan.[58] Cadogan confided to his diary 'Monday 13th July (1942): 'Lunched with A. (Eden) in his flat. J. F. Dulles there ... J.F.D. the woolliest type of useless pontificating American ... Heaven help us!'[59]

That summer there was a return match. Dulles, as

chairman of the Trustees of the Rockefeller Foundation,[60] invited Toynbee to the US. Through the Council on Foreign Relations Dulles arranged speaking engagements for Toynbee to its branches. After New York, Toynbee spent two weeks in Washington with the State Department. Toynbee's message there, and on his whirlwind tour of US cities, was to encourage America to end its isolationism, be active in world affairs, and subordinate national sovereignty to a world government.

That autumn Henry Van Dusen, President of the American Commission for a Just and Durable Peace, arranged a New York dinner party for Toynbee to meet Henry Luce, the influential publisher of 'Time' 'Life' and 'Fortune' magazines. Like many others Luce was bowled over by Toynbee. Thanks to Luce, after the war when Toynbee's abridged version of his 'A Study in History' was published, Toynbee became a cult figure in America. He appeared on the front cover of 'Time' magazine with the headline, 'Our civilisation is not doomed'.[61]

On 18th March 1943 Dulles held a New York press conference to announce the Delaware Six Pillars of Peace. Naturally they proposed a federal and regional world structure, and the end of the 'uncoordinated independence of some 25 sovereign states' in Europe.[62] Copies were sent to every minister of religion in America.

William Temple, as the new Archbishop of Canterbury, gave the same idea the full weight of his authority shortly before he died in 1944: the future of Europe should include 'the creation and development of common institutions and agencies, in the social and economic as well as the political sphere, to give effect to these common purposes and to embody the growing sense of European unity.'[63]

A *Spider In The Web*

Visser 't Hooft of the WCC sat like a spider in the middle of a web linking all the churchmen in occupied Europe with those in Britain and the US, and European and British federalists with resistance groups in occupied countries. Over and above the defeat of Nazi Germany, they all had one thing in common – the creation of a United States of Europe.

't Hooft had created a double role for himself. Known to his WCC employers, he co-ordinated and developed ideas for the post-war world. Unknown to them, because it would have severely compromised both neutral Switzerland and the Churches, he helped the Dutch resistance.

He ran a courier service known as the 'Swiss Road'. A centre in the Netherlands collected pamphlets and other information and using forged identity cards and microfilm, couriers brought the material to Geneva where, hidden inside books, it went to Spain, then to Portugal and then London.

By 1943 the Swiss Road was a regular service used both for material on the future of Europe, so close to 't Hooft's heart, and for intelligence for the paramilitary forces. Much of the material, forwarded all round occupied Europe, came from the Temple/Toynbee Peace Aims Group in Britain and from Dulles' group in the US.

Within his home country, 't Hooft tried to push the cause of a United States of Europe. Via contacts in Amsterdam he formed 'a political committee of the Swiss Road' of people who were in close touch with one of the underground newspapers, 'Vrij Nederland'. As 't Hooft put it in his memoirs, there was 'the less obvious battle for the minds of men which had to be fought in the occupied countries and for which resistance leaders needed all the help that could be given.'

By January 1944 such a wealth of material was getting through to the Netherlands from London that 'Vrij Nederland' started a second paper, 'International Information Papers'. It reproduced articles from Layton's 'Economist', for which Fabians like Barbara Ward wrote.[64]

Among his countrymen 't Hooft overdid his role in promoting a United States of Europe: he was regarded with grave distrust by Queen Wilhelmina in London. 't Hooft felt he had been misunderstood.

When an Allied victory was certain 't Hooft set up a 'Reconstruction Department' in Geneva to plan for the new Europe. In the spring of 1945 John D. Rockefeller Jr, invited 't Hooft to a private meeting and gave him $1 million for his ecumenical work. (Dulles was the chairman of the trustees of Rockefeller's Foundation).

't Hooft was in regular contact with most resistance movements especially the Dutch, the few German resisters, including von Trott, the Italians led by Altiero Spinelli who were using his house for meetings, and through Soutou and others he kept in touch with French groups in the South of France like Frenay's Combat.

Connected to this same network was John Foster's brother, Allen Dulles, who from 1943 was the head of the Office of Strategic Services (OSS) in Geneva. As he explained in his book 'The German Underground', he was very much aware of the views of the resistance leaders and the sort of Europe they hoped for. After the war Dulles was to be director of the CIA and president of the CFR.

A Post-Script: Benelux Is Born

For all the planning by Federal Union in London, by Arnold Toynbee, J. F. Dulles and their friends and the resistance movements, the only structure to emerge immediately after the war was Benelux.

Belgian socialist politicians took the example of the Prussians' Zollverein, which had forced German union via the backdoor, to create a customs union of Belgium, the Netherlands and Luxembourg. The Dutch were reluctant to the point of embarrassment and the Luxembourgers, already economically tied to the Belgians, had no choice.

Among the 15,000 Belgians exiled in wartime London, the socialists were the only coherent political group so there was no serious opposition to their plans. Their powerful leaders included a former and a current chairman of the Socialist International who opposed Belgium's short independence;[65] the Prime Minister, Hubert Pierlot and the then Foreign Minister, Paul-Henri Spaak.

Spaak was the prime mover. He had rapidly risen to power in pre-war Belgium. He had joined the Government at 35, was Foreign Secretary at 37 and Prime Minister at 38. He came from a political family. His maternal grandfather, Paul Janson, was the 'most renowned Left-winger nineteenth century Belgium had known' and did well enough to buy a chateau just over the border in France.[66]

That in one sense was going home: Janson was the grandson of a Parisian who had fought under the Tricolour during the French revolution. Spaak inherited a Jacobin tradition – anti priests and anti kings.

In 1927 the young lawyer wrote, 'The Socialist revolution is our ideal . . . we accept neither the principal of private property . . . nor that of a wage earning class . . . nor that of the bourgeois family which passes on wealth, nor that of the Fatherland . . . our Socialist aims to destroy and extirpate them.'[67] A Marxist, he co-operated with Communists but was against Stalin's suppression of freedom of thought. Over many years Spaak was to move from Marxism to a more liberal position, social democrat in his terms, but still far to the left of Anglo-Saxon liberalism. On a 1964 visit to

Yugoslavia, two years before he retired from politics, he admired Tito's 'Socialist experiment'.

Early in 1941 Spaak and the other three members of the Belgian Government-in-exile set up a 'Commission pour l'Étude des Problèmes d'Apres-guerre'. Its quick first draft recommended limiting sovereignty. By August 1943 and its fifth report, it backed a Western European economic group. The ambitious Spaak announced the result a month early.[68]

The idea was an extension of the economic union which Luxembourg and Belgium had signed on 25th July 1925.[69] Tiny Luxembourg, surrounded by major powers, had been part of the German Zollverein until the First World War and was the only Zollverein state not to be part of the German Empire. After the war the Luxembourg government thought they could not continue alone economically, and preferred a link with France because they had protected agriculture in common. For political reasons that was not possible. In the 1920s and 1930s Luxembourg and Belgium worked towards a common market for goods and services.[70]

Not all Belgians felt the same way as Spaak. Some argued for an Atlantic Alliance in which small nations would have a part to play. Frans van Cauwelaert, the Catholic President of the House of Representatives, wrote, 'The European nations are incompatible in too many ways for close interdependence to be possible. There are differences of language and culture, religion and manners, types and traditions of government . . . Above all there is the justifiable desire to prevent the loss of our independence and our freedom . . . through gradual enslavement by one or more Powers seeking, as would be inevitably the case, to exploit the European Union to their own ends.

'All systems of federation have one common fundamental defect. They all necessarily involve the subjugation of the small nations to the great Powers. The former only achieve

peace at the price of their freedom.' All the states and principalities of Germany could attest to that.

Van Cauwelaert argued that Belgium was not a 'frontier
province of a continent with its centre in Berlin and Vienna,
she forms a gateway to the Atlantic'. He added 'If one day
Europe were to be united under a single master, she would
turn against America. What is to be done? The new international order for which we are thirsting must be established
on a wider basis than that offered by a European
federation . . .'[71]

The Dutch agreed with him: the weight of Dutch opinion
was behind an Atlantic organisation and a new form of a
League of Nations. The unenthusiastic Dutch Foreign Minister, Van Kleffens, recognised that the Netherlands would
have to give up its pre-war policy of neutrality; he wanted
military alliances and to remain close to Britain. No European arrangements alone could withstand a new German
aggression. In a European group the Dutch would be dependent on the larger power, France. Like van Cauwelaert, the
Dutch were afraid that a European organisation would lead
to a Franco-German tyranny. They favoured confederation
or co-operation with their Belgian neighbours, and perhaps
with the Scandinavians as well.

Paul Rijkens, the chairman of Unilever, played a leading
role among London refugees running a debate about the
future in the 'Vrij Nederland' resistance newspaper he had
founded. A group of 200 specialists set up in early 1941 by
Rijkens at Unilever to study every aspect of national life,
rejected the idea of a United States of Europe. So too did the
Dutch Government.[72]

Only Pieter Kerstens, the Minister for Economic Affairs,
favoured Benelux. Long negotiations led to a monetary agreement on 21st October 1943 fixing an official rate for the
florin and the Belgian franc. Just after the Belgian and

Netherlands Governments returned home they signed an agreement on 5th September 1944 at La Haye creating the Benelux customs union. They described it as a transition to a political union.

The Dutch, reluctant partners, ignored the agreement until March 1947 when, under pressure, they made a few half hearted concessions to the Belgians. In June 1948 they agreed an economic union and set a timetable but did not implement it. Under fierce pressure from the Dutch Parliament they renounced the agreement.[73] Only in 1958 was the Benelux Union eventually signed. By that time much water had gone under the European bridge.

CHAPTER 4: THE AMERICAN TRIGGER

War-time Lobby Groups

Early in the Second World War the Americans began to plan for peace. Naturally they intended the new world would be both congenial and advantageous for America. Uniquely much of that planning process was carried on outside Government but with Government blessing. The process was dominated by a network of friends and colleagues, mainly Ivy League graduates with law degrees. These men frequently moved jobs between university teaching, business and government, so extending the network.

Dominant among them were the two Dulles brothers, John Foster and Allen. J. F. Dulles operated through the American Federal Council of Churches and had close links with Arnold Toynbee and his Peace Aims Group in Britain and with like minded resistance leaders in occupied Europe all connected via Visser 't Hooft in Geneva. Allen Dulles, in the OSS, had links to the same groups. The brothers dominated the small but prestigious Council on Foreign Relations (CFR) of which they were founder members.

Although the CFR was a private organisation – like its alter ego Chatham House – its members had much more influence with the upper echelons of the State Department than did the elected Senate Committee on Foreign Relations.

Between early 1940 and 1945 the CFR sent 682 memoranda to the State Department funded by $300,000 of grants from the Rockefeller Foundation. Under President Harry Truman, the first post-war president, forty-two per cent of the top foreign policy jobs were held by CFR members.[1]

Many of the CFR network were also members of the three other influential lobby groups which were to play a key role in the creation of Europe. The oldest of these groups was the National Planning Association founded in 1934 by the lawyer, and later US Supreme Court Justice, Felix Frankfurter.[2] Born in Vienna, Frankfurter was taken to the US as a child. His family were poor and the highly intelligent Frankfurter worked hard to reach Harvard. While teaching there during the First World War he became a close friend of Harold Laski, ten years his junior. Laski and Frankfurter shared political views of the far left. Both wanted to smash the British Empire and then contain the nation states within a world organisation.

At Oxford University Laski had joined the Fabian Society. He became a world renowned Professor of Political Science at the London School of Economics and was well known as an outspoken Marxist. He was on the executive committee of the Fabian Society between 1921 and 1936, its chairman from 1946 to 1948 and on the executive of the Labour Party from 1939 and its chairman in 1945.[3]

Between the wars Laski and Frankfurter frequently exchanged visits and ideas. Laski was also a friend of President F. D. Roosevelt. On one of his visits to Britain as a Visiting Professor at Oxford University for the academic year 1933 to 1934, Frankfurter was introduced by Laski to the first Fabian front organisation, Political and Economic Planning (PEP) which had been formed in 1931.[4]

The Fabian idea was to gain influence through organisations which crossed the political spectrum. PEP deliberately
did not publish membership lists so that anyone could feel
free to serve on it. PEP's findings were made public under
the name of the organisation, never the individuals. Importantly only some of its members were Fabian socialists
though, unknown to many of its members, they had founded
it and continued to guide it. To give it influence it included
Liberals and Conservatives. Some businesses were persuaded
from time to time to give funds or lend their names and
respectability.[5]

From the first PEP promoted Government regulation of
the whole of industry and agriculture, the nationalisation
of large land areas and of electricity generation. In Britain
that pattern of organisation was to be repeated many times,
for example with Federal Union and later the Federal Trust
which today is promoting ever increasing powers for the
European Union and a major education programme in
schools and universities to 'enhance the European dimension
in the curriculum'.[6]

On his return to the US Frankfurter started an American
version of PEP, the National Planning Association, and with
regular visits across the Atlantic the two groups kept in
touch. The NPA spawned more groups, and deliberately the
link with the Fabian Society became ever more clouded. Soon
after the NPA came the Business Advisory Council (BAC)
which promoted central planning and a partnership between
the state and large businesses along the lines of Roosevelt's
New Deal. In 1941 the Committee for Economic Development (CED) was founded. There have been many more since.

While some Americans, like Frankfurter, were driven to
propose a united Europe by their left wing politics others
thought in terms of security or of business. The most vocal,
the Republican J. F. Dulles had a consistent policy towards

Europe. He wanted to see a unified Europe, one state, and wanted to eradicate the nation states because in his view they caused wars. As he said in a speech in London in 1943: 'The continent of Europe has been the world's great fire hazard. Now the whole structure is consumed in flames . . . from a purely selfish standpoint any American program for peace must seek a form of federation of continental Europe.' That was the general tenor of the many memoranda from the CFR to the State Department throughout the war.

American businessmen were fully aware of the importance of Continental Europe to US trade: exports to Europe just before the war were just over forty-one per cent of all US exports. For America to prosper after the war and achieve full employment a vigorous European economy was essential. They wanted to reduce tariff barriers and other anti-American trade devices like Imperial Preference. Those who were members of the CFR and the other lobby groups put their point of view forcefully to the State department.

While Cordell Hull was Secretary of State the Dulles' point of view gained little ground. Cordell Hull feared the effect of a European power bloc which could encourage other power blocs to develop and free trade would be undermined. He influenced President Roosevelt who was in any case sympathetic to the USSR which he did not want to alienate. Roosevelt believed that his ally the USSR would help to rebuild Europe; the US and the USSR would be the two major powers in the world.

The Bear Advances 1942 – 1945

None of those on either side of the Atlantic who had planned before and during the Second World War for a European superstate had the political power to replace the failed Nazi

United States of Europe. A cataclysmic event was needed. The USSR provided it and America responded.

Those Americans who had argued fruitlessly for a federal Europe then had the chance to start the process of eradicating the nation states from Europe. Within three years of the end of the war a United States of Europe was American policy. In that short time American foreign policy moved from one extreme to another, from sharing the peace with a former ally, the USSR, to an acknowledgement of a Russian military threat.

The USSR knew exactly what it wanted to achieve: to free the Motherland, and create the deepest possible belt between Mother Russia and the rest of the world. To do that it used all its resources, diplomatic, military and subversive. From the time of its victory at Stalingrad at the end of 1942, the turning point of the war, the USSR first fought to recover its own lands from the Germans and then to threaten German occupied central Europe.

Unlike Roosevelt, Winston Churchill was well aware of the Russian threat.

During the war the Central European countries knew there was little hope of a truly independent future. The old Austro-Hungarian Empire had been a relatively benign overlord in which many races lived together in harmony but after its death in 1919 most only had a short independence before being conquered by the Nazis. Now they were under threat again from the East.

If the politicians exiled in London had understood President Roosevelt's attitude early in the war, then they would have known that they had no hope of freedom. Led by the great General Wladyslaw Sikorski of Poland, they spent their exile devising ways to regain their independence, and talked of re-creating a version of the old Austro-Hungarian Empire. Sikorski mooted wider associations from Scandinavia to the

Aegean Sea. He and Edvard Benes of Czechoslovakia talked to eight other countries[7] and ran a series of committees which increased in number as the talks continued. They reached no conclusions.

On his first visit to the US in March 1941, General Sikorski told President Roosevelt of his attempts to create Central European federations. He returned a year later hoping for support. By that time the American Government was paying closer attention to the role of the USSR after the war but was still sympathetic to the USSR. The Poles did not know that.

In December 1942 Sikorski wrote to Sumner Welles of the US State Department, an advocate of a federal Europe, 'I was struck the other day by the boldness of your conceptions on the problem of Federation. The Polish Government has constantly championed the ideal of Federation . . . I advocated co-operation between lesser states of Europe as well as the establishment among them of federated blocks, which would entail a voluntary limitation of State sovereignty.'[8]

Dr Joseph Retinger, Sikorski's right hand man, organised about twenty meetings on European unity between October 1942 and 1944 with all the exiled Foreign Ministers in the Polish Prime Minister's office. Retinger said that although the meetings were not publicised, J. F. Dulles, 'then only the representative of the United Churches of America', heard of them; 'I remember spending several hours with him and discussing . . . the general idea of the unity of Europe'.[9] Retinger also organised the 'New Europe Circle' of exiled civil servants with eighteen nationalities including representatives from Federal Union. At one of their public luncheons the Belgian Prime Minister, Paul van Zeeland, announced the plan for the Benelux Union.

The Russians were against a united Europe. They used every device, fair and foul, to stop a bloc on their own doorstep, whether it was an alliance of central European states or a United States of Europe. Any union to Russians minds, paranoically worried about encirclement and invasion, would only be a small step to a military bloc threatening its Western border.

When the idea of a united Europe was raised during the First World War, the exiled Lenin had replied, 'A United States of Europe . . . would be possible only as an "agreement between the European capitalists" and "only for the purpose of jointly suppressing Socialism in Europe." '[10] Naturally Lenin meant a Europe controlled by Russia. In 1930 Stalin had actively campaigned against Briand's proposal for a Europe of sovereign states calling it 'a bourgeois movement for intervention against the Soviet Union'.

So when the exiled governments of Eastern Europe in London planned a Central European federation, not surprisingly Stalin and Molotov, his Foreign Minister, resumed the offensive with an iron fist thinly disguised in a velvet glove. They worked on the weakest link, the Czech Prime Minister Benes and under duress, he cracked.

The Russians increased the pressure. In January 1943 they told Benes that any Czech union with Poland was a nonstarter. In the April Stalin broke off diplomatic relations with Sikorski's government, recalled his Ambassadors in London and Washington and threatened to make a separate peace with Hitler. The fearful Benes dropped discussions with the Poles. Stalin tested Western resolve by starting to put pressure on the Allies: he talked of Eastern and Western European spheres of influence with Poland in the Eastern half.

The excuse the Russians used was the Germans' announcement in April 1943 of the discovery of the graves of 10,000 Polish officers and NCOs shot at Katyn. The Germans accused the Russians. The Poles knew that was true. Stalin accused the Germans. For nearly half a century many in the

West believed the Germans were guilty. Stalin condemned the exiled Polish Government for falling for German propaganda. Soon afterwards the Russians formed a Polish National Committee. A year later, as their own armies advanced westwards, they started to pull the strings of their puppet government in Poland.

On 4th July 1943 General Sikorski died in an aeroplane crash and his death left a big gap in Polish politics to the benefit of the USSR. As suddenly as Sikorski died, the inter-Governmental activity in London stopped.

As the war went on Britain's power was weakening compared to that of its two major allies. Churchill's persuasive voice was often ignored. Churchill was totally dedicated to destroying the Nazis, then to restoring the European balance of power – to some an outdated concept. To stop the USSR advancing beyond its pre-war frontiers he was prepared to negotiate with it but he knew the Allies had to act early in the war when at their most united and the USSR unsure of the military result. Churchill knew Hitler's defeat would create a vacuum at Europe's heart which the USSR would fill if the West did not back the countries of Middle Europe. He supported a Danubian federation.

At the Teheran conference in November 1943, primarily devoted to D-Day planning, Churchill's solution to the German problem harked back to the nineteenth century. Prussia should be isolated and a Danubian, and also perhaps a South German, Confederation formed. Stalin opposed it.

According to Charles Bohlen of the American delegation, Stalin wanted Germany, 'to be broken up and kept broken up . . . the result would be that the Soviet Union would be the only important military and political force on the Continent of Europe.'[11] Stalin had tacit support from Roosevelt who suggested dividing Germany into five parts under the United Nations.

Everyone feared the possible revival of Germany. Stalin told Churchill that he thought Germany would recover within fifteen to twenty years. Churchill replied 'that the world must be made safe for at least fifty years. If it was only for fifteen to twenty years then we should have betrayed our soldiers.'

By the time of the Yalta conference in February 1945 and just before Roosevelt's death, the Russians' policy towards Europe was at last raising concern in the American Government. The balance of American opinion was tilting towards rebuilding Europe and against Russian expansion westwards. By then it was far too late to undo the effect of Roosevelt's pro-Russian policies. The war was nearly over and there was no practical way to stop the Russian advance through central Europe. Roosevelt needed Russian support to win the war in the Far East.

With victory in sight, Poland dominated seven out of eight plenary sessions. Churchill was increasingly anxious about the USSR's intentions towards Europe and told the American President that '*it was undesirable that any more of Western Europe than necessary should be occupied by the Russians*'. By that time Poland was already in the USSR's sphere of influence.

The Big Three agreed on Poland's frontiers, but not clearly enough. The new western border of Poland would be the Eastern Neisse river. The USSR was to renege on its undertakings at Yalta on Poland: its armies and its influence were to roll westwards – to the Western Neisse river. It was a catastrophe. Churchill commented, 'One day the Germans would want their territory back, and the Poles would not be able to stop them.'[12]

The Big Three agreed to divide Germany into four zones. Again Churchill tried to resist the arbitrary and quick dismemberment of Germany without any reference to its history, peoples and economy. He tried to revive the balance of power by advocating restoring France as a great power.

Churchill wrote after the war, 'We all deeply feared the might of a united Germany. Prussia had a great history of her own. It would be possible to make a stern but honourable peace with her, and at the same time to create, in modern forms, what had been in general outline the Austro-Hungarian Empire, of which it has been well said, "If did not exist it would have to be invented" . . . But vast and disastrous changes have fallen upon us . . . The Polish frontiers exist only in name and Poland lies quivering in the Russo-Communist grip. Germany has indeed been partitioned but only by hideous division into zones of military occupation. About this tragedy it can only be said IT CANNOT LAST.'[13]

Before the Potsdam conference of July 1945 Churchill again expressed his anxieties about Russia. He doubted that President Truman was convinced by the Russian threat and sent him a telegram (in which he used the phrase 'An iron curtain is drawn down upon their front') emphasising his fears about Russia, especially with a prostrate Germany leaving the way open for the Russians to advance to the Atlantic. He urged Truman to come to an understanding with Russia before the Allies lost military strength.

After the war the USSR continued its advance to build a barrier protecting the Motherland. The USSR over-ran the three small and indefendable Baltic States and was handed large parts of Poland. Poland was arbitrarily picked up and moved westwards into Germany; the German provinces of Silesia and Pomerania became largely Polish. Twelve million Poles and Germans were caught in the wrong country. The USSR continued to undermine the 'independent' Governments of Poland, Czechoslovakia, Romania and Bulgaria.

Some leading Americans agreed with the Roosevelt line that Europe was 'finished', Russia would take over. The

British Government was split: some British Labour Ministers sympathised with Russia. Churchill, by then in opposition, renewed his calls for the freedom of Eastern European countries.

America Vacillates 1945 – 1947

For a long time George Kennan of the US State Department, an expert on the Soviet Union, was a lone voice calling for America to stand up to the Russians before they created their buffer zone of Central European states.

In the first months of peace, Secretary of State James Byrnes tried an increasingly difficult balancing act. The Americans wanted independent and democratic central European states and were appalled by Russia's brutality. But they also harked back to wartime comradeship with Russia. The two positions were incompatible.

First the Americans tried the 'soft' approach – tough talking. Then they withdrew Lend-Lease. Finally they had to recognise the reality of a Communist regime in Poland. Yet they still talked of free trade with Poland. The US was not prepared to use its power, and certainly not its armed forces, to back the independence of Central Europe.

The British were increasingly irritated by the vacillating Americans. In November 1945, Lord Halifax, the British Ambassador to the US, wrote to the Foreign Office of 'this wishful attitude about American-Soviet relations . . . America is behaving like a lumbering young giant, racked by indecision, troubled by a guilty conscience and uncertain about how long his strength will endure.'[14]

The USSR was not the only major international headache for the US. George Kennan wrote of the first two years after the war, 'We were not even clear in our minds whether we wanted (the) German economy rehabilitated. Sometimes we thought we did. Sometimes we thought we didn't. Sometimes we just agreed to disagree among ourselves.'[15] In their own zone in Germany the Americans had only two priorities, denazification and democracy. There was ferocious debate on whether or not Germany should be reduced to an agricultural state and its industry dismembered. While that argument raged nothing was done to rebuild Germany and survival problems mounted.

America havered and the USSR menaced the countries on the fringes of its own empire. It was only in February 1946 that any notice was taken of Kennan's fears about the USSR. His well publicised Moscow telegram, outlining Russian strategy, led to his recall and a two year ascendancy in Washington. Kennan showed that American and Russian aims were irreconcilable. He predicted that Soviet policy would be 'to use all means to infiltrate, divide and weaken the West ... including foreign communist parties, diplomacy, international organisations, starting false trails to divert and probing weak spots.' In the long term he forecast that Communist Russia had within it the seeds of its own decay.[16]

On 9th February 1946 Stalin made a big rearmament speech. The next month, Churchill declared: 'From Stettin in the Baltic to Trieste in the Adriatic an iron curtain has descended across the continent.' Churchill wanted to free Eastern Europe and contain Russian advances to the south, in Iran and Turkey. In the US his views were considered radical. In Britain one hundred and five Labour MPs called on the Government to dissociate itself publicly from Churchill's aggressive speech. A year later most were to recognise Churchill was right.

His bluff called, Stalin reacted furiously. He claimed the governments of Central Europe had aided and abetted Germany when it attacked the USSR. The iron curtain fell further.[17] Then Stalin tried and failed to create a southern buffer zone by taking control of Yugoslavia and Greece. By July 1946 there was a gulf between the US and the USSR.

Stalin's many allies in the West increased the tension. In Belgium, the number of Communist representatives doubled from their pre-war level to twenty-three including two ministers, and then four in 1946. In France the Communists were the strongest single party.[18] In Italy a quarter of the Constituent Assembly were Communists, with two million members in the country. When the sympathetic socialists were taken into account, the pro-Soviet Left was overwhelmingly dominant nearly everywhere in Europe.

A starving Western Europe looked vulnerable to an invasion from the East. Many cities in Germany and Britain were partially rubble; so too in France, Belgium and the Netherlands. Everywhere there were refugees, twelve million Germans alone, desperate for food, clothes and housing. UNRRA was keeping many millions alive. Industry was shattered. Everything was in short supply and rationed, or no supply at all.

The final blow was the weather. The winter of 1946/47, the worst in living memory, made a bad situation desperate. It started in the fourth week of January 1947. In England the January monthly average temperature of minus 1.9°C was the lowest ever recorded. Ice formed on the sea along the East coast. Some places had no sun for a month. Snow ploughs got lost in the drifts which in some places was eight metres deep. It went on for over two months. On mainland Europe it was worse, much worse.

Then the snow melted and the flooding started. Especially in the Low Countries, many starved to death. Live stock drowned or starved, seed for the next year could not be planted in flooded fields. There was not enough energy to run industry. Economies were breaking down.

The Marshall Plan 1947

A combination of events galvanised the US to make a U-turn on foreign policy. In the January, General George C. Marshall replaced James Byrnes as Secretary of State. That same month the British gave sudden notice of withdrawal from Greece and Turkey which they could no longer afford to support. That raised fears of an imminent Communist take-over.

General Marshall responded quickly with a planning team which recommended American aid. President Truman's statement on the aid did not dwell on specifics, ' . . . it must be the policy of the United States to support free peoples who are resisting subjugation by armed minorities or by outside pressure'. Known as the Truman Doctrine, it ended American isolationism.

On 28th April 1947 General Marshall came back from a futile Council of Foreign Ministers in Moscow with no answer to the thorny problem of Germany's administration. Fearful of the Communists, the British and Americans wanted to revive the failing German economy. The Russians, busy dismantling plant and shipping it home, wanted a supine Germany. France wanted to replace Germany as the leading industrial power in Europe: it demanded to annex the Saar, guaranteed German coal exports to feed its own steel industry and international ownership of the Ruhr.

Within twenty-four hours of his return home Marshall authorised George Kennan to set up a Policy Planning Unit.

So fast was the response that the first qualification to be in the team was availability. Kennan was the most experienced member with diplomatic postings to Berlin and Moscow though his perspectives were narrow. His wartime calls for a stand against the USSR had ignored any military need for Russia's support in order to win. His Berlin posting led him to be pro-German and unlike many in Europe, he saw no long term danger in rebuilding Germany.[19] Joseph E. Johnson was an academic;[20] Colonel Charles H. Bonesteen III a regular soldier, in the Army Department; Jacques Reinstein, an economist with a knowledge of Germany; and Carleton Savage had been Cordell Hull's assistant.

In mid-May Will Clayton, the under-secretary of State for Economic Affairs in the State Department, returned from Europe with an alarming report after the freezing winter, 'It is now obvious that we have grossly underestimated the destruction to the European economy by the war.' He wrote that a support plan, 'should be based on a European economic federation in the order of the Belgian, Netherlands, Luxembourg Customs Union.'

Within a month the report of Kennan's committee was ready and on 5th June at Harvard, General Marshall announced it as the Marshall Plan. The report made three assumptions: that the USSR posed a substantial and immediate threat to Western Europe; the US should fund the reconstruction of Europe by regarding it as one unit, not independent sovereign states; and West Germany should be rebuilt as a buffer against the East.

Marshall aid was a most generous impulse. The timing was also critical as UNRRA aid had run out in March. It also suited American self-interest: American jobs and prosperity relied in large measure on trade with Europe. Kennan believed that Germany should be revived as part of a prosperous Europe which would act as a pull on the Soviet satellite countries. And Western Europe's prosperity would prevent a Russian take-over.

Yet the Marshall Plan went far beyond aid, trade and defence. Kennan asserted ' . . . one of the long term deficiencies of the European economy as a whole was its excessive fragmentation, the lack of competitive flexibility in commercial exchanges, the lack, in particular, of a large consumers' market. By insisting on a joint approach, we hoped to force the Europeans to begin to think like Europeans, and not like nationalists, in their approach to the economic problems of their country.'[21]

Reduction of trade barriers was one thing. What the Americans were contemplating was quite another. Treating Europe as one unit rather than as sovereign states has had unparalleled repercussions.

Too late, Kennan woke up to what Germany's victims in Europe knew all too well: rebuilding it as a buffer state would give German politicians the upper hand.[22] That point was not missed in Germany; it could play the Americans off against the Russians. It successfully played this game until over forty years later it achieved the reunification of West and East Germany.

The Americans went on the offensive. In one respect only were they prepared to take a back seat: Europe must produce its own plan so that the Europeans would not be antagonised. That done, American pressure for a United States of Europe was to be relentless. American insistence on a new organisation to administer Marshall aid raised the obvious question. Why not use the UN, which America said it was backing? The Americans did try the UN route first but only to manoeuvre the Russians into refusing US help. The Americans did not want to be seen as the guilty party.

In July 1947 sixteen European nations met in Paris to discuss the Marshall Plan. They talked all summer, set up a customs union study group, but soon abandoned it because of the sovereignty issue.

American pressure never stopped and every country objected to it. The British, Dutch, Norwegians and Swiss were especially against any suggestion of supra-nationality. Bill Tomlinson[23] at the American Embassy in Paris argued for the union at every turn.[24] The British Foreign Secretary,

Ernest Bevin, briefly backed it, but a customs union conflicted with the Sterling area. By the end of September a compromise report was sent to Washington with only lip service paid to the American vision of a European economy.

Then inadvertently Kennan raised the stakes. As the European nations opened talks, Kennan published an article in the CFR journal 'Foreign Affairs' signed only 'BY X'. The article became the talk of Washington. Kennan argued, as he had before in unsung internal Foreign Service papers, for 'long term patient but firm and vigilant containment' of the USSR. He wanted Russian force to be answered with counter-force around the world.

Kennan later admitted[25] he had been careless in his phraseology. His article read as though the USSR posed a serious military threat to the West. Kennan did not believe that the Russians wanted war with the West. He meant an economic and political threat.

As panic took hold in Washington, the State Department swung in favour of a united Europe to counter the USSR, and away from piecemeal aid. Under-secretaries Will Clayton and Dean Acheson changed sides. The American Government adopted Kennan's containment policy, as it became known.

Congress was hostile to the European nations' August request for the huge sum of $28 billion over four years. So President Truman side stepped Congress and set up three fact finding committees, of which the most important was chaired by Averell Harriman. The Harriman Committee's weighty report of 7th November proposed halving the amount of aid needed and removing trade barriers within Europe.

For nearly four months the battle for the Marshall Plan raged through Congress. Most Congressmen were against handing over American money. Steadily a group of lobbyists made some headway against the majority, but still they did not have enough support.

In December 1947 Senator Arthur Vandenberg, another Dulles' ally and chairman of the Senate Foreign Relations Committee, championed a reduced Marshall Aid budget of $17 billion. Cries of 'waste' and 'bold socialist blue-print' greeted it, especially from the Republicans. Vandenberg stressed the issue of containment of the USSR which overcame some hostility to giving a socialist Britain yet more cash.[26]

Help for the Marshall Plan lobbyists came from an unexpected quarter. Faced by the nightmare of an American-backed Europe on its doorstep the USSR was subverting the nations on its western border. Tension rose, retaliation followed. On 30th December 1947 the Russians forced King Michael of Romania to abdicate and declared a Romanian People's Republic. On 25th February 1948 the USSR organised a coup in Czechoslovakia and the Communists took control. Two weeks later Jan Masaryk, the great Czech leader admired throughout the Western world, was assassinated.

Banner headlines in the newspapers proclaimed the next world war less than three years after the last one. At once all American resistance to the Marshall Plan vanished. On 14th March the American Senate voted overwhelmingly for the Marshall Plan, followed on 31st March by the House of Representatives. Aid was reduced to $4 billion, a fraction of the original demand.

A Close Run Thing

If the Russians had not organised the Czech coup the Marshall Plan could easily have been stillborn. Without the authority and power of the US, a United States of Europe would probably have remained a pipe dream of the fragmented, ill-funded groups in Europe.

And without the orchestrated lobbying of the few who steered the Marshall Plan through Congress the plan would probably have failed at an early stage, too early to catch the tide created by the Soviet coup in Czechoslovakia. Most of the lobbyists had been involved in planning for the peace from the early days of the war and were members of the four inter-locking groups: the Council on Foreign Relations, the PEP, the NPA and BAC. To back the Marshall Plan they served on committee after committee and spent days testifying before the Congress.

Just before the Marshall Plan was first thought of, as early as 22nd March 1947, the few Congressmen who had long backed the idea of a unified Europe came out into the open. With the outside encouragement of J F Dulles, Senators J William Fulbright, Elbert D Thomas and Representative Hale Boggs introduced parallel resolutions in the Senate and the House asking that: 'Congress favor the creation of United States of Europe within the framework of the United Nations.'

Both resolutions passed overwhelmingly and were widely publicised by journalist Walter Lippmann. The year before the influential Lippmann, with close links to the British Fabian society dating back to the Woodrow Wilson era, had proposed in the 'New York Herald Tribune'[27] 'not less than an economic union' in Europe. Now he repeated the call in the 'Washington Post' with two columns urging the 'unification of Europe.'[28]

When put in context it is not so surprising that George Kennan's report which was conceived and written during the month of May 1947, only two months after those resolutions had been so overwhelmingly passed by the Congress, should be founded on the idea of a United States of Europe – so much more than just plain aid.

Averell Harriman, who chaired the most important committee to which Truman had delegated the debate when he was blocked by the Congress, was then Secretary of Commerce and dominated the Business Advisory Council (BAC).[29] He had been a member of it since its foundation thirteen years earlier. Whether Harriman realised it or not, BAC was dedicated to bringing together businessmen, public officials and academics to achieve a slow but steady transition to socialism.

Half the members of the Harriman Committee were members of the BAC, the National Planning Association (NPA) or the Committee for Economic Development (CED). The CED and the NPA also convened special committees on Marshall Aid. Both were chaired by the same man, Wayne Taylor. Taylor and Paul G. Hoffmann, the president of Studebaker and a founder of CED, presented the CED's findings to Congress.

Yet another private group, the Committee for Marshall Aid, worked closely with government officials to promote the Marshall Plan. Of the nineteen people on its executive board, eight were members of the Council on Foreign Relations.[30] They included the CFR president Allen Dulles, and Philip Reed, chairman of the multi-national General Electric.[31]

So it went on: names and committees all interlinked, all lobbying for the Marshall Plan.[32]

Back Door Economics

The American lobbyists found a counter-part in Europe and they renewed friendships made during the war. The European League for Economic Co-operation (ELEC), a group of economists, was the brain-child of Comte Paul van Zeeland, the former Belgian Prime Minister, who in war-time exile had backed the creation of Benelux. He used his time out of office to promote European unity.

Speaking to a small French group in October 1945, van Zeeland proposed a back door to European union: 'I suggest that we should tackle the problem from a specific and limited point of view. We shall avoid needless difficulties if we adopt an economic approach . . . We shall soon find moreover, that economic issues cannot be separated from political and social ones . . . a regional grouping . . . must go straight for radical solutions, namely a customs union and a monetary union.'[33]

Van Zeeland's soft economic option echoed that of others like the Germans and rapidly became the preferred approach. It was a means to an end.

Van Zeeland rapidly secured support from his former colleague, Paul-Henri Spaak, still the Belgian Foreign Minister. During 1946 and early 1947 van Zeeland travelled widely to set up small, national sections of elite economists. The most successful were those in London, Paris, and Brussels.

He renewed contact with the erudite Dr Joseph Retinger, formerly Sikorski's right hand man. He in turn talked to Major General Sir Colin Gubbins, who had run the Special Operations Executive and naturally knew the former resistance leaders. Retinger acted as go-between and fixer and could not have been bettered at it.

Sir Harold Butler a former director of the International Labour Organisation (ILO), led the thirty strong London group some of whom were also to join Churchill and Sandys committee.[34]

The committee included Lord Layton of 'The Economist' newspaper; and the Conservative MP and future Prime Minister Harold Macmillan; the Fabian architect of the welfare state, Lord Beveridge; MPs Leslie Hore-Belisha, Peter

Thorneycroft, and Henry Hopkinson (Lord Colyton); and the leading economist, Roy Harrod.

In France, van Zeeland's friend Daniel Serruys, by then retired from Government service, knew everyone in the field of economics and brought in top people[35] including the future Prime Minister, Etienne Giscard d'Estaing.

Van Zeeland was keen to establish early links with sympathetic Americans. So in early 1947 Retinger had a long talk with Averell Harriman, then the American Ambassador in London. They had first met in London during the war. Retinger said that Harriman 'strongly believed in European unification', and was personally responsible for the tremendous support the Americans gave to ELEC.[36]

Harriman introduced van Zeeland to his friends in the US. Most were long standing members of the CFR or one of the other three groups which since early in the war had lobbied for a united Europe.

In New York van Zeeland met Adolf Berle Jr, Franz Leemans and Nelson Rockefeller.[37] Berle, a top lawyer and former Assistant Secretary of State from 1938 to 1944, had been one of the triumvirate who had introduced President Roosevelt to the New Deal. He led the new group which included Russell Leffingwell, a senior partner of J. P. Morgan and former chairman of the CFR;[38] David Rockefeller; Alfred Sloan Jr, chairman of General Motors; Charles Hook, president of the American Rolling Mills Company; Sir William Wiseman, a partner with bankers, Kuhn Loeb;[39] and George Franklin.

Not surprisingly J. F. Dulles was among those who helped the most. He even agreed to ask Molotov, the Russian Foreign Minister, if the USSR wished to join a truly European wide organisation. Molotov replied 'they were all for the unity of Europe on condition that it would be united under Russia.'[40]

So when General Marshall proposed his Plan in June 1947, the London economists, briefed by their American friends, were waiting to welcome it. In reply they called for the abolition of restraints on trade, listed practical ways for the French, British and American Governments to channel aid and added, 'Once the benefits of Continental planning have been demonstrated to everyone, the way may be opened to more far-reaching projects.'[41]

Churchill Provides The Hook

The Americans lobbying for an integrated European economy needed a good deal more help from Europe than could be provided by the economists' group alone. Just as the spur for the Congress' approval of the Marshall Plan came from the unexpected quarter of the Soviet Union, so from another surprising quarter support came to overcome European dislike of American coercion. Winston Churchill backed a united Europe. He was stepping outside the mainstream of British opinion, but only to gain advantage for his party.

Neither of the two main British parties, Labour or Conservative, favoured giving up sovereignty, including Britain in a United States of Europe, or compromising the British Commonwealth. During the war Churchill and his Government easily succeeded in defeating the attempts of Toynbee and his lobbying friends to have any influence on national politics – a contrast with the US.

For Labour, Hugh Dalton, on the National Executive Committee, feared 'Europe' would damage the Sterling area and Imperial Preference. The Labour Party thought a United States of Europe could be a bloc to oppose the USSR, but the Party was co-operating with the Russian Government. Labour did support American defence and aspects of the

Marshall Plan, but not the European integration the Americans were demanding.

In any case Labour, after a landslide victory in 1945, was busy pursuing a social revolution. Any European adventure would be merely a diversion from the main task. The ambitious young secretary of the International Department of the Labour Party, Denis Healey wrote, 'To the extent that the internal structure of a given state satisfies the need of the workers within it, to that extent its socialist party will tend to put the national interest before international solidarity.'[42]

Churchill, leader of the Opposition, could therefore afford to present the Conservatives as the party of Europe and he did so nine months before the Marshall Plan. Churchill championed European union as a buffer against the USSR, and wanted a revived European economy to help eliminate the enmity between France and Germany.

On 19th September 1946 at Zurich Churchill called for the creation of 'a kind of United States of Europe' under Franco-German leadership. With the USSR threatening Central Europe Churchill recalled: 'We all know that the two world wars which have passed arose out of the vain passion of a newly-united Germany to play the dominant part in the world . . .' He called for Germany's punishment but added 'We must look to the future . . .'

'I am now going to say something that will astonish you. The first step in the re-creation of the European family must be a partnership between France and Germany . . . The first step is to form a Council of Europe . . . Great Britain, the British Commonwealth of Nations, mighty America, and I trust Soviet Russia . . . must be the friends and sponsors of the new Europe and must champion its right to live and shine. Therefore I say to you: Let Europe arise!'

A summary of Churchill's speech, published in all the main European newspapers, caused a sensation. Perhaps Britain, to whom so many looked for leadership after the war, was to move towards a united Europe. For years afterwards the debate continued: had Churchill been in favour of a United States of Europe as the federalists proposed? Did he see Britain as part of it? The federalists say yes, but the truth is otherwise. As Clement Attlee – the then Labour leader – said, Churchill was playing party politics.[43]

Conservatives Unite With Marxists

In Europe, Churchill's support came from decidedly non-Conservative quarters and unlike Churchill they were in earnest. Churchill's superb oratory of 'Let Europe Arise!' inspired the far left group, the revolutionary European Union of Federalists (UEF). Unlikely alliance though it was, Churchill's group and the UEF made common cause. What was not surprising given their totally incompatible positions was that they broke apart. Yet for two years the British Conservatives and the Marxist-orientated Europeans worked together.

The UEF was by far the largest of the left wing pressure groups for a united Europe which had formed after the war. While most groups were tiny, the UEF had a membership of 150,000, mainly in France and Italy. The UEF arose from the secret meetings in Geneva in 1944 organised by the Dutchman, Visser 't Hooft of the World Council of Churches, and the Italian Communist, Altiero Spinelli.

Its intellectual roots went back to the French revolution. Its Dutch leader, Hendrik Brugmans, had worked briefly for the resistance movement.[44] Brugmans wanted to make Europe a third force between the 'totalitarian socialism' of Stalin's USSR and the 'anarchic capitalism' of the US. He supported 'the great Russian revolution.' Europe, he thought, would gain from large scale socialist planning. The contrast with Churchill could not have been greater.

The French and Italians had completely opposite views of the "Europe" they were fighting for. The French, led by the academic Denis de Rougemont and the Russian Alexandre Marc formerly of the Toulouse resistance group, Libérer et Fédérer, diplomatically paid lip service to the idea of a superstate, but what they really wanted was an international organisation to reflect 'pre-existing social realities'. They meant there should be representatives from every walk and class of life as the philosopher of Proud'hon had preached and the Paris Commune carried out.

The two Italian leaders, Altiero Spinelli and Ernesto Rossi, wanted a superstate as they had argued from their prison island, Ventotene, and later from Switzerland.

Building on Churchill's speech, his son-in-law, Duncan Sandys, worked hard to launch the British United Europe Movement (UEM) in grand style at the Albert Hall in London on 15th May 1947.[45] Sandys called for 'a loose association of states similar to the British Commonwealth.'

Duncan Sandys was an extremely able administrator and diplomat. Just after resigning from the Foreign Office in protest at the British Government's policy of appeasing Germany, he had been elected a Conservative MP in 1935. That year he married Churchill's daughter, Diana. Disabled while fighting with the Norwegian Expeditionary Force in 1941, he became a Government Minister for the rest of the war.

The fund raiser for the new movement was the chairman and creator of ICI, Lord McGowan, assisted by a new and energetic recruit to ICI from the Treasury, Paul Chambers, who later became ICI's chairman. They invited industry leaders to fund raising lunches at which Churchill spoke, and produced enough cash to keep the group going for its first year.

Despite Churchill's authority, the UEM had only a slight

influence in Britain and never made it clear what they meant by 'Europe'. There was no membership. Its newsletter had a circulation of 2,000, and 'Europe' was never a major issue in Britain other than briefly in late 1947 and early 1948 because of the Marshall Plan.

The prospect of substantial American funding for economic recovery motivated all the groups to try to join forces. The only serious disagreement was between Sandys and Count Richard Coudenhove-Kalergi. Before the war Coudenhove-Kalergi had been alone with his Pan Europa movement. In June 1946 when he returned from war-time exile in New York, he found he had rivals. Given his experience Coudenhove-Kalergi thought he should be the leader of all pro-Europeans.

But Pan Europa was by then a dated organisation with few specific proposals. Coudenhove-Kalergi quickly realised he would have to change tack. After discussions with the British MP, R. W. G. Mackay, he decided on the idea of uniting all European parliamentarians.

By early July 1947 he had a sufficient response to call his first conference in Gstaad, Switzerland, where he lived, followed by a major conference in the September with 114 MPs mainly from France and Italy. He wanted a European Assembly to bring in a United States of Europe.[46]

Faced with stiffening competition Duncan Sandys tried a pincer movement with a new French organisation, Conseil Français pour l'Europe Unie. The editor of 'Le Monde', Professeur René Courtin, led it. Sandys portrayed his own group as less integrationist than his rival and thought Coudenhove-Kalergi wanted all the limelight.

To try to agree on a common line in answer to the Marshall Plan Sandys and Retinger arranged for all the major international groups to meet in Paris on 20th July. Almost immediately Coudenhove-Kalergi's group walked out. The rest joined forces to form what was later called the European Movement.[47] Winston Churchill and Robert Schuman were joint presidents. Sandys chaired it, with Retinger as secretary.[48]

That September (1947), when Sandys and Retinger went to Coudenhove-Kalergi's first meeting of his European parliament in Gstaad to try to win his support, they were inspired to launch a large scale campaign for a Congress of Europe. They thought the Hague would be a suitable place to host 750 delegates for a week. The Hague Congress developed Churchill's and Sikorski's war-time idea of a Council of Europe about which Churchill had made a radio broadcast on 22nd March 1943 with little response.

Their big problem was the lack of money to stage such a large meeting. The Dutchman, Pieter Kerstens, the instigator of Benelux, stepped into the breach by raising ninety per cent of the money from Dutch organisations. For the next eight months Sandys and Retinger worked round the clock.

An Unholy Alliance?

The alliance between the Conservative Sandys and the socialist Retinger was curious though the times were unusual. Sandys, following Churchill's lead, was as concerned about the fate of Eastern Europe as he was about that of Western Europe, so some of Retinger's appeal must have been his total concern for his home country of Poland.

Retinger came from a professional Polish family. After his father's death Count Wladyslaw Zamoyski became his guardian. The Zamoyskis were one of the oldest and wealthiest families in Poland. Under his patronage Retinger spent his youth in the salons of Paris. In the 1920s he was a member of the National Executive of the Polish Socialist Party. His secretary of later years said he was a 'fervent socialist'. His political life was chequered – he was asked to leave France, was not welcome in Britain, and spent some impoverished years in South America. With the outbreak of war Retinger went to Britain and in June 1940 on his own initiative persuaded Churchill to give him a plane to fly to Bordeaux to bring General Sikorski to London to regroup. Until Sikorski's death he remained close to his side pulling strings behind the scenes. He played on mystery and liked to be an eminence grise.

Retinger always put Poland first. After Sikorski died in 1943 he had volunteered to make his first parachute jump into occupied Poland despite his age of 57 to try to discover what the Poles thought about the advancing Russians.

Why did Sandys battle for a united Europe, and a Europe to include Britain? In the late 1940s Sandys was an important figure in the fight for a united Europe. Without Sandys' organisational abilities the Hague Congress could not have happened. That proved to be the starting point for a chain of events leading to the European Coal and Steel Community.

Following his own advice, Sandys spoke in vague terms but there is little doubt that he was a federalist. Sandys believed that given the recent war there should be one European defence force and no national armies. Political union with a common citizenship and an elected parliament would naturally follow economic union, but it would take time. He saw no conflict with Imperial Preference or the British Commonwealth. A European customs and currency union would naturally include the Commonwealth. The key to success would be the balance of France and Britain against Germany.

Sandys intended the Hague Congress to encourage governments towards the long-term goal of European unification by fostering every kind of inter-governmental discussion, and by creating the habit of thinking of Europe as a whole.

That achieved, national sovereignty could be given up step by step. He proposed regular Ministerial conferences, a permanent secretariat to carry out joint studies, and the launch of a popular campaign. Sandys decided that the political, economic and cultural reports prepared beforehand for agreement at the Congress should be deliberately couched in vague terms so that agreement would easily be reached and then they could be tightened up after the conference.[49]

Sandys knew how radical most of his associates were. As early as February 1947, the heads of the revolutionary UEF wrote[50] to Sandys to ask for his committee's views on their proposals. Brugmans and Marc spelt out their beliefs: the surrender of sovereignty; and European-wide planning of production, consumption and exchange. They were concerned about the impact on the USSR of creating a Western European bloc and dividing Europe into two parts. They wanted Russian fears to be allayed. There could be no doubt they wanted a socialist United States of Europe, sympathetic to the USSR. The UEF leadership also included Spinelli, who had moved only slightly to the right from his erstwhile Stalinist position. He made no secret of it.

Nor was Sandys the only Conservative allied with the Marxists. The British members of the economics group, ELEC, included Conservatives. It is quite possible that unlike Sandys, few fully appreciated what their continental colleagues intended or, if they did, doubted that they would have the power to achieve it. They may have thought it was much more likely that Britain would be the leader of Europe. Further, the economists' skills were badly needed to sort out the major problem of currency convertibility which was crippling European trade and recovery. The British certainly hoped to join Western Europe and the Commonwealth into a massive trading area.

Most of the French and Belgian members of ELEC were

socialists, as were most of Coudenhove-Kalergi's Pan Europa group. They had no hesitation about giving up sovereignty and moving towards a superstate. They were explicit about their plans for a United States of Europe and had been formulating their ideas over many years.

A booklet was published in May or June of 1947 under the banner 'Design for Freedom' by twenty-four mainly Conservative MPs, led by Peter Thorneycroft of ELEC.[51] The writers had hoped that the 'good' Hitler had done to make Europe one economic unit would be preserved. They praised national economic planning, such as the socialist Monnet Plan in France, and wanted to abolish tariffs within Europe as the Marshall Plan envisaged.

They added, 'no government dependent upon a democratic vote could possibly agree in advance to the sacrifices which any adequate plan must involve. The people must be led slowly and unconsciously into the abandonment of their traditional economic defences, not asked, in advance of having received any of the benefits which will accrue to them from the plan to make changes of which they may not at first recognise the advantages to themselves . . .'

Some Conservatives may have been beguiled by Churchill's leadership, but he was playing party politics for all it was worth. He tried to ban members of the Labour Party from the United Europe Committee. He even went as far as to lead his supporters from his room in the House of Commons across the road to Number 10, Downing Street to persuade the Prime Minister, Clement Attlee, of the case for European unity.[52] Attlee had been in favour of the Benelux Customs Union, and was later to favour Schuman's plan for the European Coal and Steel Community. But like Bevin, Attlee did not think they were practical for Britain.

Long before he returned to power as Prime Minister in 1951, Churchill realised that the movement he headed was moving fast in a direction he could not follow. Though some were bewitched by the power of his oratory and misunderstood his aims, over the years Churchill was consistent in his view that some kind of unity of Europe was right, but not for Britain, which should only be 'a friend and sponsor'. Certainly his contemporaries, like Spaak and Attlee, recognised his position. He believed in what he called the three concentric circles interlinking Britain and the US, Britain and Europe, and Britain and the Commonwealth. The link with Europe was the least of the three.[53]

Labour's Position

The British Labour Government was resentful of Churchill's growing success and could not compete with his reputation. It therefore distanced itself from the Hague Congress. Divided only by party politics Churchill and Bevin, the Labour Foreign Secretary, had very similar views.[54]

The only speech any member of the Labour Government made in favour of European unity was in January 1948.[55] Ernest Bevin, the Foreign Secretary, appeared to back European unity but his words were carefully chosen to appeal to the Americans whose support he needed for a military alliance in a worsening international situation. When Bevin backtracked, Dean Acheson commented, 'his health (was) failing and his judgement with it.'[56]

Bevin had major anxieties: he wanted to keep the American link but was afraid that the US would retreat into isolationism; he wanted Western European defence which had been proposed in the latter stages of the war, and he did not want Britain to be just lumped in with other European countries when Marshall aid was distributed. It had given up so much to save Europe.

Bevin was disillusioned by Britain's war-time experience of

Europe, of those unreliable allies. He put his confidence in the US. He told the MP Henry Usbourne, a world federalist, that Britain must remain a sovereign state, backed by America, because a federal parliament in Strasbourg, faced by Russian troops, would vote to capitulate. 'Hitler could never take over this island ... but the Russians might take it over by a vote in a European Federal Parliament without our being able to fire a single shot.'

Bevin's view of the unreliable European allies was widely shared in Britain. Lord Garner said of Britain's war-time European allies, 'Some of them had let us down. Some of them had fought against us. All of them were seen in 1948 to be liable to communist intervention.'

On the specific issue of a unified Europe, Bevin had three worries: 'being united with the Continent without taking the Commonwealth into account; the delicate question of sovereignty;' and the 'differences between the political systems of the five countries'.[57]

While the Labour Government distanced itself from the Hague Congress, many individual Labour MPs backed European unity. On the eve of the Congress, nearly a hundred Labour Members signed an All Party motion proposed by R. W. G. Mackay and Robert Boothby (Conservative) for a European federation 'based on common citizenship, representative institutions and human rights, with powers including foreign affairs, defence, currency and trade', and twenty-seven Labour MPs went to the Hague Congress.

In March 1948, the Socialist International met in Surrey with delegates from thirteen parties from Marshall Plan countries. Guy Mollet, on behalf of the French socialists, proposed a big European campaign among socialists to back the Hague Congress. The British Labour Party stalled for time. A month later, Léon Blum, leader of the French socialists, tried again, but the Labour Party refused to come to the Hague and dissuaded others from going.

The issue was raised afterwards at the Autumn 1948 Labour Party Conference when Fenner Brockway proposed co-operation with other socialist parties to achieve a United States of Europe. The Chancellor of the Exchequer, Hugh Dalton, dismissed such theoretical federalism in favour of practical British functionalism.

The banker, Sigmund Warburg, tried to put pressure on the Labour Government to lead a European union. Warburg, who had fled to Britain from Germany before the war, was one of a long line of German and East European immigrants who thought Britain should be part of an organised unified Europe (Professor Zimmern was another). Never at home in Britain, a country he admired but did not understand, Warburg thought that 'without a great Germany there will never be stability in Europe. Britain and Germany together could build a united Europe which would quickly overtake the US.'[58] Unwittingly, that view had much in common with that of Adolf Hitler. Warburg never gave up, but used his considerable influence to persuade the Americans to finance the building of a United States of Europe. His closest contact was the American, George Ball.

The Hague Congress went ahead without the Labour Party and turned into a political platform for the Conservatives. Their supremacy was short lived. They were to be quickly ousted by their European socialist partners.

The Hague Congress May 1948

The Hague Congress met between 7th and 10th May 1948 with Winston Churchill in the chair and eight hundred individuals there by invitation only. All prominent figures, they included eighteen former Prime Ministers and twenty-eight former Foreign Ministers.

Everyone favoured creating a United Europe. Most wanted a radical federation, while the British, following Sandys' lead, promoted a more pragmatic approach with vague goals.

The Congress resolved that 'the time has come when the European nations must transfer and merge some portion of their sovereign rights so as to secure common political and economic action for the integration and proper development of their common resources.' That included Britain; but most of the British delegates did not.

Churchill advocated some sacrifice or merger of national sovereignty in a step by step approach to political unity – not for Britain of course. Paul Ramadier echoed that, calling for the gradual establishment of institutions and no federalist revolution. On the other hand, Coudenhove-Kalergi wanted 'an immediate and radical solution', a constituent assembly. Brugmans of the UEF called for the overthrow of 'the dogma of sacrosanct national sovereignty'.

R. W. G. Mackay, aligned with Coudenhove-Kalergi, added 'I don't think it greatly matters whether you talk of a surrender of sovereignty, of a merger of sovereignty, of a transfer of sovereignty or of an enlargement of sovereignty, so long as it is quite clear at all times that the individual states of Europe are giving up some of the rights to exercise powers which they cannot exercise without interfering with the other states of Western Europe.'[59]

The importance of the Hague Congress cannot be overestimated. Its resolutions set the scene for the next fifty years and formed the outline for all the later treaties on Europe: the European Coal and Steel Community, the Treaty of Rome, the Single European Act and the Maastricht Treaty. Above all the Congress approved the long term goal of an economic and political union, including a defeated Germany.

The issue of a European Assembly raised temperatures. A directly elected Assembly was rejected. Neither the French nor British Governments supported it. Harold Macmillan (Conservative) and R. W. G. Mackay (Labour) argued that to agree on the terms of such an assembly and elect one within a year, let alone six months, would be impracticable.

After the Congress, rifts started to appear. The revolutionary UEF was disappointed that the idea of 'living forces' (representatives of all walks of life) was not part of the proposed European Assembly. They thought a two speed Europe was likely: an inner federal group and the outer states with preferential relations, that is Britain. Eventually British reluctance could be overcome.[60]

The balance of power began to swing away from the British. The addition of two small revolutionary groups[61] boosted the French socialists in the European Movement so that when the first of the follow-up conferences began in February 1949 the federalist bias was even more marked.

The British did not want an effective European Assembly but Paul Ramadier, who returned to the French Cabinet in September 1948, secured French agreement for it. He put the proposal to the other five governments. Both France and Belgium wanted a Consultative Assembly of Parliamentarians and a Council of Ministers.

The prospect of American money had focused French attention on European integration. Now Frenchmen were talking of integrating Germany into a European union led by France. That dominated French thinking for the next forty-five years. The make-up of the post-war French Assembly added impetus: most of them were new to national politics and eighty-five percent had been in the resistance movements with their strongly federal influence, yet only one or two per cent of all French had been active resisters.[62]

Britain, seeking a compromise, proposed a Council of Ministers to keep decisions in the hands of elected governments. In the late autumn of 1948 negotiations began behind the scenes, chaired by Edouard Herriot. The French Ambassador in London, René Massigli, was told to press the British for 'the nucleus of a federal organisation'.[63] Just before Christmas, the negotiators agreed on a Council of Europe and a European Consultative Assembly of Parliamentarians.

Bevin for the British vetoed it. In mid-January 1949, the French Foreign Minister and joint president of the European Movement, Robert Schuman, visited London to threaten that France would go ahead without Britain. At the end of the month, the proposal was endorsed by the Council of Ministers of the Brussels Pact. Britain abstained.

A year after the Hague Congress, the Statute of the Council of Europe established a Committee of Ministers and a Consultative Assembly, but with advisory powers only. The British Labour Government was scarcely involved: as Sir Stafford Cripps said to an American preaching Anglo-French union, 'How would you like it if we asked you to go to bed with Brazil'.[64]

Bevin, the Foreign Minister, remarked, 'We've got to give them something and I think we'll give them this talking shop in Strasbourg, the Council of Europe'. He commented later 'if you open that Pandora's box, you never know what Trojan horse will jump out'.[65]

CHAPTER 5: CREATION

American Domination

In June 1947 under the banner of Marshall Aid the goal of a United States of Europe through economic union had became US Government policy. In March 1948 Congress had endorsed it. Those Americans who had lobbied hard for Marshall Aid cash to be tied to a political programme then made sure they were in charge of executing the policy.

Senator Arthur Vandenberg vetoed both Acheson and Clayton of the State Department to head the new European Co-operation Administration (ECA) which ran the European Recovery Program (ERP). He backed Paul G. Hoffmann, the founder of one of the inter-linked lobby groups, the CED. Hoffmann then deliberately reduced the State Department's influence. Averell Harriman, who had played such a leading role among the lobbyists, became the ECA special representative in Paris.

Once the ECA started operations in Paris in the summer of 1948 the battle between the Americans and the British continued non-stop. At every opportunity the Americans at the ECA tried to limit national sovereignty and to force open the British Empire and Commonwealth to American trade by making sterling convertible into dollars. The British fought them every step of the way. The British were not alone. American pressure was resented by every other European country.

Equally, the Americans were disappointed that the talks which had started in July 1948 between sixteen European countries had taken nine months to come to a conclusion and merely produced a co-operative group, the Organisation for European Economic Co-operation (OEEC). Co-operation was not what the Americans wanted: they wanted Europe-wide planning and the integration of Europe's economies to increase production.

The Americans thought Britain was the key to their new Europe and their tactics reflected that. They were anxious that the British representative in Paris on the OEEC committee should be of Ministerial rank to give extra status to the OEEC. Yet Britain was not to have special status and treatment in return. Its authority was merely to be used for American ends. As General Marshall's under-secretary[1] commented, 'The special wartime position for Britain would be inconsistent with the concept of West European integration and other objectives of (the European Recovery Programme) ERP.'

The most belligerent Americans were those based in Europe and the most forceful was Harriman, the ECA special representative in Paris. A British civil servant remarked: 'Apparently Harriman thinks himself such a swell that he cannot have truck with anyone unless they are Ministers.' He added that nobody on Harriman's staff could possibly understand why the Foreign Ministers of sixteen sovereign states 'were not prepared to travel to Paris to have the honour of meeting Mr Harriman.'[2] Attempts to make the OEEC stronger were dubbed the 'Harriman problem'.

Another British official recorded Harriman's imperious comment to him that the British Government 'over-rated the importance to us of the Commonwealth and the Sterling Area and that we would probably do much better for ourselves by making up our minds to integrate at once with Europe.'[3] To those who worked at the ECA from around Europe and the US, its primary role, unspoken but all pervading, was to create a unified Europe.[4]

Unrelenting American pressure caused Bevin, the British Foreign Secretary, to protest at the way American officials presumed 'to interfere with the way we conduct our business in this country.'[5]

Secret Funding

To further their policy of European integration the Americans financially backed those Europeans who, after the Hague Congress of May 1948, argued for integration. It was expensive enough to run that Congress, but to run an even more elaborate organisation was beyond the resources available to any of the major groups. Without outside funding the Hague Congress would have been the end of the matter.

Coudenhove-Kalergi had been the first to go to America for money just before the Congress started. With Allen Dulles and Bill Donovan, he founded a committee[6] to publicise the issue in America and to provide cash. Unfortunately for

Coudenhove-Kalergi, that summer Sandys and Retinger took the same route. With Winston Churchill heading their organisation, and the success of the Hague Congress behind them, Coudenhove-Kalergi was outmanoeuvred.

The Americans naturally switched support to Churchill, whose prestige was unrivalled. A propaganda organisation, the American Committee on United Europe (ACUE), was formed, with offices at 537 Fifth Avenue in New York. General William Donovan was the chairman, Allen Dulles the vice chairman and Thomas W. Braden managed it.[7]

The top three positions were all held by past or present members of US intelligence. During the war, 'Wild Bill' Donovan had masterminded the Office of Strategic Services (OSS)[8] and continued to work for the CIA as a consultant until 1955; Dulles, the war-time head of the OSS in Geneva, had recruited Braden as an OSS field officer – both worked in the fore-runner to the CIA and later the CIA itself. Most of those on the committee were either other intelligence officers, like Walter Bedell Smith, or lobbyists for the Marshall Plan. They included Senator Fulbright who had proposed the resolution in favour of a 'United States of Europe' in March 1947; and Paul G. Hoffmann, head of the ECA.

They all had one aim: the rapid integration of Europe. As the international situation worsened the concept of European integration developed a stronger defence angle: one unified and revived Europe would both control Germany, deter the USSR and act as a cornerstone for the new NATO. To do that the ACUE funded any group or individual supporting the cause. Those receiving money had to favour rapid integration and political authority for the Council of Europe.

In March 1949 Churchill himself visited Donovan in New York to ask for support. His emphasis continued to be on liberating Eastern Europe. He told the Americans, 'there can be no permanent peace while ten capitals of Eastern Europe are in the hands of the Soviet Communist Government . . . They send their delegates to our meetings and we know their feelings and how gladly they would be incorporated in the new United Europe . . . We therefore take in our aim and ideal, nothing less than the union of Europe as a whole.'[9]

Three months later, Sandys wrote to Donovan asking for more money. He said £80,000 would keep the organisation going for another six months and fund the next Assembly. His concern, and that of the Americans, was that the financing should be kept secret. They did not want the Russians to make political capital out of it.

The Americans saved the European Movement which would otherwise have collapsed after the Hague Congress. They supported the first Council of Europe at Strasbourg, and the preparatory conferences at Brussels and Westminster in early 1949. They contributed $28,360 in 1949 and $30,665 in 1950 (over a quarter of a million dollars a year at today's prices), which came partly from government and partly from private sources.

The ACUE's funding from the Government accelerated during the 1950s and it gave a total of $3 million in that time (over $30 million at today's prices) principally for propaganda. The organisation was disbanded in 1960, though CIA involvement in the cause of European union carried on.

It is important to note that the ACUE was a semi-overt operation. What have not been made public are the covert operations, interlinked with the activities of the ACUE, by which the US sought to implement its policy on Europe. The ACUE was almost certainly the small tip of a large iceberg.

As Altiero Spinelli later wrote, 'American influence has been applied continually and with increasing momentum in favour of a unification of Europe'. He rightly called it a 'decisive factor' and went so far as to suggest that after the war the Americans could have annexed Europe but chose to bring it federation instead.[10]

America Backs Revolution 1949 – 1950

Backed by American money, Duncan Sandys and Dr Joseph Retinger of the European Movement organised a series of conferences with a strongly federal bias. In February 1949, in Brussels, they set out the aims and structure. Two months later, at Westminster, the Economic Committee set the long term objective of the creation of a Common Market, with a public institution for steel, coal, electricity and transport.

In July, the Legal Committee under Pierre-Henri Teitgen proposed a European Convention on Human Rights. In December, the Cultural Committee passed resolutions to set up a European Cultural Centre in Geneva led by Denis de Rougemont and Raymond Silva; a College of Europe in Bruges to educate the future administrators of Europe under Professor Hendrick Brugmans; and a European Centre of Nuclear Research.

In June 1950, social policy was laid out emphasising the need for a political authority. In September 1951, Germany's place in Europe was debated, and in January 1952 the issue of the countries of Eastern Europe was addressed. Harold Macmillan chaired a group on a supranational policy towards the USSR and its satellites.

Many items in the conferences had a socialist pedigree, usually of long standing, some based on Fabian plans going back to the 1920s. The College of Europe was proposed in a Political and Economic Planning paper of August 1944 for educating the elite of Europe: 'the universities of Europe . . . must play a central role. It would be important to set up at the same time . . . one or more special European Staff Colleges for the training of Europe's key administrative personnel.'[11]

A year after the Hague Congress the European Movement staged the first session of the Council of Europe in Strasbourg on 8th August 1949. It lasted for a month, with 185 delegates from twelve countries. Paul-Henri Spaak, the Belgium Foreign Minister, was elected President, with Lord Layton and Winston Churchill, vice Presidents. Those who went said it was more like a festival than a conference. 25,000 people gathered in the main square of Strasbourg to hear speeches by Churchill, Spaak and others.

The main call was for a European Political Authority with limited functions but real powers and an independent secretariat, in fact all the machinery of an embryo state. Delegates also wanted economic union, a serious examination of the Ruhr problem and co-ordination of Europe's basic industries.

The movement was rapidly accelerating away from intergovernmental co-operation, and the British were finding themselves on difficult ground. Harold Macmillan, the future British Prime Minister, circulated an amendment to the statute of the Council of Europe suggesting that 'the Committee of Ministers should be an executive authority with supranational powers: the Committee shall have its own permanent secretariat of European officials.' That was clear enough but Macmillan told the Conservative Party conference two months later, in words that sounded like a fudge, 'there is no question, at least to my mind, of constitution-making, still less of Federation. Why even in the Commonwealth and Empire we have made no rigid constitutional framework, still less can we do so in Europe.'[12]

Duncan Sandys wrote just after the conference, 'there must be created some form of European Political Authority, capable of formulating and executing a truly European policy . . . the Assembly must acquire . . . the means of exercising a decisive influence . . . otherwise (it) will become a meaningless debating society.'[13] He proposed that the Committee of Ministers should have more power, and then the Assembly too would be more powerful. Eventually, he said, a unified Europe would evolve.

The British Government was equally clear in rejecting any loss of sovereignty. The gulf with the five federalist-minded Continental countries deepened. At the November 1949 meeting of the Committee of Ministers, Britain and the Scandinavian countries rejected the increase of powers and agreed to admit Germany only as an associate member.

Denis Healey of the Labour Party noted with disapproval that the undemocratic European Movement controlled the Strasbourg Assembly. It was outside any government control. Sandys, he noted, was still 'pulling the strings' behind the scenes.[14]

Sandys responded quickly to the crisis with an ad hoc committee to create a European Political Authority consisting of twenty-one leaders of the European Movement. Led by UEF members Brugmans and Spinelli, the French, Italians and Dutch wanted even more: an immediate federal authority with defined powers.

The few British, wedded to what became known as the functionalist or evolutionary approach, wanted a slow increase in joint action through common institutions without transferring sovereign powers straight away. Lord Layton thought a Federal Pact of the continental variety would not have public support. He and Robert Boothby MP agreed that the Council of Europe should be saved by supporting the pragmatic steps of a Court of Human Rights, currency convertibility, and economic co-operation. The use of joint sovereign rights to achieve these practical aims would lead, one day, to a more formal union.

Henri Frenay of the UEF suggested a compromise two-speed Europe. Those who wished should sign a Federal Pact straight away and other states could have preferential relations with the federation.

With American backing the federal process was moving far faster than either Sandys or Churchill could have envisaged and certainly well beyond Churchill's own thinking on Britain's role in the proposed Europe.

The Labour Government remained implacably opposed to any British involvement in a federal venture making sure that power in the new Council of Europe lay with the Council of Ministers, thus neatly side-stepping the attempt to create a nascent political authority.

By June 1950 the British-led European Movement was breaking up: the UEF withdrew from its executive committee. The Americans of the ACUE immediately refused further funding. Donovan and Braden came over to see what was happening for themselves. It was obvious that the British were not prepared to go down the federal road and were making it difficult for the others to make progress.

Spaak told Braden that he could do nothing on his own, but if he had American support he would lead the movement and displace the British. The Americans were under the mistaken impression that with the British out of the way federation would be just around the corner.[15]

The ACUE, run by CIA officers, backed Spaak. In effect he was their willing agent of influence. Indeed later Braden tried to persuade his CIA colleagues to use Spaak, with whom he had become very friendly, as an agent in a clandestine operation in the US – one which had nothing to do with European Union. He was turned down within the CIA.

Britain refused to agree to any modification of the Statute of the Council of Europe. Sandys was isolated. He resigned as chairman of the European Movement's international executive, with only the slightest push from the Americans. Later, in November 1950, Spaak took over and, backed by the Americans, the headquarters of the European Movement was moved from London and Paris to Brussels. It has stayed there ever since.

Again backed by the Americans Spaak and a new secretariat began a programme of propaganda to back a free trade area with a single currency and for the automatic debate of Council of Europe resolutions in national governments.[16]

The British Refuse America's Terms

At the diplomatic level a year of fruitless pressure left the US State Department with serious doubts that Britain would ever play the central role to create a United States of Europe. If Britain did not give up any sovereignty and stood aside, all the other European countries would be too weak to control the Germans.

British resistance soon reduced the American plan for fast economic union to a limited one of removing trade barriers, realigning currencies and co-ordinating national policies. From late 1948 onwards the Americans had had some support from Belgium and Luxembourg which wanted an immediate customs union, and the French who were prepared to move to a limited union.

Yet the months passed and the problem of non-convertible currencies loomed ever larger and with it the fear of economic stagnation playing into the hands of the Communist parties and thus of the USSR.

It was time for reassessment. George Kennan, author of the Marshall Plan, now concluded after three months work that he and his colleagues had been wrong, unification was not necessary after all for Europe to recover economically but it was necessary to solve the German problem by tying it into Europe.

Kennan found Britain's reluctance to take part in European union 'both serious and compelling', given its position on the Atlantic seaboard, and its overseas involvement. The way to involve the British might be to include the Americans and the Canadians too. Kennan's sympathy for Britain went only so far: he thought the British government and politics were 'seriously sick' and in dire need of support.[17]

Kennan assumed, but did not commit to paper, that the French would now head the movement towards political unification. America's military commitment would remain intact until 'replaced by other security arrangements in Europe'. The strongest reason for tying Germany into Europe was withdrawing American troops. Germany would stay outside NATO and unarmed.

The talks, which duly opened in Washington in September 1949 between the Americans, Canadians and British, were dominated by the latest sterling crisis. Dean Acheson of the State Department won the argument against the US Treasury who thought the British were after another hand-out to fund the welfare state. Acheson was prepared to settle for no more than British co-operation over European unity. He combined a belief in unity with the view that British and American interests were largely identical.

With only a few heated exchanges, a tripartite organisation was agreed. Importantly Britain would be regarded as exceptional and not forced into a European union; and it would be able to include sterling countries in the liberalisation of intra-European trade. So Britain gave way on devaluation. On 18th September 1949 sterling was devalued by a hefty thirty per cent.

The new era was short lived. The French, not fully consulted beforehand, were dismayed by the threat of an Anglo-

American coalition and feared they would be left alone to face the Germans. On top of that, they had of course had no advance warning of sterling's devaluation which put paid to their months of planning for a regional economic union called many things from Fritalux to Little Europe. The situation was worse than ever.

The Americans' optimistic view of the British reaction to the talks soon turned out to have been misplaced. The British feared a Continental union would be protectionist and harmful to British trade. Even worse, if Germany were to be included it would eventually dominate the union. If it were excluded it might drive eastwards and possibly into the arms of the Russians. A union had nothing in its favour.

America's Ambassadors in Europe opposed Acheson's apparently conciliatory views. They concluded that America must stop being 'so tender with Britain.'[18]

The ECA pushed for the quick creation of supranational institutions including a monetary authority and a trade commission. Hoffman, the ECA head, in a high profile speech to the OEEC council on 31st October 1949 said openly for the first time that Europe would have to be integrated into a single market. Planning should be completed by the following year.

The Americans tried to strengthen the OEEC as the way to integrate Europe, still expecting Britain to co-operate while not herself becoming part of the union. Britain would not co-operate.

America therefore turned its back on the British and looked to the French to lead the European union. With governments in France often not lasting more than a few months – the longest serving Prime Minister of the Fourth Republic was Guy Mollet with sixteen months – the Americans needed a stable organisation or individual with whom to deal.

There was one man who, exceptionally for a Frenchman,

had an attachment for Americans, and had worked with American businessmen for thirty years counting many of them among his close friends – Jean Monnet.

Monnet And Frankfurter

In the First World War Jean Monnet's first adventure away from his family's brandy firm in Cognac was as the French representative on the Allied Executive Committees for the re-allocation of common resources. At the Paris Peace Conference in 1919 he met the Dulles brothers. John Foster in particular became a life long friend. Their friendship continued when Monnet, aged only 30, became the second in command at the new League of Nations. For a time Monnet was drawn back to Cognac to save his family brandy firm from bankruptcy, and that done he ran the Paris office of a small American finance house, Blair and Co. He joined John Foster Dulles in projects to lend money to Poland and Romania. In the late twenties and early thirties, Monnet got to know a network of American businessmen, mainly friends of Dulles, including Averell Harriman, John McCloy, Donald Swatland, and Henry Stimson.

A quiet job in Cognac with the family firm would not have satisfied Monnet. He was never happy with the status quo and preferred grand projects to minor ones. He was a man of great charisma and presence and very determined. His natural inclination was to operate behind the scenes. He thought his lack of oratory precluded him from entering politics.[19]

When the Second World War broke out Monnet returned to his previous war supplies job but this time in charge of operations in London. He persuaded Churchill that he was the man to be sent to the US to arrange critical war supplies for the Allies. With his usual lack of modesty Monnet described in his 'Memoirs' his great success, apparently against the odds, in securing supplies from the Americans. He failed to mention the substantial help he received from the American Supreme Court Justice, Felix Frankfurter. He met Frankfurter soon after he arrived in Washington in August 1940 and described their relationship in his memoirs as a deep one.

Monnet owed Frankfurter a great deal. Frankfurter made sure Monnet remained in the US after American critics pointed out that he was not in favour of de Gaulle.[20] Frankfurter was the key to Monnet's supplies for the Allies, the 'Victory Program' and 'Arsenal for Democracy' of 1941. Every day they were 'plotting strategy, sharing information, and trading gossip'. Frankfurter was even re-writing Monnet's memos. Their war-time partnership was a huge success. Monnet could certainly not have done it without Frankfurter and his network of so-called 'boys'. Monnet in effect became another of Frankfurter's 'boys' and a particularly close one.[21]

Felix Frankfurter was to be one of the central figures in the conception and birth of the European Union. He was a life long socialist who over many years used his position as a Supreme Court Justice to amend the constitution subtly in the direction of socialism.

In the US Frankfurter had exceptional influence. At Harvard he had struck up a close relationship with Louis Brandeis. Unlike Frankfurter, Brandeis was a multi-millionaire. In 1916 Brandeis became a Supreme Court Justice. The two began to work in tandem, but unofficially.

Both Brandeis and Frankfurter abused their positions as Supreme Court Judges. From behind the scenes, and using Frankfurter, Brandeis advised President F. D. Roosevelt throughout his Presidency to further the socialism of the New Deal. Roosevelt made Frankfurter a Supreme Court Judge in

1939 in recognition of services rendered, and most of the services were extra-judicial. Both judges interpreted the constitution for their own political ends. In 1930 Frankfurter wrote that, through the due process of law, 'justices could read their own economic and social views into the neutral language of the Constitution.' Not long before he died in 1965, he regretted abusing his judicial position.

One biographer explained: 'Felix Frankfurter learned the art of being an extra-judicially active member of the Supreme Court at the knee of Justice Brandeis. It now appears that in one of the most unique relationships in the Court's history, Brandeis enlisted Frankfurter, then a professor at Harvard Law School, as his paid political lobbyist and lieutenant.'[22]

The two created intelligence networks of 'boys', Frankfurter's pupils from Harvard, whom over twenty-five years he and Judge Brandeis placed in government and judicial positions. The 'boys' acted as their eyes and ears and could on occasion carry out their policies. David Lilienthal, head of the Tennessee Valley Authority in the 1930s, was one of them: he carried out the pioneering project in creating a major nationalised electricity scheme which had been masterminded by the London Fabians. One of Frankfurter's closest – and lifelong – friends was the leading Fabian, Professor Laski of the London School of Economics. Frankfurter had started the National Planning Association inspired by the Fabian Political and Economic Planning group.

By the time of the war the number of Frankfurter's 'boys' ran into three figures. As a biographer commented, 'This adroit use of the politically skilful Frankfurter as an intermediary enabled Brandeis to keep his considerable political endeavours hidden from the public. Not surprisingly, after his own appointment to the Court, Frankfurter resorted to some of the same methods . . .'[23]

A glance at Frankfurter's diaries shows that nearly every

day of his life he was manoeuvring to achieve some political end or other. After Britain declared war on Germany, Frankfurter agitated for America to go to war to back his British friends, pushed for Lend-Lease and, to pay for, it claimed the price of the independence of India. He wrote to Lord Halifax, Britain's Ambassador to the US, 'The rooted feeling of America is that India is Britain's victim.'

Even before he met Frankfurter Monnet was close to many in Frankfurter's network[24] and Frankfurter introduced him to more. With their wives they met for dinner roughly once a week for over two years. For the rest of the war, including most of the critical nine months he spent in Algiers rebuilding his French political contacts and was briefly a member of de Gaulle's Provisional Government, Monnet and Frankfurter were in almost daily touch.

Monnet's Plan And The Birth Of The ECSC

Immediately after the war, and backed by de Gaulle, Monnet was in a strong position to put his plan to rebuild French industry into operation. He gathered a small team together. Most had been with him in Algiers and most were to stay with him for years. In Algiers the team had planned 'an economic union going well beyond a mere customs union' and 'a single economic entity in the coal-and-steel producing areas spanning the French, German, and Belgian frontiers.' Monnet had recommended ending European national sovereignty to the French provisional Government.[25]

Monnet's Plan was a French version of the New Deal. That may not have been a coincidence. Monnet and Frankfurter may well have discussed it and Frankfurter, one of the first campaigners for the New Deal, may have inspired it.

French industry was in a desperate plight after more than a decade of decline and destruction: under the premiership of Léon Blum in the 1930s, industry owners had lived in fear that their workers would take over the factories – it was not a time for investment and renewal. Then it had suffered grievously under the German occupation.

Partly because of Monnet's American friends and the existence of his Plan, France had the biggest share of Marshall Aid, more than Britain with its larger economy. In fact a quarter of all American equipment deliveries to Western Europe, measured in dollars, went to France.

The emphasis of the Plan, which Monnet ran for seven years, was on steel, partly because that had been Germany's engine of war. Two thirds of French steel was produced in Lorraine (built up under German ownership between 1871 and 1918) using coking coal from just across the border in the Ruhr and French iron ore. The Germans controlled French production by manipulating the prices of coke and freight.

Despite the war-time devastation of German industry it was steadily recovering. As supplies of Swedish iron ore improved the Germans became less and less dependent on supplies from France. Equally the recovery of German industry boosted German steel production. That in turn increased home demand for Ruhr coke.

France's iron and steel exports were increasingly unnecessary to Germany. In time Germany would have no dependence on France for steel production. Monnet's overriding aim was to move fast to merge the two countries' interests before Germany recovered fully, enabling France to take over the industrial leadership of Europe. He was also aware that one day, inevitably, Germany would rearm.

Under the Monnet Plan Germany would be forced to disgorge ten to fifteen million tons of coke a year from the Ruhr and five million from the Saar. In December 1946 France effectively annexed the Saar, then within its zone of occupation, by putting a tariff frontier around it.[26]

In April 1949 and devised jointly by Monnet and Will Clayton of the American State Department the US, Britain, France, Benelux and Germany agreed to create an International Ruhr Authority. This would allocate coke between France and Germany and regulate steel output.

But it was not enough to relieve the tension between a Germany beginning to recover its political strength and French designs on European leadership. Matters came to a head in January 1950, when the French Foreign Minister, Robert Schuman, made his first official visit to Germany. It was a disaster. The sticking point was French *de facto* control of the Saar. That Schuman had grown up in Metz under German control, had studied law with Chancellor Adenauer in Bonn, fought in the German army and only entered French life in 1918 aged thirty-two, when Lorraine was returned to France, had no softening impact upon the Germans.

Chancellor Adenauer's strident publicity campaign to regain the Saar and control steel production in the Ruhr was wearing the French down. The French had no chance of controlling either for any length of time. Urgent and extreme action was needed.

In secret Monnet and his team wrote the blueprint for the first building block of the United States of Europe. It was conceived and driven outside the French Government and civil service, and outside normal democratic channels. No-one in the French Government was consulted. Monnet had a separate office in the rue de Martignac in Paris, within a stone's throw of the Quai d'Orsay and the main Government buildings.

Monnet regarded surprise and secrecy as key: they were techniques he employed throughout his life. He may well have believed it was essential to take the French Government by surprise and not allow time for the usual disagreements to grow. He certainly thought the issue should be kept out of the normal diplomatic channels between France and Germany.

According to his memoirs, Monnet implied that he had thought up the outline of the plan alone in the Alps where he had spent the second half of March 1950. On 16th April his team agreed to merge French and German coal and steel interests. The next day they produced a first draft which ended 'This proposal has an essential political objective: to make a breach in the ramparts of national sovereignty which will be narrow enough to secure consent, but deep enough to open the way towards the unity that is essential to peace.'[27] The next eight drafts left that out but the purpose remained.

On 20th April the proposal was put to Bernard Clappier, the French Foreign Minister's chief of staff, who took a week to reply. On 3rd May Robert Schuman raised it in the French Cabinet. It was agreed at the next Cabinet on 8th May. That same day Schuman sent a personal letter to Adenauer, so urgent that it was brought into a German Cabinet meeting. In it Schuman said that his aim was 'not economic but highly political.' Adenauer agreed to Monnet's proposal with alacrity.[28] Monnet's bombshell of the European Coal and Steel Community was dropped at an international press conference that evening.

The European Coal and Steel Community, or the Schuman Plan as it was named, was thought up and agreed in just three weeks. Historians agree that Monnet was its author.

Yet there were parallels with the Franco-Anglo Union plan of 1940, apparently the creation of a few days work, which Monnet claimed as his own. That was the work of others led by Professor Toynbee and had been in preparation and negotiation for a year. Monnet had been willingly used.

Monnet was an imperious man with huge dynamism. That

he was a hard and relentless taskmaster both on himself and those around him was softened by his magnetic, enthusiastic personality. One of his assistants wrote that he 'read few books and was suspicious of erudition based on second hand beliefs.'[29] Monnet may have been the fixer, not the author.

For several years the ideas on which the European Coal and Steel Community were based had been widely discussed in different forums, for example among the economists of ELEC. The year before they had proposed a public body to control coal, steel, electricity and transport.[30] That had been agreed at the Westminster Conference.

Those ideas were brought to fruition by Monnet just when the French were increasingly anxious about a strengthening Germany, and the Americans had run into serious resistance both from the British Government and from Duncan Sandys of the European Movement.

According to Lord Roll, a British civil servant at the centre of negotiations for many years, the pressure to integrate was 'never even slightly relaxed by Jean Monnet and some Americans.'[31]

What was being created went far beyond a coal and steel community.

It deliberately had all the attributes of an embryonic super-state with institutions to match: a High Authority, a Common Assembly to be called the European Parliament, and a Court of Justice, Justice Frankfurter's particular speciality.

The intention was that national governments' influence would not last long though the ECSC still maintained the palliative of direct links. The new Court of Justice would slowly and steadily impose change on national governments. The Court would act as the mechanism for creating the new state, just as the American Supreme Court had increased the centralisation of the US at the expense of the states. The simplicity of the plan was its brilliance.

There is no proof of Frankfurter's direct involvement in the ECSC: Frankfurter left diaries, which he may have intended to be published, but he destroyed many of his papers, probably deliberately.

In 1957 the European Court of Justice was to become the centre-piece of the Common Market embodied in the Treaty of Rome. It has been the paramount mechanism for taking sovereignty from the nation states and giving it to Brussels. No further treaties were needed – they have merely speeded up the process. The judgements have just rolled inexorably on. That may well be Frankfurter's legacy.

Germany And America Back The ECSC

The European Coal and Steel Community suited Chancellor Adenauer. His propaganda campaign for a united Europe was merciless: he used every opportunity to put pressure on France. That way he thought Germany would regain its sovereignty and remove the occupying powers.

Two months before the ECSC was announced, Adenauer had proposed a merger of France and Germany – of their economies, parliaments and citizenship. He gave an interview to the American journalist, Kingsbury Smith[32] proposing that Franco-German political union should be open to the British, Italians and Benelux. He repeated the message in three further interviews within a month.[33]

He sent Professor Erhard to Paris on a reconnaissance mission. According to one biographer, Erhard 'carried the German proposals typed on the notepaper of the great Vereinigte Stahlwerke, the huge steel cartel nominally broken up by the Allies.'[34] Adenauer's closest adviser on the ECSC was Dr Robert Pferdmenges, a former member of the steel works' supervisory board, so he carried the powerful steel lobby with him.

Adenauer was backed by John McCloy, the outspoken American High Commissioner in Germany, an old friend of Monnet and 'partner' of Frankfurter for whom he had acted as a trouble-shooter early in the war when in charge of political and military matters in the War Office.[35]

On 18th October 1949, McCloy had suggested in 'The Times' that the International Ruhr Authority might be extended to the whole of Western Europe. Despite his own enthusiasm for unity, McCloy was being manipulated by Adenauer and, to his regret, was often pushed farther than he intended.[36]

As Schuman's note to Adenauer said, the coal and steel community was political. From the start the French and Germans never intended to include the British. If the British chose to join after the main terms had been set that was all well and good. The British were not to be given the chance again to debate the framework in case the aim of political union was watered down and became mere co-operation like the Council of Europe.

Dean Acheson, who had become the American Secretary of State in the January, inadvertently highlighted the lack of consultation with the British. He visited Paris on 7th May 1950 en route to London for a NATO conference the following day. Schuman told him about the plan, which Acheson understood he and Monnet had developed in secret. According to his autobiography that was the first Acheson had heard of it. He immediately informed President Truman by telegram.

Acheson was embarrassed when he arrived in London because the British had no idea of what was afoot and assumed Acheson had connived in it. The British were only formally informed after the world was told at the press conference, when the French Ambassador, René Massigli, called on the British Foreign Secretary, Ernest Bevin.

Acheson, though he was Secretary of State, probably genuinely did not know. He had been deliberately sidelined for the job of running the ECA by Senator Vandenberg to limit State Department influence. Acheson rebuffed attempts by the ECA in Paris and Donovan of the ACUE to pressurise the British to pursue European federation. He thought it was up to the British whether or not federation was in their interest and that of the Commonwealth. Acheson would only urge, not force.

Bevin reacted furiously to the news and immediately suspected a French-American plot. Press reaction was mixed. Two papers, 'The Economist' and the 'Daily Express', realised that the motives behind the ECSC were political and not economic. The 'Daily Express' editor wrote, 'It would be the end of Britain's independence'. The rest of the press took the plan at its economic face value.

While Clement Attlee, the Prime Minister, welcomed the Franco-German reconciliation in the House of Commons, he added Britain would wish to study the economic consequences, and that there could not be a 'commitment to the acceptance of the principles in advance.'[37]

That was exactly what Monnet wished to avoid. The British note to the French said, ' . . . if the French Government intend to insist on a commitment to pool resources and set up an authority with certain sovereign powers as a prior condition to joining in the talks, His Majesty's Government would reluctantly be unable to accept such a condition.' Britain asked for a special position at the ECSC negotiations. The French refused. In one of the many notes which flew between London and Paris, Monnet explicitly wrote that the aim was 'partial fusion of sovereignty'.[38]

Both Monnet and Schuman told the British they would go ahead without them if necessary. Britain's involvement was no longer essential, because of the new political triumvirate of France, Germany and the US. That reversed the position of the first five years after the war.

Monnet visited London five days after the first announcement as no-one else fully understood the details.[39] It was a transparent attempt to paper over the massive cracks in Franco-British relations.

Monnet also called on some of his old friends for their views, including Geoffrey Crowther, the editor of 'The Economist'. Crowther was another friend of Frankfurter.[40] It is noteworthy that 'The Economist', backed by Lord Layton, supported European unity from those first days and, as will be seen, pushed hard for Britain's entry. While some of 'The Economist' writers thought Britain should be a member, the Liberal Layton at the time did not.

On 1st June, the French tried a compromise of semantics with the British; they suggested the merging of some sovereignty as an 'objective' not a 'resolve', wording that was less binding. The British, given only twenty-four hours to reply, proposed a meeting of Ministers. Monnet and Schuman refused because the principle of supra-nationality would not be likely to remain intact. The French were not going to give the British any room to negotiate. After that they heaped opprobrium on the British for failing to take part.

The director of the British Iron and Steel Federation told a government working party that the issues for the new High Authority would go far beyond the coal and steel industries themselves, for example to tariffs, wages and plant location. Governments would have to implement ECSC decisions.[41] He had hit on the central dilemma of the ECSC for the British Government – the loss of sovereignty.

The British Labour Party published a booklet, 'European Unity', on 13th June which embarrassed the Party because of its lack of enthusiasm. But Denis Healey and Hugh Dalton had drafted it some months before. A Labour Government, they said, had a sovereign right to pursue democratic socialism. They did not want a supra-national authority to impose agreements: the need was for 'international machinery to carry out agreements which are reached without compulsion.'[42]

The Conservative Party was no more in favour of the ECSC than was the Labour Party. The exceptions were a few Conservative MPs in ELEC: Harold Macmillan and fellow members wrote to 'The Times' urging British acceptance of the Schuman Plan. He thought the concept of sovereignty had changed and compared the Plan with the pooling of information and resources in NATO, a comparison which has been made many times since.[43] In his autobiography Macmillan said he thought Britain could have changed the terms of the Schuman Plan to make it inter-governmental. That was wishful thinking.

The House of Commons' two day debate on the Schuman Plan was overshadowed by the prospect of war again – North Korea had just invaded South Korea. Inevitably the ECSC was seen in the light of defence concerns. Most Conservatives playing the party line thought Britain should join the discussions on the Schuman Plan. Much of the argument concerned peace, reconciliation and, as Edward Heath, the future Prime Minister, said in his maiden speech the need to tie Germany into a united Europe.

Churchill's speech to the House showed the French were right to think the British would not want to give up sovereignty and given a chance would alter the substance of the Plan. Churchill countered Macmillan's concept of pooling sovereignty. Referring to Britain putting its armies under SHAEF for the limited and specific purpose of winning the war, he said, 'no-one suggested that General Eisenhower should have had the power to say what units of the British army should be suppressed and disbanded, or how they should be raised or remodelled . . .'

While many MPs recognised the aim of a federal Europe, it was obviously so far off and not a serious issue. They gravely misunderstood the intent of France and Germany, let alone the US. They apparently had no idea of the international network which had led to the ECSC. Most speakers were naive enough to believe that the Schuman Plan did not conflict with the interests of the Commonwealth. Most of the debate was to be repeated many times during the next forty-five years.

Monnet realised that few British MPs understood the intent of the Schuman Plan. At a press statement during the Paris conference of the Six, he insisted on a supra-national approach: 'over and above coal and steel, it (the Plan) is laying the foundations of a European federation. In a federation, no state can secede by its own unilateral decision'.[44] Germany's Dr Hallstein endorsed this, 'The German Government reaffirms that the importance of the Schuman Plan is above all political. In this context economic problems, substantial as they may be, are secondary.'

Macmillan did not give up. He did not understand that there was no room to negotiate. With fellow Conservative MP David Eccles, he proposed another plan at the Second Strasbourg Assembly in August 1950 to make a coal and steel authority responsible to a Council of Ministers and linked to national Parliaments. The new project would allow any member state to withdraw if it gave twelve months notice.

Monnet emphasised he was against the right to withdraw; he wanted a fusion of powers, not a balance. Reynaud asked Macmillan to withdraw his amendment because the treaty signing was only a few weeks away. By that time of course the CIA officers running the ACUE had already decided the

British were to be removed from the leadership of the European Movement because they were not 'federal'.

Two years later, in March 1952, the then Conservative British Government was to try again with the Eden Plan to subordinate the ECSC to an inter-governmental Council of Europe tied to national parliaments. A few agreed, but not those who mattered: Adenauer, Monnet, the French Government and the guiding Americans.

The detailed negotiations for the ECSC took about six months. Each country had national interests to protect: the Italians wanted to expand their high-cost steel production; the Belgians had massively inefficient coal mines; the Germans were reluctant to abandon cartels. Adenauer resisted the strong Ruhr lobby in the higher interest of removing all Allied control from Germany. The existence of the ECSC was to allow Germany to re-establish a Ministry of Foreign Affairs and have diplomatic relations with foreign countries.

Some French were fearful of German hegemony: 'Why offer Germany what it would have imposed upon us if she had definitely defeated us?' said one.[45] Their voices counted for nothing.

The Treaty establishing the European Coal and Steel Authority was initialled on 19th March 1951, and took just over a year to ratify. In August 1952 the new Community began work in Luxembourg with Jean Monnet, an unelected official, its first President. The common market for coal opened the following February and that for steel in the May.

In his opening speech Monnet stressed that the new Community merged part of each nation's sovereignty with the High Authority which could take decisions binding throughout the Six. The Community had the power to levy taxes, was responsible to a European (not a national) Assembly, and to a European Court of Justice. He added, 'these institutions are supranational and, let us not shrink from the word, federal.'[46]

The ECSC was designed to be a regulated and centralised organisation, not a free market. The pattern was repeated later with the Common Market and then the Single Market. The ECSC's many inadequacies were partially obscured by a thirty year steel boom. In any case, since its purpose was political, its economic failings were quietly buried.

From the start the Germans defeated the anti-trust articles, a notable American interest.[47] Despite the treaty and the Allied break-up of the great Vereinigte Stahlwerke into thirteen firms, the German steelmasters remained a cartel. By 1959 the Thyssen family had regained control of a quarter of the Ruhr's crude steel production and other steel groups had reformed. In France by 1958 six groups with interlocking ownership controlled seventy-six percent of French steel production.

Four Years Of Defence Debate

On 25th June 1950 the North Koreans invaded South Korea and President Truman committed American troops, not just to repulse the invasion but to free North Korea from Communism. Truman needed to increase the American army fast and send new troops to Europe in case the Russians surged westwards. Fearful Ruhr industrialists even advertised in Communist Party newspapers in Eastern Europe in case the USSR should gain the upper hand in Germany.

Three days after the fighting started, the Americans slashed the European Co-operation Administration budget by $208 million.[48] Not surprisingly European union ran a very poor second to defence. The ECSC negotiations were at a delicate stage and a major war could have destroyed them.

On 12th September 1950 the American Secretary of State,

Dean Acheson, dropped a bombshell. He proposed to create ten German divisions within NATO and have sixty divisions in Europe altogether. The Americans would send four. The Americans proposed a united command, not a separate German army and a German general staff.

The rest of NATO agreed and waited to see how the sensitive French would react. German divisions rang all the alarm bells in France, and a NATO solution was unthinkable because it would give Germany equal status.

The Radical, François Quilici, said in a National Assembly debate, 'The Americans will leave one day. But they will have re-created and developed German power over our frontier . . . The story, the sad story, is beginning again.' The socialist, André Philip, replied that 'the only way to ensure that a new Germany shall not dominate Europe is to see that Europe dominates the Ruhr.'[49] Schuman for the French Government would go no further than a German paramilitary police force.

An integrated European army had already been debated in August in the Council of Europe in Strasbourg and formally proposed by Winston Churchill, then still in opposition and playing politics. He later famously said 'I really meant it for them and not for us' adding a European army would be a 'sludgy amalgam'.[50]

An integrated army suited the federalists who dominated the Council of Europe and had been discussed from the earliest days. André Philip remarked that its creation would be 'financed by a European fund fed by European taxes.'[51] The problem was that only five years after the end of the war few could support German participation.

Afraid that the ECSC might not survive this crisis Jean Monnet quickly proposed extending it to defence – a European Defence Community (EDC). It was called the Pleven Plan after the then French Prime Minister, René Pleven. Monnet used his ECSC team to draft the terms: a European

Defence Minister would be responsible to a Council of Ministers and a Common Assembly; German troops would be integrated at the lower battalion level rather than division level; and German soldiers would wear a European uniform. As many sensibilities as possible would be allayed. But it was obvious that the Germans would be treated as second class citizens, not what Adenauer wanted.

Adenauer was always pushing ahead of the possible. He had been campaigning for a European Defence force for some time, especially in the US.[52] It was all part of his non-stop strategy to regain German sovereignty, abolish the Allied High Commission and make Germany an equal international partner.

Monnet wrote, 'the federation of Europe would have to become an immediate objective. The army, its weapons and basic production would all have to be placed simultaneously under joint sovereignty. We could no longer wait, as we had once planned, for political Europe to be the culminating point of a gradual process, since its joint defence was inconceivable without a joint political authority from the start.'

Felix Frankfurter, his American mentor, always recommended caution and slow change, if necessary waiting for years to effect a revolution. After forty-five years of integration European defence is only now being seriously proposed. It is a huge leap and one that cannot be disguised for what it is.

No-one was keen on the EDC. Only briefly did Monnet see it as a way out of a difficult situation. It was too early to add such an emotive building block in the slow creation of Europe and he soon turned his attention back to the ECSC.

The State Department was worried that the Pleven Plan would detract from the fighting ability of NATO, and its political structure would take years to sort out. The French,

British, Dutch and Belgians were all reluctant to give up any sovereignty on defence. When the Pleven Plan was put to the French National Assembly in October 1950, the watering down process started at once.

The EDC would have faded away had not the Americans, despite their reservations, seized upon it as a way of appeasing the French, whom they did not understand, and rearming Europe against the Russians.[53] Once the potential threat from the USSR began to escalate, West Germany was assured of an independent future.

That dealt Adenauer an excellent hand. He could afford to shed his previous position of aggressively playing all sides off against each other and become the co-operative European statesman. He remarked, 'The creation of a Europe which is politically strong is the only path leading to the recovery of Germany's Eastern territories, which remains one of the essential goals of our activities.'[54]

Germany was the only country to benefit from the EDC proposal: part of the deal was to be the restoration of German sovereignty. In May 1951 Germany was admitted to the Council of Europe. Steadily it regained all the aspects of a sovereign state.

Adenauer pushed harder at the opening door: Professor Hallstein (Adenauer's 'personal assistant' in the Foreign Office) demanded German entry to NATO.[55]

Germans had a mixed reaction to rearmament. The military expected a renaissance and immediately demanded the renunciation of collective war guilt, the release of war criminals, and equal status for German soldiers in the new European army. Adenauer had already been having private meetings with senior officers of Hitler's Wehrmacht and other military contacts, the former German armed forces had cause to believe their time was about to come again.

On the other hand Kurt Schumacher, the SPD leader,

fought the EDC hard and bitterly. During twelve years in Nazi concentration camps he had been brutally treated, losing both an arm and a leg and was dreadfully disfigured.

Among the general population there were substantial reservations and unease which were to grow as the years passed.

The British Foreign Secretary, Anthony Eden, pushed for the two Communities to be inter-governmental under the Council of Europe. Monnet successfully lobbied his friends in Washington to defeat that.

Spurred by the Americans, eighteen months of negotiations led to the Bonn Convention on 26th May 1952.[56] The UK, France, West Germany and the US agreed to restore West German sovereignty provided the EDC treaty was not just signed but ratified by all signatories. Only Germany and Benelux ratified it. The Italians prevaricated and the French were split.

Too Soon For Political Union

For a short time, mainly during 1952, the 'Europeans' tried to push beyond an EDC to political union with the European Political Commission. Altiero Spinelli and André Philip of the revolutionary UEF proposed a constitution for a United States of Europe with all the major state functions under a European executive.

Spinelli bitterly reflected on British guardianship of the European question. 'There was no talk of federation, transfer of sovereignty, supranational institutions . . . but instead an abundance of platitudes and generalities concerning a generic 'union', the heritage of a common civilisation, solidarity against communism, a permanent resolution of the Franco-German question and so on.' Spinelli thought Churchill and the British had duped the Americans over the Marshall Plan so the idea of a United States of Europe would eventually fade into the history books.[57]

The US State Department had reservations about the European Political Commission: it was going too far too quickly and could sink the still unratified EDC treaty, a forecast which proved correct.

It may have been a case of the ACUE and the CIA, which did not necessarily move in tandem with the State Department, putting on pressure to move quickly to federation. The ACUE was funding the UEF which proposed the Commission and Spaak became the chief spokesman for it.

Spaak had resigned in December 1951 as president of the Council of Europe after it had been limited to an intergovernmental group by the British. Spaak probably made the move to the UEF in agreement with the Americans of the ACUE as he certainly had when he resigned from the European Movement, again frustrated by the British.

Spaak asked two American Professors, Carl Friedrich and Robert Bowie, to draft a European federal constitution. Friedrich, a world federalist, had already been commissioned by the ACUE to write a comparative study of federalism in Australia, Canada, Germany, Switzerland and the US.[58]

In August 1952, Monnet now at the ECSC planned a draft treaty for a European Political Community to be the umbrella for the ECSC and the EDC with responsibility for economic policy and co-ordinate foreign policy with a common market for goods, capital and people. 10,000 French mayors added their signatures and the Germans readily agreed.

A European Political Authority and a European Parliament were just what Adenauer wanted to further Germany's return to sovereignty and respectability. He said the new institutions would secure lasting peace with France. Adenauer's campaign was backed by fellow German speakers and Catholics,

Schuman from France, and De Gaspari from Italy with the support of Catholics from Benelux.

Liberals from all over Europe attacked Adenauer for trying to create a 'Little Europe' of French, Germans and Italian Catholics centred on the Rhine with similar boundaries to Charlemagne's Empire. Adenauer's European vision naturally excluded the British, Scandinavians and other Protestants especially East Germany under Russian domination. Despite laying ritual claim to the Eastern Lander, Adenauer could never allow German re-unification which would destroy his Catholic power base. When international tensions briefly relaxed after Stalin's death in 1953 the USSR considered returning East Germany – it was a liability to them. Adenauer did not reply.

'Little Europe' proved to be an aberration though it achieved the twin German aims of regaining sovereignty and international power. The Bismarck tradition of a relationship with Russia, and if necessary a lesser link with the West, still had a wide appeal in Germany.

Pope Pius XII backed the Catholic 'Little Europe'. During the war he had been carefully sympathetic to the idea of European union and afterwards he encouraged the emergence of a right wing and Catholic Germany as a key to a 'Little Europe'. His household was largely dominated by Germans.[59] One of the Pope's officials and a close friend, Dr Luigi Gedda, had helped to defeat the Communists in the 1948 Italian elections. Gedda had CIA funds via the American Embassy in Rome.[60] When he switched to support a 'Little Europe' more CIA money was forthcoming.

During 1952 the European Political Commission was debated in the French Cabinet and the ECSC. Some enthusiasm continued into 1953. Amid dissension it died when the French rejected the EDC.

The EDC Dies

Thawing relations with the USSR after Stalin's death in March 1953 and the end of the Korean war four months later should have killed the EDC proposal. Yet the debate continued for more than a year fanned by J. F. Dulles, the new US Secretary of State from January 1953. An advocate of destroying the European nation states for nearly all his life, Dulles had led the American campaigners for European federation but he had had no official political role. Now he was in a supreme position to act.

Dulles virtually alone increased international tension. Where his predecessor, Dean Acheson, had been careful not to push hard for the EDC in case the French thought they were being forced into a corner, Dulles had no such scruples. He used the stick rather than the carrot.

In his first television speech to the nation as Secretary of State he said: 'if . . . there were no chance of getting effective unity (of Europe) and if in particular France, Germany and England should go their separate ways, then certainly it would be necessary to give a little rethinking to America's own foreign policy in relation to Western Europe.'[61]

Dulles repeated his threats several times during 1953, in particular to the French and often face to face. The next year he used 'shuttle diplomacy' – a first – visiting Europe at least once a month. His threats were counter-productive.

Worse, Dulles' dogmatic campaign for the EDC threatened the fledgling ECSC. Monnet had to ask him to visit the ECSC in Luxembourg for a day to show his support. Dulles agreed to a permanent American representative to the ECSC, his supporter David Bruce with Bill Tomlinson as his deputy.[62]

When Monnet visited Washington to receive a degree in May and June 1953, his backers turned it into the nearest thing to a State visit.[63]

Monnet's friends from the lobby groups dedicated to one Europe included Allen Dulles, now head of the CIA; John McCloy, the former High Commissioner for Germany and now chairman of the Chase Manhattan Bank in New York;[64] George Ball with his law firm Cleary, Gottlieb, Friendly and Ball; and Walter Bedell Smith, now at the State Department, a member the ACUE and formerly head of the CIA.

Monnet met General Donovan, chairman of the ACUE. He dined at Brook's Club with his old friends and mentors Felix Frankfurter, George Ball, Adolf Berle, all long standing backers of a United States of Europe. The next day J. F. Dulles introduced him to President Eisenhower.

Monnet confidently told the Senate Foreign Relations Committee on 5th June of his faith in a United States of Europe. The newly published draft treaty of a European Political Community would, he said, mean the federation of Europe. Monnet used his considerable charm to make his 'State visit' an overwhelming success. Such was his authority that the Americans believed him. The US was now visibly backing a United States of Europe.

By August 1953 Churchill knew the EDC had no more life left in it, but Dulles could not let go. He was goaded by the thought, not shared by the British, that Germany bereft of sovereignty might slip into the Russians' sphere of influence. With Adenauer there that was extremely unlikely, but doubtless he cleverly used this possibility in conversation with his friend Dulles. Under Dulles the alliance with Germany replaced the old 'special relationship' with Britain.[65]

Dulles' dogmatic belief in the EDC had blinded him to its folly. As he told Spaak, 'United States policy had since, 1946, been based on the hope that one day western Europe would unite.'[66] Dangerously he listened only to his supporters, Monnet and Spaak.

In the French National Assembly debate of October 1953,

widely discussed in the French press, Michel Debré put the
Gaullist Case against the EDC: 'The profound problem is
the German will to expand, and this phenomenon far sur-
passes all the quarrels of France and Germany. Today's
problem is not German hostility toward France . . . It is the
unity of Germany, its reunification, the recapture of the lost
territories . . . Our policy is clear: to prevent Germany from
preparing for re-conquest, and then going beyond that. Our
policy must be to bind it, to act as a brake, a moderating
element . . . not only does the European army not bind it, it
increases the German danger.'[67]

Nearly a year later, the final passionate French debate on
the EDC took place at the end of August 1954. The French
defeat at Dien Bien Phu (Indo-China, now Vietnam) on 7th
May after fifty-six days of fighting, and the American failure
to reply to French requests for help, critically affected the
outcome. The EDC was defeated by 319 to 264 with 43
abstentions. Every party was split except the Communists
who opposed it. The elder statesman, Edouard Herriot, who
had led support for Pan Europa in the late 1920s, declared:
'For me (it is) the end of France . . . Beware of having to
regret an act you would not be able to repair, an act you
would not be able to take back.'[68]

The French sank the EDC just as they would probably
have sunk the ECSC had not Monnet sprung it on them.

Immediately after the death of the EDC, Eden succeeded
with his own plan – an old fashioned alliance. He revived
the 1947 Brussels Treaty on defence and turned the Western
Union into the Western European Union (WEU), now to
include Italy and Germany. The WEU was made subservient
to NATO and so a transatlantic alliance controlled arms
production. Germany would not be allowed to manufacture
atomic, biological or chemical weapons and would be limited

to twelve divisions. With that insurance policy, Germany regained its sovereignty and became a member of NATO.

A British commitment proved to be the breakthrough. Britain pledged that the four British divisions and its tactical air force would not be withdrawn from the Continent except in 'an acute overseas emergency.' If the British had not guaranteed troops, Germany would have remained occupied by the Big Four. The new treaties were rapidly ratified and on 5th May 1955 the Western Allies recognised the new Federal Republic of Germany. Eden had saved the Atlantic Alliance.

Monnet told David Bruce who passed it on to Dulles that the British plan was a 'camouflage and dangerous decoy because it would give the impression that European unity can be achieved without transferring powers of decision to common institutions.'[69]

Adenauer had an additional bonus from the death of the EDC. It ended the plan to Europeanise the Saar which the French had annexed. Two years later the Saar population voted overwhelmingly to re-join Germany. That was endorsed by the 1957 Treaty of Rome.

For the first ten years after the war France had had a hold over Germany. When German sovereignty was restored in 1955 that hold was dramatically weakened. From then on France had to become more and more vociferous in negotiations. In the end it was bound to lose.

Three Ways To Unity

With the end of both the European Defence and Political Communities the ECSC could easily have faded away. Britain showed no inclination to join and just opted for associate status. The French Prime Minister, Mendès-France, disliked the idea of negotiating with a High Authority, not a real state. The ECSC was cumbersome: proceedings were held in four languages and it was physically split between Strasbourg (the Assembly) and Luxembourg (the Court). Many practical problems emerged because of the different tax systems and production laws. Monnet was accused of being a lame duck president – he had fallen ill after only six months in the top job.

Yet almost at once, in the autumn of 1954, three new initiatives were underway each designed to further the ultimate cause of a united Europe: the Common Market, the Action Committee for a United Europe and Euratom.

The Common Market initiative was begun by the Dutch Foreign Minister, Dr J. W. Beyen. He wrote to his close ally Spaak suggesting a substantial and immediate broadening of European integration, not the slow sector by sector approach. Known as the 'Benelux Memorandum', Beyen's paper deliberately replaced the emotive words 'United States of Europe' by 'Economic Community'. His proposals had been in circulation for a long time. They were discussed by Federal Union in London at the beginning of the war and at the 1949 conferences organised by Sandys and Retinger.

Beyen said he devised the Common Market with some supra-nationality to guarantee the irreversibility of Dutch-German relations, a guarantee disliked by his Cabinet colleagues. When Holland had become part of the Nazi EEC the Germans had deliberately made Holland dependent on Germany by giving its important agricultural products only one market – Germany.

Beyen believed it was necessary to give up some sovereignty to preserve the nation state against its former German occupier. Perhaps his war-time Nazi sympathies helped him to take a more positive line towards the Germans than most Dutch were able to do. While Beyen had been at the Bank for International Settlements in 1939 he was denounced in the British House of Lords for his 'well known Nazi sympa-thies'.[70] Then in 1940 he had joined the board of Unilever which, like many large companies, had substantial frozen Reichsmark credits in Germany and could be open to Nazi blackmail. Most did not succumb: Beyen may have done. The continental manager of Unilever in London was also suspected of having Nazi sympathies. Beyen went on to be a leading Dutch banker and then Foreign Minister.

Within a month of receiving Beyen's suggestion for inte-grating Europe, Spaak met Monnet informally in Paris in October 1954 and the two agreed that the way forward must be through the less contentious economic field. Monnet himself was never keen on the Dutch Common Market approach[71] perhaps because it did not have the American parentage he valued. Nonetheless Monnet started to drum up support for the economic approach to union. He spent the autumn of 1954 talking to the leaders of the six ECSC countries.

On 11th November 1954 Monnet handed in his resig-nation as president of the ECSC. John McCloy reported to Felix Frankfurter that 'Mendès-France had given the impression that a certain return to nationalism was in the air and Jean feels this should be counteracted.' Dulles thought he should have fought on.

The Beyen plan was put to the ECSC Council of Ministers in February 1955. The small Benelux countries saw a Common Market, in which they would play their part, as a counter to the threat of a Franco-German link which might either have excluded them altogether or reduced their influ-ence to a minimum.

For Germany the Common Market could be another step towards international respectability and might ultimately lead to German control of Europe. In the short term it was a bargaining counter to make France return the Saar to

Germany. Germany saw the Common Market as an extension of the Zollverein or customs union, which had been deliberately conceived to subordinate the many German states to Prussia. It could be used again to unite Europe in Germany's favour with an immediate concentration of power in the Ruhr. If Britain stayed outside it would be isolated, just as Austria had been nearly one hundred years before, and then ultimately it would be forced to treat for terms. That was prescient.

The Action Committee

In the New Year of 1955 Monnet suggested the second initiative, a group called the Action Committee for a United States of Europe. It was to be influential for twenty years until Monnet's health faded.

The Committee was a clever idea: government representatives were included yet they acted in unofficial capacities. The Committee worked across governments yet was not directly responsible to any of them. It had the authority of thirty political leaders from six countries (the British joined in 1968), twenty major parties, and the ten most powerful trade unions. In France, where governments had a short life, Monnet's Action Committee had a particularly powerful influence.

The Committee was made up of representatives of parties and trade unions with a distinctly socialist bias. Employers were notable by their absence, so too were individual delegates. That deliberately cut out another prime mover of European union, Altiero Spinelli: he and Monnet did not get on. Monnet also deliberately excluded the Communists and Gaullists who were the strongest opponents of federalism.

The ACUE partly funded the Committee though the Americans complained that Monnet 'concentrated deliberately on labour and socialist elements'.[72]

Its large permanent team had a strong and continuing impact because the committee itself only met once or twice a year. It published resolutions to steer Governments' European policies. The letter of invitation to thirty-three delegates stated that the goal of the Committee was a United States of Europe.[73] The new committee was not formally established until 13th October 1955 because Monnet still had to serve out his time as President of the ECSC.

Euratom

While Monnet was building his Action Committee, Frankfurter gave him another project, a third initiative, to restore the flagging fortunes of 'Europe'. Frankfurter introduced Monnet to another of his 'boys'. Max Isenburgh, the deputy legal counsel of the American Atomic Energy Commission, happened to be in Europe on a Rockefeller Senior Fellowship.[74]

Isenburgh advised Monnet that the way to extend the ECSC and keep the European momentum going was to establish a new Community for the peaceful use of atomic energy. Atomic energy was then the exciting technology of the future. Monnet took to this idea with enthusiasm as he had to Franco-Anglo Union and the ECSC and made it his own. One of Monnet's team, Louis Armand, did most of the detailed work on the treaty for the peaceful use of atomic energy and was to become the first President of Euratom. Monnet used Spaak – the better speaker as he thought – to present the case to the ECSC to relaunch 'Europe'.

Euratom had a secondary function: it was designed to prevent the Germans from developing an independent – and thus threatening – atomic energy industry.

Euratom, which had substantial American backing, was never to achieve the great success which Frankfurter and Monnet expected. From 1959 the price of oil and gas fell sharply, partly thorough the discovery of new fields, and made atomic energy uncompetitive.

Messina And The Treaty of Rome

To further the Common Market and Euratom, Spaak and Beyen suggested to the Prime Minister of Luxembourg, Joseph Bech that the Foreign Ministers of the Six should meet. Backed and paid for by the ECSC, they arranged a conference in Messina in Sicily. The place was chosen to support Gaetano Martino, the Italian Foreign Minister, facing an election in his home constituency.

As ever, the French were cautious.[75] The Benelux three were impatient for success. So too were Martino of Italy and Hallstein of Germany. The British Foreign Office thought 'nothing would happen and sent a civil servant, Russell Brotherton, as an observer'. According to the Conservative MP, Peter Thorneycroft, author of the 1947 booklet advocating that the British give up economic sovereignty, Brotherton was 'a brilliant civil servant. In so far as the light of European union was carried at all during that period (early 1950s), it was due to him.'[76]

The Messina conference was a quick affair lasting just two days – 1st and 2nd June 1955 – with delegates staying twenty-five miles down the coast at Taormina. Few reservations were expressed. Pinay for France was concerned that the tariff barrier protecting the new community from the rest of the world should be high enough and wanted the other Five to raise their wage rates so France would not be handicapped. Martino stressed the need to harmonise taxes and social security contributions.

The conference accepted Spaak and Monnet's proposals for the Common Market and Euratom. Plans were included for a European network of inland waterways, motorways, electrified railways and for cheaper electricity.

The Six called for 'a new stage in the building of Europe . . . (with a) first step in the economic sphere . . . to work for the establishment of a united Europe by the development of common situations, the progressive harmonisation of their social policies. Such a policy seems to them indispensable if (Europe is to) maintain its position in the world, regain its influence and prestige and achieve a continuing increase in the standard of living of her population.'

Monnet had an odd role at Messina. He stayed away in Luxembourg, but was constantly on the telephone to sway the French and German socialists who had previously blocked the European Defence Community.

In the last days of his Presidency of the ECSC, Monnet seemed to have second thoughts and wanted to stay on but the French government vetoed him at Messina. René Mayer replaced Monnet on 10th June.

To turn the Messina Resolution into a treaty Spaak headed a committee which took two years to negotiate. It included national delegates[77] and representatives from the ECSC High Authority. When the negotiations looked in danger of stalling, Monnet sent a small team led by Pierre Uri to the South of France to work in peace on the Spaak Report – the forerunner of the Treaty of Rome.

But as ever, France had the most serious doubts. Agriculture was as important to France as it was to Holland. Over a quarter of French worked on the land and produced sixteen per cent of French GDP. That was significant enough but importantly the farmers were over-represented in parliament. Further France was producing huge surpluses, especially of cereals, amounting to forty per cent of the Community's total agricultural production from only twenty per cent of the Community's arable land.[78] Two of Monnet's team convinced the French farm leaders that they would have a protected outlet for their grain and sugar beet surpluses.[79]

Three events during 1956 accelerated negotiations. In the January most of the Gaullists – the 'anti-Europeans' – lost their seats at the French general election and power swung to the socialists led by Guy Mollet. On 26th July Nasser seized the Suez Canal immediately raising fears of an oil shortage. That helped the Euratom discussions. Tension rose again when the Hungarian uprising of 25th October was brutally put down by the Warsaw Pact forces.

Germany and France were the centre of negotiations. With tensions high at a key meeting on 6th November 1956 Adenauer agreed to Mollet's economic conditions. Above all Adenauer wanted political integration and judged that France's agricultural demands posed little threat to the German economy. So Adenauer accepted French demands for minimum prices to protect the home producer which would eventually be agreed by weighted majority voting. Any hint of free trade in France was anathema, the French economy had to be protected

The free trader German Economics Minister, Ludwig Erhard, challenged the deal. 'Le Monde' reported his views: 'France has considered the Common Market project solely from the point of view of protection of its economy and cares little for true freedom of trade. The result will not be a market with free competition, but an economic burden for Europe.'[80] Erhard's objections did not last long: if there was a German advantage he would trim his views on free trade. He rightly saw that the EEC was a step towards a European Zollverein which could only benefit Germany.

During the negotiations Monnet and the Six made a number of overtures to Britain, but its interests were no more compatible with this stage of 'Europe' than they had been with the ECSC or the EDC. Spaak suggested in his memoirs[81] that the Common Market negotiations worked because they were inspired by a common political goal. It was one which Britain did not share then and does not share now.

The Treaty of Rome was signed on 25th March 1957 in the Sala degli Orazie Curiazi of the Capitol. The detailed treaty had 248 articles, plus annexes and protocols to set up the European Investment Bank and the European Court of Justice. It was, as Monnet, said a staging post on the way to a 'more important revolution which was still to come – a political revolution'. It was the opposite of free trade, a trading bloc or customs union with an external tariff barrier to the rest of the world.

The Preamble started with the determination 'to lay the foundations of an ever closer union among the peoples of Europe.' Under Roman law the Preamble is the intent of the law by which disputes are interpreted, unlike British Common Law under which it would have no significant meaning.

Majority voting, as used in the ECSC, was key just as it had been in the Prussian's Zollverein. It was refined by a weighted vote devised by Uri to balance the interests of the smaller and larger countries. France, Germany and Italy had four votes each, Belgium and the Netherlands two and Luxembourg one. Under the Treaty of Rome no one state would be able to hold up the rest.

To start with twenty-five areas were covered by qualified majority voting rather than unanimity. It was the beginning of the ratchet towards majority voting on every issue. The national veto was a short term measure only. Today the national veto has nearly disappeared.

The Common Market was to be introduced in three stages of four years each. Its main points were the elimination of internal customs duties; the erection of a tariff barrier around the Community; the free movement of people, services and capital within it; the creation of a Common Agricultural Policy; and a common transport policy. Common rules were to be introduced on competition policy and tax; laws were to be harmonised. Economic policies were to be co-ordinated and a Social Fund set up. A separate treaty established the European Atomic Energy Commission.

The first President of the Commission was Walter Hallstein, well liked in the US. Sicco Mansholt, the Dutch socialist Minister of Agriculture, was one of the Vice Presidents. He had conceived a fore-runner of the Common Agricultural Policy.

The new European Economic Community (EEC) achieved early successes. Duties were lowered faster than the treaty dictated and the Common External Tariff (CET) – the outer tariff wall – was quickly in place. With the reduction of internal tariffs, French and German trade within the EEC doubled between 1958 and 1962.

Large businesses responded by setting up offices to lobby Brussels – inevitably they became part of the Brussels' system.

But agriculture caused grave problems. By 1960 French surpluses were even bigger. The French government tried and failed to restrict production: farm income was rising more slowly than non-farm income. The French farmers rioted. The German Government wanted to open German markets to French produce but German farmers resisted. Eventually the French were to be satisfied by the Common Agricultural Policy.

Yet there was a big potential prize. Monnet's United States of Europe Action Committee declared in October 1958: 'Tomorrow's political unity will depend on making the economic union effective in the everyday activities of industry, agriculture, and government. Little by little the work of the Communities will be felt ... Then, the everyday realities themselves will make it possible to form the political union which is the goal of our Community and to establish the United States of Europe.'[82]

Adenauer echoed that declaring it was a step towards the 'realisation of political union.'[83] On 1st June 1958, General de Gaulle returned to power in France. Their optimism was to be short lived.

Crisis As De Gaulle Resists The Tide

At a surprise press conference in September 1960, de Gaulle pushed his Trojan horse into the enemy camp. He proposed regular co-operation among the Six in the political and defence fields. It was music to Monnet's ears. De Gaulle easily persuaded the Five to join a committee chaired by the French diplomat, Christian Fouchet.

But instead of promoting the end of the nation state, Fouchet used the pretext of a stronger foreign policy to try to remould the EEC and make it inter-governmental, ending majority voting. A committee of civil servants in Paris would by-pass Dr Hallstein's Commission in Brussels with its Commissioners under oath not to take instruction from national governments under article 157 of the Treaty of Rome.

The Fouchet Plan came to a head in May 1962 when de Gaulle bitterly attacked a Europe of 'myths, fictions and pageants' and Brussels with its 'stateless people' and its technocratic jargon. He accused the US of being Europe's federator.

French politics fell apart with five Ministers resigning and 296 deputies – nearly half – signing a 'European manifesto'. The six Heads of Government did not meet again for six years. In Brussels Fouchet is still a term of abuse.

Despite the crisis, de Gaulle cemented a Franco-German alliance. The elderly Adenauer made a State visit to France at the end of 1962 and both leaders reviewed troops on the fields of Charlemagne and knelt before the High Altar of Rheims Cathedral. De Gaulle told his German hosts on his State visit to Germany 'Sie sind ein grosses Volk.' In January 1963 the two signed a Treaty of Friendship. Franco-German reconciliation, eighteen years after the war, seemed to be a triumph.

As a respectful farewell to Adenauer the Bundestag agreed to the treaty. The Bundestag carefully added a preamble of German aims including self-determination, reunification, a unified Europe, co-operation with the US and an integrated NATO army. The NATO clause stung de Gaulle. One of de Gaulle's Cabinet later wrote 'American pressure had won and de Gaulle knew that 'The Continent of Europe' was mortally wounded.'[84]

Whatever the outward appearance, de Gaulle's many attempts to woo Germany away from the United States were always doomed to failure. America and Germany were locked together. Both feared the USSR; both wanted European union. De Gaulle was outgunned.

The crisis came to a head when Brussels made three proposals: to have its own resources to fund the Common Agricultural Policy (CAP) from the Common External Tariff (CET); to give more budget powers to the European Parliament; and, worst of all from de Gaulle's point of view, to introduce majority voting into the Council of Ministers (the main decision making body of the EEC which under the Treaty of Rome deliberately began as an intergovernmental group only).

On 30th June 1965 de Gaulle withdrew from Brussels altogether. The Empty Chair crisis was the most serious challenge to Brussels which has yet happened.

The negotiations to set up the Common Agricultural Policy were still underway – they took from 1962 to 1966 in a series of marathon meetings to deal with the massive agricultural surpluses, mainly French. By the end of 1964 the critical EEC grain price had been decided, far higher than it should have been, enabling inefficient farmers to stay in business and raising food prices to the consumer. The next step was to finalise the financing of the CAP including majority voting.

Hallstein, the President of the Commission, had put the new proposals to the Assembly first and to increase its own powers the Assembly had readily agreed them. By the time the proposals came to the Council of Ministers there was little room to manoeuvre. De Gaulle said he had been forced into a corner by Hallstein.

Six months of behind the scenes bargaining failed. De Gaulle was not going to give in to majority voting and federalism. To lessen the authority of the Commission and reduce its independence he sacked the head of Euratom, Etienne Hirsch, for not following Paris's orders. The new German Chancellor, Kurt Kiesinger, then agreed to remove Hallstein as head of the Commission. That was a blow to Monnet who correctly regarded the Commission as the key to a supranational Europe – the beginning of a European Government.

In January 1966 the Six settled the majority voting problem with the Luxembourg Compromise. Its interpretation was not clear: France thought that when an important national interest was at stake negotiations must continue until every country agreed, however long it took; the other Five thought agreement should be reached within a reasonable time.

For another seventeen years the veto was used many times and held back a federal Europe. It ended during a challenge from the British Prime Minister, Mrs Thatcher, in 1982. Even today many do not realise that the veto has long since gone and the full terms of the Treaty of Rome now apply.

De Gaulle shared Churchill's concept of a Europe which stretched from the Atlantic to the Urals but his Europe excluded American influence. For both views he had wide support in France. He wanted a balance between French led Western Europe and the USSR with Eastern Europe; both France and the USSR were nuclear powers.

De Gaulle believed 'the construction of 'Europe' . . . would only result in hitching Europe behind the American wagon . . . *America is not part of Europe*, he exclaimed. *That is what the map shows!* From this sprang his rejection of Atlanticism . . . which increasingly separated him from supporters of a 'United States of Europe': people like Spaak, Luns, and finally the Germans themselves.'[85]

In March 1966 France withdrew from NATO which left Germany to chose between the US and France. That was no choice: Germany remained in the US camp.

For all his efforts de Gaulle could only hold back the tide of 'Europe' for so long. He did not have the option to pull France out of the EEC because of the strength of the French farming lobby. Nor could he prise Germany away from its long term alliance with the US. Equally he could not remove American involvement with Europe. He did succeed in stopping Britain from joining the EEC but only in his life time.

"About turn"

CHAPTER 6: THE BRITISH 'U' TURN

Macmillan Reverses British Policy

From the end of the war until 1960 Britain was certain that a supranational European authority of any kind was not for it. Britain said "no" to the European Coal and Steel Community, "no" to the European Political Community, "no" to the European Defence Community, and "no" to the European Economic Community.

Yet in the space of a few months the British government did a complete about-face. All previous refusals to give up any sovereignty were pushed to one side. What had changed?

Anthony Eden resigned as Prime Minister after the Suez debacle in January 1957 and was succeeded by Harold Macmillan. Macmillan had had a long flirtation with the idea of European union. The impending existence of the new Community itself imposed a strain on the British Government. The European hawks in the American Government kept up the pressure and propaganda for Britain to be part of the new Europe, a pressure which increased with the Presidency of John F. Kennedy.

All these things combined to create an atmosphere in which a wishful-thinking British Prime Minister succumbed, turned his back on the Commonwealth and deviously embraced European political union.

Macmillan's Record 1938 To 1957

Macmillan solved political problems with corporate solutions. He had published 'The Middle Way' in 1938 after the Depression but when dalliance with Communism was still widespread. His book included a number of references to Fabian publications and generally drew on left-of-centre literature of the time.[1] He asserted that 'the great majority of the people quite clearly regard the depression and crisis as a transitory and fortuitous occurrence. This is of course a profound error.'[2]

His answer was to nationalise some of the means of distribution, impose a minimum wage, create a National Economic Council and a National Investment Board. It was, Macmillan said, 'planned capitalism', if he had been honest he would have said it was a British 'New Deal', the Fabian programme to introduce socialism.[3] The economic crisis to which Macmillan was responding was already receding, partly thanks to rearmament.

Macmillan first met Jean Monnet in London in 1940. In Algiers in 1943 they cemented their friendship when Macmillan was a political adviser to General Eisenhower. Monnet wrote, 'Macmillan and I used to take refuge in Tipasa, a seaside village some 45 miles west along the coast road. There, walking among the Roman ruins near the sea, we quietly made plans for the future.'[4] His words, with a more short term emphasis, were echoed in Macmillan's autobiography.

Macmillan had been a founder member of the small European League for Economic Co-operation (ELEC) set up by Count Van Zeeland in 1947 expressly to introduce political union by the economic back door. Van Zeeland and his colleagues from mainland Europe wanted to give up national sovereignty in favour of a socialist superstate. Most of the British members had a more pragmatic attitude and hoped to improve Europe's devastated economy though Peter Thorneycroft, the Conservative MP, with others wrote a booklet advocating that Britain give up its economic sovereignty.

Did Macmillan understand the motives of some of his colleagues in ELEC and the strength of their Continental organisation? At the least he was beguiled by the situation of the day – a hungry Europe devastated by war, and the hope that political union was so far off that it might never happen. On the other hand he was described by federalists as one of them, 'a committed European.'[5] A united Europe probably appealed to Macmillan's penchant for the grandiose solution.

At the 1948 Hague Congress Macmillan may have ignored the fact that most of the European Movement wanted one state. A politician first and last, Macmillan had said one thing to his European audience and another to his Conservative Party Conference. In May 1951, Macmillan and ELEC organised a conference to discuss closer economic integration between the Commonwealth and Europe. It concluded 'Everyone would benefit immeasurably'.[6] That conclusion could not have been more wrong.

One of his influential ELEC colleagues, Paul-Henri Spaak of Belgium, repeatedly said that if only Britain would join the Common Market it could write its own terms. That would never have been the case. The pressure from Spaak, from Monnet and the Americans was constant, but the incentives they used were false.

In his autobiography,[7] Macmillan bemoaned Britain's refusal to join the European Coal and Steel Community. He assumed that Britain could have led the ECSC. In that too he was sadly mistaken. Britain was deliberately sidelined to avoid dilution of the federal agenda. In the Parliamentary debate on the ECSC, Macmillan suggested that the concept of sovereignty had changed, that it could be pooled and cited NATO as an example. It was an example used many times over the coming decades, but as Churchill remarked in the House of Commons, NATO did not have 'the power to say what units of the British army should be suppressed and disbanded, or how they should be raised or remodelled.' "Pooling", as R. W. G. Mackay said at the Hague Congress, was and is a euphemism for handing over sovereignty.

As an alternative to the European Defence Community, Macmillan proposed a confederation led by Britain and organised along Commonwealth lines, not a federation. He feared if Britain did not lead Europe, then one day Germany would, with the even greater danger that Germany might side with Russia. He agreed with fellow ELEC member, Lady Rhys Williams, that to remain a world power Britain had to join with Europe, otherwise it would either be isolated or become another American state.

Macmillan's paper[8] on the future of the Council of Europe, written whilst he was Minister of Housing in 1952, was swiftly rebutted by the Foreign Office: 'Mr Macmillan's proposals overlook two important points. The policy of the six countries participating in the Schuman Plan and the EDC is to achieve European unity on federal lines. Their long term objective is to create a European political authority . . . There is no indication that these countries would be prepared to accept an intergovernmental approach to European unity as a satisfactory alternative, even if the UK joined.'

The FO pointed out that Macmillan had overlooked that NATO incorporated continuous consultation between governments, dealt 'on an inter-governmental basis with defence, economic affairs, production' and was expanding into other areas as well. NATO was 'an association of states which has evolved in some direction further than the Commonwealth . . . and has the added advantage of Canadian and United States participation' – an Atlantic community.

Macmillan's policy towards Europe reversed that of Churchill and Eden. It dominated the Conservative Party in his generation, the next two generations as well.

Yet in 1959, despite the humiliation of Suez three years earlier, scarcely a Conservative MP returning to the House of Commons with a majority of 100 seats had any thought of joining a federal Europe. The same was true of most members of the Labour Party. Eighteen months later Britain was knocking on the door of Europe.

Plan G, The Sixes And The Sevens

The British Government's first response to the proposed protectionist Common Market was to try to include it with other OEEC countries in a wider free trade area – a project known as Plan G. When Macmillan first became Prime Minister in 1957, he enthusiastically pursued Plan G to try to make the EEC institutions inter-governmental just as he had tried to do to the Council of Europe in the early 1950s. Led by Reginald Maudling negotiations for Plan G went on for two years from October 1956, only to end abruptly when General de Gaulle vetoed the idea.

In December 1958, Dr. Erhard visited Macmillan, accompanied, as Macmillan reported in his autobiography, by 'a lot of "tough" Germans'. Erhard asked that no further meetings of the Maudling Committee be held until the end of January – after the new Common Market was to start. Macmillan refused. Erhard replied that the date of 31st January was a requirement, not a negotiating position.

The Americans were puzzled by Plan G. Some, like J. F. Dulles, the Secretary of State, did not want any dilution or disruption to plans to create European political union. Others worried that the new Community would be protectionist against American trade at a time when American trade surpluses were going down. That fear was dispelled when the new Community lowered its trade barriers for the first time in January 1959.

The British were left without any influential friends working in their interests. Plan G was dropped and the Swedes proposed a more limited free trade belt surrounding the new Community, the European Free Trade Area (EFTA). The Outer Seven were Britain, Norway, Sweden, Denmark, Switzerland, Austria and Portugal. EFTA had no strong central institutions, and agriculture and fishing were deliberately excluded. It started in January 1960.[9]

The Americans were uncertain about EFTA. They were against it because unlike the EEC it had no political content – it was all about trade. They were for it because it favoured free trade.

But the British were left in no doubt about the Americans' true concerns. Douglas Dillon, the American Under Secretary of State, on a tour of European capitals, told top British civil servants in December 1959 that 'while we would not oppose the EFTA arrangement we could not view it with any great enthusiasm because it did not have the same political content as the EEC and would mean discrimination against our exports.'[10]

The battle of the Sixes and Sevens followed. The Six, under pressure from the Seven and from the GATT[11] negotiations, accelerated their tariff reductions.[12] The economies of the Six were booming. To make the psychological pressure worse for those outside, the Six talked of raising their outer tariff wall, the Common External Tariff, so making their own situation even better and those outside even worse. The GATT countries complained and were given a few sops: the EEC quota increases were extended to all GATT members.

Macmillan was worried by the Six's acceleration of internal tariff cuts. In March 1960 he went to France to ask General de Gaulle not to carry out the cuts – a fruitless and humiliating mission.[13]

The British believed de Gaulle was a fellow spirit because, he wanted co-operating nation states. When Michel Debré visited de Gaulle in Colombey-les-Deux Eglises to discuss his misgivings about the Treaty of Rome in 1957, de Gaulle said 'What difference does it make? When we are back in power, we'll tear up these treaties.'[14]

The reality was rather different. As the Americans were quick to realise, de Gaulle was in no position to tear up treaties, however strongly he felt about independent nation states. French farmers and French trade unionists, in particular, had a vested interest in continuing with the EEC. All he could do was to ensure France led Europe, and there was no increase in federalism.

In October 1959 Macmillan wrote a summary of the British situation to his Foreign Secretary, Selwyn Lloyd: 'Clearly one of the most important tasks of the next five years will be to organise the relations of the United Kingdom with Europe. For the first time since the Napoleonic era the major continental powers are united in a positive economic grouping, with considerable political aspects, which, though not specifically directed against the United Kingdom, may have the effect of excluding us both from European markets and from consultation in European policy. For better or worse, the Common Market looks like being here to stay, at least for the foreseeable future. Furthermore, if we tried to disrupt it we should unite against us all the Europeans who have felt humiliated during the past decade by the weakness of Europe. We should also probably upset the United States, as well as playing into the hands of the Russians. And of course, the Common Market has certain advantages in bringing greater cohesion to Europe. The question is how to live with the Common Market economically and turn its political effects into channels harmless to us.'[15]

Macmillan Makes Moves

That same month Macmillan was overwhelmingly confirmed as Prime Minister in his first General Election as leader of the Conservative Party. His position in Parliament and in the country was strong. For the next three years Europe was the most important issue for the Cabinet. Macmillan did not announce Britain's intention to apply to join the EEC until July 1961. Yet at a much earlier stage he must have decided on that course of action. Exactly when is obscure. In his autobiography and from the Cabinet papers the impression given is that the decision crept up, until somehow it became inevitable. Yet Macmillan made the moves which ensured that result. He may have thought he might apply to join the EEC earlier in 1959 but he waited until he was strengthened by the General Election before making any moves.

Macmillan's first move was to appoint Sir Frank Lee as joint head of the Treasury from the beginning of 1960. Sir Frank was nearing the end of a distinguished career in the

Civil Service. He was also one of the few civil servants who believed Britain should join the EEC. When Thorneycroft was at the Board of Trade at the time of the Schuman Plan (ECSC) and pushing for British entry, he said he was 'brilliantly served by Sir Frank Lee ... one of the greatest permanent secretaries a man could ever wish to have. I wanted to take him with me to the Treasury. I believe that history would have been a little different if I had managed to do so. However, I was not allowed to do so.'[16]

Sir Frank at the Treasury was soon kite flying, testing the idea of British entry. His officials began to look at the issues; he circulated a few heavyweight politicians and civil servants with the idea of joining the EEC and then proposed it in a Cabinet sub-committee of 23rd May 1960 chaired by Macmillan. Britain had started down the road to Rome.

An important Lee supporter was the British Ambassador to Paris, Gladwyn Jebb (later Lord Gladwyn), one of the most prominent and forceful men in the Foreign Office. Jebb wrote that he only accepted the need for a supra-national solution after the ECSC in 1951. He thought it would 'prepare the way for a World Federation'. Jebb, like many British, misunderstood the meaning of Continental federalism for he wrote of Marx 'however internationalist he may have been ... his ideal society was a highly centralised one far removed from federalism.'[17]

The main argument then and in later committees was that the Six without any internal trade barriers would do even better economically, and Britain might be shut out. At the tail end of the argument was the political fear of a new and united force on the Continent having a major impact on the world stage. The proposed answer was 'near identification' or 'close association' with the Six, to join without actually formally signing up to the Treaty of Rome. Throughout, the preservation of Commonwealth interests was said to be paramount. That was lip service only. Those interests were never consulted, only over-ridden.

A further Cabinet analysis suggested that were Britain to join the EEC then the Treaty of Rome would have to be substantially amended. The foreign policy prize would be big: Britain would be a power within Europe and through Europe could remain an international power. The economic advantages of joining were assumed, never analysed nor proven. The Common External Tariff would have to be accepted. A political price was assumed but not specified. Surprisingly, the Cabinet doubted that the US would be keen on Britain joining the Six. They could not have been more wrong. That must also have represented a massive failure of intelligence or the communicaiton of it to the Government. It led to muddled thinking which has continued to this day.

The Cabinet emphasised the insurance policy of de Gaulle's view of a Europe of nation states, a toothless federation, but without recognising that the forces for a federal Europe were already stronger than de Gaulle, inside the EEC, could fight. Again they wrongly assumed that if Britain joined it would be able to mitigate the gradual loss of sovereignty. Macmillan was under no illusion but others in his Cabinet were partially lulled into a false sense of security.

Some harder heads expressed reservations. Heathcoat Amory, the Chancellor of the Exchequer, said in Cabinet, 'A decision to join the Community would be essentially a political act with economic consequences, rather than an economic act with political consequences.'[18] Sir Roderick Barclay, the head of the UK delegation to the European Commission in Brussels, spelt out the aim of the Community to unify all economic policies and the strong fear of the Six that Britain would dilute it.

After appointing Sir Frank Lee, Macmillan's second move was to be deliberately vague of purpose and avoid robust analysis. The Cabinet of the day was mainly against joining the Six. The principle, to join or not to join, backed up by a balanced analysis, was never – over three years – put to Cabinet members. Again the assumption has to be that since the issue was never confronted directly that Macmillan and his assistant, Heath, were manoeuvring politically to secure Britain's application. On one occasion Heath deliberately withheld an adverse analysis from the Cabinet sub-Committee.

Macmillan may have been partly driven by the collapse of the Paris Summit in May 1960 after Kruschev announced that his forces had shot down a U2 spy plane piloted by Gary Powers. While there was no logical connection between that and Britain's entry to the EEC, Macmillan and his political circle were prey to a deep sense of defeatism. The results of the Suez debacle, and their feeling that Britain was in inexorable decline, influenced them powerfully.

Macmillan's third move towards Europe was to reshuffle the Cabinet to be pro-EEC. In July 1960, Macmillan appointed three pro-Europeans to the Cabinet: Duncan Sandys at Commonwealth Relations, Christopher Soames at agriculture; and Edward Heath at the Foreign Office as the number two to the Foreign Secretary, Lord Home. Heath was given special responsibility for the European negotiations. All were crucial positions. Peter Thorneycroft was brought back to the Cabinet in the lesser role of Minister of Aviation. In 1947 he had written, 'The people must be led slowly and unconsciously into the abandonment of their traditional economic defences . . .'

Sandys had gone much further than any other Conservative in pursuing European unity and the European Movement would not have existed without him. At the same time he pretended to back the inter-governmental approach. He had allowed himself to be pushed so far along the road towards federalism that in the end, isolated from his British colleagues, he had resigned in favour of Spaak.

Heath held the key position. While at Balliol College, Oxford on a scholarship just before the war, he had been 'most strongly influenced intellectually by Professor A. D. Lindsay'. His relationship with Lindsay was much closer than that of most students. Heath went to Lindsay's weekly lectures on morals, but he also went regularly to his 'open house' outside the curriculum. According to Heath's biographer, John Campbell,[19] Lindsay taught a generation about democracy who might otherwise have been tempted by Communism or Fascism. That was to misunderstand Lindsay.

Professor Lindsay was a powerful man and his influence on the young and impressionable Heath may have gone much further than Campbell suggested. He was a social leveller, and did not 'toady to toffs', exactly the attitude Heath was to take when he became an MP. Lindsay, a Marxist, had joined the small team organised by his former student Professor Arnold Toynbee with William Temple, the Archbishop of York, Professor Zimmern and Bishop Bell. They had worked closely with J. F. Dulles and friends, and seized any opportunity to create a European superstate and end national sovereignty.

Heath's maiden speech in the Commons had advocated that Britain should join the ECSC to lead it. As Jean Monnet made clear, leading Europe was always an impossibility for Britain because Britain wanted what the others did not, a Europe of nation states; joining on the others' terms was the only option. Was it arrogance that caused Heath to think that Britain could lead Europe?

Heath was not given an easy time in the Commons because of his relatively humble background. His deep resentment led him to want to make his mark, almost to spite everybody, and climb to the top by whatever means he could.[20] Macmillan offered him the chance. During his seven years as a whip in the House of Commons, Heath had became close to Macmillan and was a confidant. Macmillan found Heath's intelligence network among MPs invaluable.

By the summer of 1960 Macmillan was definitely exploring how to be associated with the Six and probably to join them. The appointments Macmillan made and the talks he held suggested that, even at that stage, an application was almost inevitable; but it was to take another year.

To Sacrifice Sovereignty

Harold Macmillan noted in his diary of July 1960, 'Shall we be caught between a hostile (or at least a less and less friendly) America and a boastful, powerful Empire of Charlemagne – now under French but later bound to come under German control? Is this the real reason for 'joining' the Common Market (if we are acceptable) and for abandoning a) the Seven b) British agriculture and c) the Commonwealth? It's a grim choice.' Macmillan added later that his diary entry exaggerated the position.[21] Those were indeed the issues, and he was never to make them public. Deception became the name of the game.

When, a few years earlier, Macmillan had dined with Gladwyn Jebb at the British Embassy in Paris, Jebb's wife, Cynthia, had confided to her diary, 'I feel Macmillan has to be allowed to air his curious theories, and must be flattered . . . If one bluntly argues with him, I can see he could turn nasty. There is an almost cruel look now and then . . . I suppose this might be the flaw in his character, and why people say they can't trust him.'[22]

Fear was one motive: fear of America and fear of being locked out of Europe, as Sir Frank Lee put it. It is not surprising to find that possible alternative courses of action were never considered such as continuing with EFTA or building on the Commonwealth trading arrangements. Even the cautionary notes sounded in every Cabinet sub-committee paper were either ignored or glossed over.

With a pro-European team behind him, Macmillan embarked on consultations with the Six. His first port of call in August 1960 was Germany and Dr. Adenauer. Macmillan was wary of Adenauer, whom he said had deceived him before when he said he would back EFTA and then backed de Gaulle. Macmillan was surprised by his good reception, but then Germany and the US had a similar view on the EEC's political development. The two men discussed various ways in which Britain could be associated with the Six. It was a tentative first step towards the Cabinet committee's foreign policy objective of being in the inner circle of the EEC.

Heath, in his new job in charge of European negotiations, saw the French Ambassador and then Professor Hallstein, the EEC's first President. Hallstein made it clear to Heath that the EEC's long term aim was a federal state and full political integration. Heath noted Hallstein's assumptions that Britain would eventually join and to do so would make most of the concessions.[23] The campaign gathered momentum: Heath visited Rome in August and Paris in October to begin talks. His officials held talks with the Germans, Italians and French.

In January 1961 de Gaulle told Macmillan face to face that the Six and the Commonwealth were incompatible. Yet Heath had told the Conservative Party Conference the previous October there was no question of a choice for Britain between the EEC and the Commonwealth, Britain would not turn its back on the Commonwealth. The EEC could only gain from the Commonwealth.

In December 1960 Heath wrote to the Lord Chancellor,

Lord Kilmuir, for an opinion on how much sovereignty Britain would lose if it signed the Treaty of Rome. Heath himself thought the fear of supra-nationality was overdone, but debate within the Civil Service raised the issue.

Lord Kilmuir replied in some detail that British sovereignty would be affected in three ways:
'(a) Parliament would be required to surrender some of its functions to the organs of the Community;
(b) The Crown would be called on to transfer part of its treaty-making power to those organs
(c) Our courts of law would sacrifice some degree of independence by becoming subordinate in certain respects to the European Court of Justice.' He added that there is 'no precedent for our final appellate tribunal being required to refer questions of law . . . to another court . . .'

Lord Kilmuir ended, 'In the long run, we shall have to decide whether the economic factors require us to make some sacrifices of sovereignty: my concern is to ensure that we should see exactly what it is that we are being called on to sacrifice, and how serious our loss would be.'[24]

That assessment has never been made. Indeed Kilmuir's final question had the issues in reverse importance: the EEC was intended to be the first step to a political state using trade as the easy route to union.

Heath was left in no doubt that what was proposed was a revolution in British government. Nothing of that scale and magnitude had happened since the Civil War in the seventeenth century; and then Britain remained British. Both Heath and Macmillan deliberately ignored Kilmuir's advice on the loss of sovereignty.

Macmillan pushed ahead until the British government formally announced Britain's application to join the EEC in July 1961. At each Cabinet and sub-Committee meeting, the goal posts were moved ever more closely towards entry and away from 'arrangements' between the Six and the Seven, and Britain's 'near identification' with the Six. The advantages and disadvantages were never fully discussed and disquiet was assuaged with assurances that no immediate decision was necessary, a situation which has been repeated many times since. On 17th May 1961 Heath told the Commons that 'there was no alternative to going in'. They had never even thought of an alternative. On 22nd July the Cabinet formally agreed to apply.

Heath informed Jean Monnet of Britain's decision the day before the House of Commons was told.[25] Monnet wanted Britain to agree to the principle of the EEC first, and to negotiate the key points afterwards, just as he had over the ECSC. Everything else could be sorted out once Britain was inside. Macmillan refused.

Britain's application was warmly welcomed by the Six and especially by Germany. To Germany Britain represented a large export market which would otherwise be outside the EEC tariff barrier. An added bonus would be more trade with the British Commonwealth where Germany had very little.

For its part France kept raising the stakes. For example, when Macmillan agreed to accept the Common External Tariff, the tariff wall between the EEC and the rest of the world, de Gaulle then introduced the next problem area, agriculture. The French said progress would be made if only Britain would accept the Treaty of Rome.

Macmillan summed up a key Cabinet meeting in May 1961 with the words, '... we should have to accept the (Treaty of Rome's) underlying political objectives and although we should be able to influence the political outcome we did not know what this would be.' The assumption was that Britain would be able to block the EEC's federalist tendencies and that Britain could be a power within Europe but not outside it. Heath made much of Britain's veto in his propaganda. He never admitted that both the ECSC and the Treaty of Rome introduced majority voting with the intention that national vetoes would be phased out completely.

Dumping The Commonwealth 1961

To present the British government's *volte face* on Europe required careful handling: neither the public nor the Commonwealth was prepared for it. Only the Cabinet and a few civil servants knew what was going on until the public announcement. Hugh Gaitskell and the Opposition were shocked. Over a year's negotiations had been held in secret.

Three Ministers, Sandys, Thorneycroft and Hare were sent to each Commonwealth country in June and July 1961. They did not go to seek agreement on the likely new policy, far less to negotiate, only to inform. Yet they said that no application could succeed unless terms for the Commonwealth were met. British Ministers well knew that the only terms to be negotiated were the details of the transition from a Commonwealth Preference system to its death. The negotiations were to be dominated by those transitional arrangements, and much was made of not upsetting the Commonwealth which in reality was being abandoned. That was part of the price of EEC membership.

Not surprisingly no Commonwealth leader favoured Britain's move. Diefenbaker of Canada objected strongly. Nehru of India questioned whether Britain would gain any influence in the EEC. Menzies of Australia thought it could only weaken the Commonwealth. The African countries feared they would be cast into the same EEC mould as the former French colonies, which still smacked of the French Empire.

The Commonwealth was given no choice and no chance

to join together to challenge the British Government at a Commonwealth Conference which some Commonwealth Prime Ministers wanted. Cynically, Macmillan carried out a sounding of Commonwealth leaders, on a divide and rule basis: the answer had already been decided – the Commonwealth was to be dumped.

Commonwealth leaders were angered by the Americans who certainly did not want the British Commonwealth given any kind of privileged position within the EEC; most wanted it smashed. The Secretary of State, Dean Rusk, and his assistant, George Ball, went to considerable lengths to tell Commonwealth leaders in public and in private that they were not welcome in the EEC. The US then softened its position slightly by offering transitional help, which had some impact in Australia but not elsewhere.

British agriculture and the cheap food policy of more than a century were abandoned. The British system of importing Commonwealth food at the lowest world prices and then subsidising British farmers (deficiency payments) was to be abandoned in favour of importing expensive European food grown by inefficient farmers in a protectionist bloc.

After the Six had successfully negotiated their own Common Agriculture Policy in the Spring of 1962, they were able to reject favourable terms for the British Commonwealth as a whole. So deals had to be agreed to phase out Commonwealth food supplies – over 2,500 in all – country by country, and product by product.

For eighteen months, Heath led the negotiations to 'become full, whole hearted and active members of the European Community in its widest sense' as he told EEC member governments. Members of Parliament, the British public and the Commonwealth were not told that. In October 1961 Heath informed them that the treaty had no political obligations, only implications. He gave Ministers a formula to use emphasising that the obligations of the Treaty only applied in the limited area of trade and some social matters. Quite deliberately the Government never discussed the surrender of sovereignty: the Treaty of Rome was only another treaty.

Labour Says No

Hugh Gaitskell, the Labour Party leader, wrote to President Kennedy of his bitter disappointment and astonishment at 'the preliminary agreements reached at the beginning of August (1961)... the British Government had swallowed the whole EEC policy both on tariffs and agriculture... Heath obtained nothing but vague assurances as to what might be done in the future'.[26]

In the autumn of 1962 Gaitskell set up a committee to 'develop the idea of an alternative' to British entry.[27] The committee, organised by Harold Wilson, included Douglas Jay, Denis Healey, James Callaghan, James Meade and John Murray. Gaitskell told Murray that he wanted to safeguard British agriculture and British links with the Commonwealth. Unknown to him Macmillan had already decided to abandon them.

Gaitskell fathomed the economic arguments that Heath was bandying about and realised that membership of the EEC could limit Britain's ability to pursue its own foreign policy, its own economic planning and British control of sterling might be at stake.

Murray wrote an astute two-part memorandum which Wilson's committee unanimously accepted and which saw through Macmillan's 'negotiations'. The Government, according to Murray, was being 'devious' with the Commonwealth; 'if there was no question of political union, as we were repeatedly assured there was not, why not just have a trading arrangement?' Unlike Heath who was putting out propaganda about inevitable economic decay if Britain did not go into Europe, Murray calculated that it would cost Britain at least £500 million a year.

Another Heath argument was the benefit of a larger market for British goods. Murray called it a mirage: 'it was not as if some vast new country was being opened up to us for the first time. We were already very much in the European markets concerned. The only difference that entry would make would be that the tariff wall would disappear. But a wall has two sides and the vast industrial complex of Europe, whose efficiency was so much vaunted by Euro-zealots, would equally gain free access to our markets. We might well find ourselves with a new, large chronic trading deficit with our new partners.' Murray was proved right: that was exactly what happened.

At Murray's recommendation Gaitskell planned a Commonwealth tour for February 1963 to reinforce an alternative strategy. In January, tragically and suddenly Gaitskell died. There was no Commonwealth tour.

Not A Popular Project

Public opinion in Britain was certainly not behind a British application to join the EEC. Federal Union, run by the Fabians, stepped into the breach; since the Messina Conference they had increased their propaganda efforts. Ota Adler, one of their funders, claimed that a number of civil servants were former members of Federal Union which helped their cause.[28] Most supporters were young, some were Quakers, some Fabians or idealists wanting to prevent another war. Many were quickly disillusioned.

The Economist Intelligence Unit,[29] long a supporter of a federal Europe, published two 'unbiased' studies in 1957 and

1958 showing that British industry would be better off inside the EEC, everybody would gain. What was never admitted, and probably few knew, was that the CIA paid for those studies.[30]

Another study in 1960 addressed Commonwealth problems and their solution. Heath attended the press launch.

A dedicated group, 'Britain in Europe', was set up by Federal Union to target industry and Europe House was opened in Fleet Street in March 1958. Within a couple of years three lectures a month were being held at Europe House. When Britain announced its application Lord Gladwyn (Gladwyn Jebb), who had just retired from the FO, led the Common Market League. They were backed by two top lawyers, Lords Wilberforce and Diplock who appeared at conferences. Despite some CIA support, the League was perpetually short of money.[31]

The Common Market League had nowhere near the support given to the populist Anti-Common Market League, but those against the EEC never marshalled their arguments strongly. Fatally, they did not have strong leadership in the House of Commons.

One pro-European barrister, Dennis Thompson, later wrote that 'there were many possible objections that might have been raised by the lawyers against membership, such as the loss of legal sovereignty of Parliament, the inroads into the common law legal system ('the best in the world'), the domination of a foreign court in Luxembourg, and the making of regulations by the Commission. The only really informed opponent was Derek Walker-Smith in Parliament, but he never had much support from the Temple owing I believe much to the effectiveness of the London Leiden meetings'.[32] The meetings were organised by the Europa Instituut of Leiden in the Netherlands. The Instituut had been set up in December 1957 as part of Leiden University to study and teach all aspects of the EEC.

Contemporary politicians have described Macmillan as unscrupulous in his methods and lacking in clear thought about his policies; in his later years he became more of a radical showman. In his attitude to Europe he had shown an ambivalence since the end of the war. He was too uncritical of the federal, centralist Europe which was being created and to which, without thought of other options, he was trying to commit Britain.

Inevitably, once he had decided to apply to join the EEC Macmillan and his close colleagues had to disguise the truth of what they were doing. If the truth had been laid before the House of Commons and the British people there is no doubt they would have said no, just as the leaders of the Commonwealth had done.

Fulfilling An American Dream

Nor was Macmillan thinking clearly about America's position. Since 1947 a United States of Europe had been US policy and an influential group of Americans had been working for it for some years before. That was appreciated by the British Foreign Office, and by the leaders of both the Labour and Conservative Party. That is until Macmillan became Prime Minister. Strangely, on his visit to Washington in March 1960 Macmillan was 'startled to find how strongly the American administration backed the Common Market, if necessary to the detriment of any 'special relationship' with Great Britain.'[33] While the American position had fluctuated in intensity, that had been its direction for thirteen years. Yet the British Conservative Party felt it had been ditched by President Eisenhower.

Once J. F. Kennedy became President in January 1961, the

American attitude to Europe was reinvigorated. There were three strands to that policy: the pro-Europeans held a strong position in the new administration; yet the special relationship was not abandoned; and the US was not so set on European unity that it ignored the impact of the protectionist EEC on American exports.

Arthur Schlesinger described Kennedy's attitude: 'As for the character of that unity, he did not think nationalism altogether a bad thing. He knew that the United States would not lightly renounce its own sovereignty; this made him a bit sceptical of rigid supranational institutions in Europe. Though he had the greatest affection and respect for Jean Monnet, he was not tied to Monnet's formulas – or those of anyone else.'[34]

Kennedy's Administration was as much concerned about the EEC's tariff barrier against the US. That concern led to the long Kennedy Round of tariff negotiations which were only successfully ended in June 1967. It was the first time the EEC negotiated as one unit.

Those in favour of 'Europe' were probably stronger under Kennedy than at any previous time. The strength of their network, based on close friendships and long periods working together for a common cause, presented a more formidable advocacy for 'Europe' than the unpolished J. F. Dulles could muster as Secretary of State.

The most senior 'European' under Kennedy was the lawyer, George Ball, who moved from number three to two in the State Department. He had worked with Monnet in Washington during the war and Monnet hired him in 1945 to help draft documents. In 1947 he had moved to Monnet's office in the rue de Martignac in Paris and in secret and cramped conditions worked there periodically over a few years drafting documents. Ball then became the American adviser to Monnet when he was President of the ECSC. He stayed on after Monnet resigned as adviser to the ECSC and then went to Euratom and the EEC. Ball was thoroughly unpopular in London which limited his influence.

Ball and most of his Washington network were Frankfurter's 'boys'. They included David Bruce, Ambassador to Britain and formerly Ambassador to France, (Ball had unofficially used Bruce's Embassy to work for Monnet); Robert Schaetzel (Ball's deputy); Walt Rostow, chairman of the Policy Planning Council and his deputy Henry Owen; and John Tuthill, the US representative first to the OECD, and then to the EEC. All were close to Monnet and other members of his team. All had been involved in the European issue for many years.

The British did not realise the strength of the link between Monnet and the Americans. Monnet asked Ball to intervene with President Kennedy to pressurise Macmillan to apply to join the EEC. He did so.[35]

Monnet's Action Committee eased the lengthy negotiations: help with the technical complications came from its Documentation Centre mainly financed by the Ford Foundation under John McCloy (another Frankfurter 'boy') and helped by the Centre of European Studies in Lausanne run by Monnet's friend Professor Henri Rieben. Francois Duchêne, a Monnet protégé, did much of the hard work. He had impeccable 'European' credentials: formerly he was an 'Economist' journalist and later a director of Chatham House.

As a result of his friends, Monnet could actually contribute to American planning. His views were unattributably included in the Stevenson Report, the action programme for the first hundred days of the new Kennedy administration. The group introduced Monnet to Kennedy at an early stage of his Presidency. Monnet's agenda was to lower tariffs as a top priority, closely followed by Britain's entry into the EEC. The next stage would be more moves towards political union. The last stage, especially in view of the debacle over the EDC, was European defence. That is the stage which has only now been reached, over three decades later.

To boost 'Europe', Monnet promoted the idea of a partnership between Europe and the US. He believed it would be a partnership of equals and ultimately of one President talking to another President. In an Independence Day speech in 1962 President Kennedy said, 'The US looks on this vast enterprise with hope and admiration. We do not regard a strong and united Europe as a rival but as a partner. To aid its progress has been a basic object of our foreign policy for seventeen years.' Monnet prepared a background paper for the speech and Ball used it to advise the President.

The pro-Monnet group did not have things entirely their own way under Kennedy. The White House staff included a number of men who took a more pragmatic line including McGeorge Bundy who co-ordinated foreign policy. Bundy's deputy, Walt Rostow, summed up the dichotomy of America's policy towards Europe: could there be 'a Common Market settlement while the UK remained a national nuclear power, specially linked to the United States'?[36]

A Nuclear Defeat

It was the nuclear issue which was to defeat Macmillan's attempt to join the EEC. In the first place he cancelled Britain's independent nuclear deterrent, Blue Streak, in April 1960 in favour of a cheaper joint venture with America. That left Britain vulnerable to US policy. After Suez the US had been keen to rebuild the special relationship with Britain and signed a bilateral agreement to exchange information on nuclear warheads. Eisenhower agreed to replace Blue Streak with Skybolt, a limited range air-to-surface missile. That caused consternation in the 'European' camp in Washington, because it would maintain what they thought of as Britain's illusion of great power status.

When Kennedy met Macmillan in April 1961, he repeated Eisenhower's message that America wanted Britain to join the EEC. George Ball, accompanying Kennedy, made it clear yet again that the US saw the EEC as a political unit, not a commercial group and repeated that they were not in favour of EFTA, the free trade area, because it challenged the political unity of the Six. It was a repeat of the conversations Ball had had not long before in London with Sir Frank Lee and Edward Heath.

To achieve their aim the Americans tried to distance the nuclear issue from the EEC. De Gaulle wanted to be in the nuclear club and for France to be centre stage in Europe's defence, independent from the US. He looked to Macmillan for help but Macmillan, as requested, refused to share America's nuclear secrets with France. America did not want Europe to be completely independent of it in the key area of defence, and therefore refused to help France. The pro-Europeans in the US administration added their pressure: they did not want either France or Britain to have nuclear weapons.

The nuclear issue loomed even larger in the EEC negotiations. The Americans ran into problems with their Skybolt programme. Macmillan met Kennedy in Nassau in December 1962 to ask for its replacement, Polaris. At Nassau, Macmillan secured Polaris.

Only days before de Gaulle had again told Macmillan of his desire for an independent European deterrent and suggested co-operation between the two countries. France had joined the nuclear club the previous July when it exploded its first atomic bomb in the Sahara. Macmillan appeared not to understand the depth of de Gaulle's antipathy towards the British-American relationship.

Kennedy turned his back on George Ball's entreaties to deny Britain a nuclear deterrent because of his personal relationship with Macmillan and the close partnership America had with Britain on so many international issues. Of key importance to the Americans was the ceding of a British base for their Polaris submarines on the Clyde. Defence was always going to be a higher priority for the Americans than European union, as it had been in the Korean War, and will be in the future.

So Macmillan did not have to give in to American pleas to join the EEC. Britain could have stayed with EFTA, the Commonwealth and free trade.

Just as negotiations for Britain to join the EEC were nearly complete, on 14th January 1963 de Gaulle gave a press conference. To everyone's shock he said 'non'. Reminiscent of Churchill's remark to him in 1944, 'Every time we must choose between Europe and the open sea, we will chose the sea . . .', de Gaulle said: 'England . . . is insular, bound by its trade, its markets, its supplies, to countries that are very diverse and often very far away . . . (and) very different from those of the continental countries. How can England . . . be incorporated into the Common Market as it was conceived and as it works.' De Gaulle showed a far better under-standing of Britain than did Macmillan.

De Gaulle had two motives. He was always loath to share the leadership of Europe with Britain but he had not been strong enough either inside or outside France to say 'non' earlier. In November 1962, the National Assembly elections gave him that strength. Second, de Gaulle believed Europe should be independent of the US especially in defence, a vital point Macmillan missed. In de Gaulle's eyes, Macmillan put his relationship with the US higher than his concern for Europe.

Labour Tries Again

Harold Wilson, the Labour Prime Minister from 1963, was against British entry.[37] He favoured an Atlantic free trade community to include the Commonwealth, Latin America and Japan, very much along the lines John Murray had recommended to Gaitskell. But Wilson pursued power above else and trimmed his policies to suit. A pincer movement trapped him.

George Brown, his foreign secretary, fought hard for British membership of the EEC and would not give up: he had tenacity but not erudition. He had been a British delegate to the Council of Europe in 1951 when the Labour Party was in opposition. Although the British were then fighting any suggestion of a federal Europe, Brown had been quickly convinced that 'Europe' was the way forward and he managed to combine that with a belief in the Atlantic Community.[38]

In the summer of 1963 Roy Jenkins, a leading Fabian and a previous chairman, had chaired a Labour Committee for Europe to oppose Gaitskell's policy.[39] When Labour returned to power in 1964 twenty members of that committee were in the government, and five in the Cabinet.

In 1966 Federal Union sponsored a new campaign for a European Political Community. It was building momentum. With Brown and Jenkins pushing for Britain to join the EEC, Wilson reluctantly changed sides.

At that year's General Election, when Labour turned a small majority into a large one, all three parties were in favour of joining. Only the Conservative, Enoch Powell, made a determined stand against.

Brown persuaded Wilson to make a tour of European cities in January and February 1967 to create pressure for British membership. The tour was not always a diplomatic one with

Brown, often much the worse for drink, making extraordinary outbursts.

On 10th May 1967 the Labour Government formally applied for membership of the EEC. Gladwyn commented, 'What seems to be established is that at no time, and in no conversation with any British representative, did the General (de Gaulle) let it be supposed that he was in favour of Britain's joining the EEC.'[40] Not surprisingly in November, and for the second time, de Gaulle vetoed British membership. There was not even time to negotiate.

Brown then joined Monnet's Action Committee, as did Jeremy Thorpe for the Liberals and Sir Alec Douglas-Home, Selwyn Lloyd and Reginald Maudling for the Conservatives. Edward Heath and Roy Jenkins were to join later.

The Third Try – 1969

George Brown refused to give up. Despite the fact that a majority of the British Cabinet were opposed to British entry, Brown fought to keep Britain's application on the table. For some Cabinet Ministers it was easier to throw Brown that sop than continue the fight against a cause they thought was lost.

Suddenly the main block to British membership was removed. In April 1969 de Gaulle resigned the French Presidency and died within the year. In December 1969 the EEC member states agreed that negotiations should be reopened with Britain, Ireland, and Denmark. Norway had already re-applied in 1967.[41]

The British Government produced a second White Paper on the Common Market, this time only on the economic benefits and costs. The benefit of a much bigger and faster growing 'home' market was again lauded, an argument Gaitskell had already shown to be specious. Buried within the

February 1970 White Paper[42] is the following: 'Not only are the areas of uncertainty already mentioned very large, but the technical problems of making comprehensive and realistic estimate of the effects of membership are equally formidable.'

The paper concluded that the economic balance remained 'a fine one' and in the short term was disadvantageous. In the long term there would be the substantial cost of the Common Agricultural Policy. No quantitative answer could be given on whether those costs could be offset by what were described as the 'dynamic effects of membership'. The CBI view was accepted that the 'unquantifiable benefits of membership should in the long run exceed the balance of payments cost.' If CBI members ran their businesses on that basis then most would be bankrupt.

Despite such a flimsy economic assessment all three political parties supported Britain's third application. When Edward Heath won the June 1970 election for the Conservatives within two weeks of entering Number 10 Downing Street he re-opened negotiations.

The political argument, well rehearsed in Establishment circles, was that European economic unity was not something narrow or inward looking. Britain's own links with the Commonwealth and elsewhere in the world would help Europe to exert a greater political influence in the UN, the Western Alliance and help secure world peace. All the publicity material at the time stressed economic integration.

That was the subject of the next White Paper of July 1971.[43] It referred to 'the creation of a wider European Community of free nations, whose joint strength and influence on the world can be so much greater than that of the individual members.' There was 'no question of any erosion of essential national sovereignty.' References were also made to monetary and political union but it was easy to slide over the implications and it was almost universally believed that this was to be a Europe of nation states.

Yet Lord Wilberforce later said: 'It was Article 2 of the European Communities Act 1972 which made European legislation part of UK law. The vital article which people do not always have in mind is article 189 of the Treaty of Rome which states that a regulation shall be binding in its entirety and directly applicable in all member states. (It) terminated the sovereignty of the British Parliament and the supremacy under the constitution of the other national parliaments . . . It was not long before (the European Court of Justice) made a number of decisions which stated that European law was now a separate legal order taking precedence over the laws in individual member states . . .

'In 1972 a group of us[44] (lawyers) were consulted on this point and we had no difficulty in saying that UK law was henceforth to be subordinated to European law . . . The position was appreciated by our courts. Soon after 1960 a number of decisions were made . . . which accepted the supremacy of European law even over our statutes . . . all this was well established when we entered the Community in 1973. It must be taken to have been understood by informed people in 1975 . . . even if the media did not take pains to point it out.'[45]

That is disingenuous of Lord Wilberforce: the media did not know and Heath's Government did nothing to broadcast the legal advice they were given.

The decisions taken by the European Court of Justice between 1957 and 1972 need not have applied to Britain. Once Britain had joined the EEC it can be argued that because Britain has no written constitution, unlike all other European countries, laws already made in Luxembourg did not apply because they had not been agreed by the British parliamentary process.

Lord Wilberforce and many other lawyers have taken the view that those laws have been accepted by default. But in British law, based on Common Law, decisions by default cannot establish a precedent. That case has never been made in a British Court.

Heath was briefed in 1972 by the Law Lords Wilberforce, Diplock and Simon about the supremacy of the European Court of Justice. It was the second time he had asked the question. In December 1960 Lord Kilmuir had told him that Britain would lose some sovereignty under the Treaty of Rome but now the changes in European law of 1960 caused Lord Wilberforce to say that it was a total loss of sovereignty.

Heath had long been aware of the political aim of the EEC. At home he talked of the advantages to Britain's trade. But, as he publicly admits today, but failed to admit then, he was well aware of the full implications of the Treaty of Rome. In April 1962, soon after Macmillan's failed application, Heath addressed the Ministerial Council of the WEU in which he applauded the Political Union: 'We have all along recognised that the Treaties of Rome and Paris had a political as well as an economic objective.'[46]

In March 1967 Heath gave a lecture at Harvard[47] which was peppered with references to political as well as economic union. He thought that political union would end nationalist rivalries, that national boundaries for the new generation had no meaning and with economies of scale 'Europe' would become a first class power. He told his American audience that 'the primary reason why Britain entered into these negotiations was political, political in its widest sense'. He went on, 'In Britain a myth has become fashionable that we were concerned only with economic affairs and obsessed with minor details. Nothing could be further from the truth. The main purpose of the negotiations was political. This was made plain at the levels of Heads of Government.' Heath had never made it plain either to Parliament or to the British public.

Heath knew that economic union was merely the route to political union. He went on, 'It was therefore natural that although the primary reason for our negotiation was political the negotiation itself was mainly concerned with economic matters. And this will be so with any future negotiation.' He referred to the increasing union of fiscal policies and that a common commercial policy would come into effect by 1970. 'This means that no individual member will be able to use commercial policy as a means of carrying out its own national foreign policy.'

In a 1987 speech[48] looking forward to the next ten years Heath remained consistent. He emphasised the need for the Community to develop a unified government but pragmatically, not by creating a constitution. That government would extend to foreign policy and defence. In reviewing the history Heath asserted, 'What is so constantly forgotten is that the creation of the Coal and Steel Community was a political act for a political purpose, and that the communities are political institutions which themselves exist for a political purpose.'

Heath did not apparently understand everything. He said that the ECSC was founded to prevent further wars between France and Germany. That was certainly partly true for France but even more important was to establish French leadership of Europe before Germany regained its strength. For Germany it was the way to regain its sovereignty and ultimately to dominate Europe. For Jean Monnet and his American friends, particularly his mentor Felix Frankfurter, it might also be the start of a socialist superstate. The ECSC treaty and the Treaty of Rome, probably inspired by Frankfurter, were designed to do exactly that. Heath had apparently fallen for the propaganda which obscured the truth behind the ECSC and the EEC.

Yet his own mentor had been Professor Lindsay of Balliol College Oxford, one of the architects of 'Europe'. To what extent has Heath been influenced by Lindsay's Marxism? It is possible that the Conservative Prime Minister has been an unwitting tool of the few who designed the socialist United States of Europe.

Heath's personal ambitions may also have led him to muddled thinking about 'Europe'. Some think that Heath wanted to climb to the top by whatever means he could find.[49]

It was obvious to all who knew him at the time that Heath wanted British entry at almost any price including the end of the Special Relationship with the United States and with the Commonwealth. Britain in Europe would be able to give more to the rest of the world than Britain alone with its Commonwealth.[50]

A Propaganda Campaign

With a Prime Minister prepared to go to such lengths to achieve British membership of the EEC, little outside help would have been necessary. But some was forthcoming. In November 1968 Ernest Wistrich had taken over the 'Britain in Europe' campaign. At the time it was severely underfunded and needed a new sense of direction.

Wistrich had escaped from Poland early in the war and joined the RAF. His family had run a substantial timber business in Danzig. His political sympathies were Communist. The highly capable Wistrich revitalised the campaign and today, though offcially retired, is still a central and active figure.[51]

During 1969, when many would have thought the issue was dead, 'Britain in Europe' organised a series of country house debates with top speakers like Miriam Camps, formerly of the US State Department. She was a prolific writer with titles published by the Fabian Political and Economic Planning, Chatham House and the Council on Foreign Relations. The Ford Foundation helped to fund some of Federal Trust's activities.

In July 1969 'Britain in Europe' took over the British European Movement. Under Sir Edward Beddington-Behrens, never a keen federalist, the British European Movement had reached a low ebb; he had died at the end of 1968. The revitalised group was chaired by Lord Harlech (formerly David Ormsby-Gore) with his strong American connections, formed when he was the British Ambassador in Washington and was highly thought of by the Kennedy Administration. Sir Geoffrey de Freitas MP was his deputy with Lord Gladwyn and Duncan Sandys as vice chairmen. The group pursued the aim of a United States of Europe to include one foreign policy, one defence and one economy and a democratically elected European Parliament.

Both in the House of Commons and the country the majority was against British entry to Europe. In 1970, opinion polls were running at roughly three to one against. Wistrich's revitalised organisation swung into action. To counter the antipathy in the Commons, the European Movement spawned the Conservative Group for Europe run from its offices and largely funded by it. The Conservative Group was chaired by the MP Tufton Beamish with Norman St John Stevas doing most of the hard work on the ground to convert MPs. The arguments centred on raising living standards, social welfare, peace and improving Britain's world role.

With the European Movement (linked to Federal Union and thus to the Fabians) on the same side as the British Government it is not surprising to find that the Government's co-ordinating group and the European Movement met regularly in the Foreign Office. The campaign was given a big push by weekly media briefings at the Connaught Hotel in central London (second home to many royal families). An extra spin was given by the pop group Unity with 'Got to get in to get on'. Petula Clark, Jilly Cooper and Jimmy Greaves appealed to a wide audience and made 'Europe' sound like a safe idea.

Chatham House put on a conference to encourage the idea of 'Europe's' academic respectability. It was chaired by Sir Alex Cairncross, then the Economic Adviser to the Treasury. The papers used for the Conference came from Federal Trust, the Fabian offshoot.

Chatham House's Director, Andrew Shonfield, like Ernest Wistrich, had strong East European family connections and sympathies. Shonfield was, like his predecessor Arnold Toynbee, committed to a United States of Europe and Chatham House has never ceased to be a champion of European Union. Shonfield was also influential in the Labour Party.[52]

In the spring of 1971 and paid for by the British tax payer, the Government issued eleven free fact sheets through post offices and mailing lists as though Britain had already joined the EEC. It was to be another six months before Parliament agreed with the Government. In the House of Commons, Peter Shore described that campaign as 'very expensive and almost improper'.[53]

The two most influential papers in favour of Britain joining the EEC were 'The Economist' and the 'Financial Times' (Shonfield was a regular FT contributor). 'The Economist' had long been influenced by its owner the Liberal, Lord Layton, who was in favour of a federal Europe though was not persuaded that Britain should be a member until the 1950s. Geoffrey Crowther, its editor from 1938 until 1956 and intimate friend of Felix Frankfurter and Jean Monnet, had no doubts about where Britain's future lay, and he employed other journalists of a like mind, some of whom were members of the Fabian Society. For years 'The Economist' campaigned for the end of the British Empire, another Fabian aim.[54]

Today 'The Economist' is still supporting European Union and protectionism, while repeatedly saying that it believes in free trade. In 1995 it began a campaign to make Britain a Republic and abolish the monarchy, another Fabian aim. A subsidiary newspaper, 'European Voice', began publication in 1996 from Brussels and promotes a generally pro-Brussels point of view.

Few would think of 'The Economist' as a revolutionary newspaper but its editorials have quietly backed revolution for the last fifty years. It is an example of Fabian 'permeation and penetration' of what began as a Liberal paper. Today its world-wide influence is substantial.

The then editor of the 'Financial Times' M. H. ('Fredy') Fisher was another in a long line of refugees from Germany or farther East who, not understanding Britain's history of international trade, thought it perfectly natural that Britain should be part of an organised Continental bloc (like Professor Zimmern, Lord Roll and Sigmund Warburg). But they differed from those like Wistrich and Shonfield – their sympathies did not extend to Eastern Europe.

Fisher, born in 1922 in Berlin, escaped with his family to Switzerland in 1936. Educated in Britain he fought in the British Army. Between 1971 and 1980 he was the forceful deputy editor and then editor of the FT. It is apt that when he left the FT Fisher went to a congenial home with the merchant bankers, Warburg.

The 'Financial Times' was already sympathetic to 'Europe' because its previous editor Gordon Newton had been 'converted' (part of the Commission's promotional policy) on a

European tour in 1958 guided by Robert Schuman. The EEC funded a campaign to influence decision makers and during the sixties and early seventies about a third of its annual promotion budget was spent on Britain. Individuals, carefully chosen, were taken on goodwill trips to Brussels and Strasbourg tailored to their particular interests. That programme continues today.

The 'Financial Times' is still broadly sympathetic to Brussels but not all its experienced journalists share that view. Therefore it has a more balanced presentation.

Negotiations And A Packed House

In October 1970, with the public relations war well under way, the Government started talks with the EEC. Heath himself led on Europe, with Geoffrey Rippon in charge of the detailed negotiations. Negotiations were simplified because of the previous Macmillan application and with the Common Agricultural Policy fully operational there was little room for Britain to manoeuvre on terms. A five year transitional period was allowed for industry and agriculture to accept Brussels' terms.

From the start Heath was aware from bitter experience that the key to negotiations was the relationship with France. Underlying all was the French fear that Britain would seek to destroy the EEC. Britain would have to join on French terms or not at all.

Many press commentators were not at all certain that the negotiations would succeed – a reasonable point of view since they had already failed twice. Particular sticking points were sugar exports from Barbados and Mauritius to Britain when the EEC was already self-sufficient in sugar. Should New Zealand lamb and butter continue to be exported to Britain? Sterling could not remain as a reserve currency. What should Britain contribute to the Community budget? The biggest problem of all was Britain's right to fish in what were still its own territorial waters. So thorny was that problem that it was not resolved before Britain entered the Common Market.

The breakthrough came when Heath spent two days with President Pompidou in Paris on 20th and 21st May 1971. It was only their second meeting, the first was at General de Gaulle's funeral. Overnight the climate changed. On his return Heath made a statement to the House of Commons saying that nothing of significance should be inferred from those talks but from that time negotiations quickened, pessimism among the negotiating team was dispelled, and a positive air was obvious in the corridors of the House of Commons.

Pompidou himself explained to the French people in a television broadcast what had taken place in Paris. The translation includes:

'When I arrived in Office (1969), Europe was . . . in deadlock. Our partners in the Europe of the Six could no longer accept that Great Britain be left out . . . Once the negotiation was open, because I do not believe in basing foreign policy on lies and hypocrisy . . . we had to put our questions frankly. And that was exactly what happened . . . when I had my long talk with the British Prime Minister.

'So I put the question in the clearest possible way. First, I said: you accept the thing which lies at the very root of the Common Market, namely the Community Preference, whereby members obtain their supplies in the first place from the Community? And the British Prime Minister confirmed in the clearest possible terms what had, in fact, already been said publicly by the British representation in Brussels.

'Second question: on the functioning of the institutions and the unanimity rule (the Luxembourg Compromise) to which, as you know, France is essentially attached . . . the British Government answered yes, and in fact confirmed its answer publicly.

'Third, the monetary question: Sterling has at present special status, known as that of the reserve currency . . . I obtained from the British Prime Minister an undertaking . . . the Pound would become a currency like the others and would therefore participate in what we are trying to achieve: the creation of a European monetary union.

'Fourth question, which was probably the most important of all: I asked the British Prime Minister what he thought of Europe, in other words, whether Britain was really determined to become European, whether Britain, which is an island, was determined to tie herself to the Continent, and whether it was prepared consequently to loosen its ties with the ocean towards which it has always looked. And I can say that the explanations and views expressed to me by Mr. Heath are in keeping with France's concept of the future of Europe and, incidentally, in keeping with what Mr. Heath has been publicly saying for years.'

Some years later an MP wrote to Heath asking if that translation was correct. Heath would only say that talks between heads of state are held in confidence.[55]

The June 1971 negotiations quickly agreed on sugar, sterling's role as a reserve currency was to be run down gradually but without any set dates, and only fishing was outstanding. After the summer recess the government's publicity campaign swung into top gear. The final debate in the House of Commons took six days at the end of October.[56] The Conservatives were split on the issue of sovereignty and the Labour Party on the terms.

Sir Alec Douglas-Home led the debate for the Government. His arguments for entry centred on the known costs; the willingness of the CBI to rise to the trade challenge of Europe;

the opportunity to influence political developments with the safety of the veto under the Luxembourg Compromise (but he did not say it only temporarily reversed majority voting); and the increase in security for Britain. Other pro-EEC MPs spoke of the fear of being outside 'Europe', of the futility of thinking Britain could go it alone and of the chance to shape the Europe of the future.

Only a few MPs from both major parties understood the issues and were courageous enough to speak out. Sir Robin Turton (Conservative): 'Parliament would become a rubber stamp of Brussels;' under article 189 of the Treaty of Rome 'all those directives and regulations already made or to be made will be binding on this House.' He quoted the European Commissioner, Herr Dahrendorf: 'The Europe which the people have created has become an illiberal and bureaucratic leviathan obsessed with harmonising things for the sake of harmonisation.'

David Stoddart (Labour) said he had not had one letter in favour of Britain's entry in his large post-bag and talked of 'the Prime Minister's fanatical obsession . . . who had made up his mind to go in on any terms irrespective of the damage that was done to this country and to its economy . . . Surely Hugh Gaitskell was right in 1962 when he said that we cannot overcome 1,000 years of history in five minutes.'

Gerald Nabarro (Conservative) said the 'sovereignty issue was scantily dealt with in the 1971 White Paper' and quoted Andrew Alexander writing in the 'Daily Telegraph' on the White Paper's denial of any loss of sovereignty as 'A plain lie. There is no other word for it.'

On costs, Denis Healey (Labour) pointed out that 'if . . . we accept the Common Agricultural Policy, not only do we give the Six access to the largest food market in the world, but we must pay high prices for our food instead of the low prices we pay now for Commonwealth food – whereas the

Six did not face this penalty when they set up the CAP: they have always paid high prices.' Peter Shore (Labour) remarked that the cost to Britain of the CAP at £400 million to £700 million a year and rising fast would mean paying £300 million a year 'to France in perpetuity and about £100 million a year to Holland'.

On protectionism Joan Lestor (Labour) asked, 'how (can) an organisation like the EEC which everybody agrees is based on a protective tariff wall to which this country must agree as part of the price of entry . . . can be said to be outward looking.' Peter Shore (Labour) saw through Frankfurter and Monnet's plan to create one state which would evolve through the judgements of the Court of Justice without realising its source.' We have been asked,' he said, 'to make a prior commitment to accept, not merely the Treaty and the regulations made under it, but all the emerging policies under the heading of economic and monetary union.'

When it came to the vote the Labour Party repeated the three line whip of 1966. The Government won by 356 to 244 (the vote in the House of Lords had already been won by 451 to 58).

The Conservatives were allowed a free vote. But Heath, a former party whip, had chosen all 150 members of his Government on their willingness to vote for 'Europe'. Two had slipped through the net; both resigned. Sir Teddy Taylor said that Heath had taken him for a pleasant walk in the garden of Number 10 and asked him 'Why throw up your career?'[57]

That was packing on a scale that even Harold Macmillan had not followed – he had merely chosen some key members of his Cabinet for their European credentials. Of the back-benchers, Healey remarked in the Commons' debate that after 'three months of solid arm twisting by constituency associations . . . very few Conservative MPs have not already succumbed to this torture.'

Labour too had problems. Despite the three line whip Roy Jenkins, Shadow Chancellor and Deputy Labour Leader, led 68 Labour MPs into the "yes" lobby. Jenkins did not feel he had to resign until six months later over the issue of a referendum. Only in 1996 did a British television pro-gramme[58] reveal that Jenkins' Labour group and the Conservatives Whips had secretly worked together to make sure that each division gave the right result. Jenkins coyly said on camera that the intrigue had been kept from him.

At the time Michael Foot (Labour) spoke out strongly, 'At one time everything depended on the full-hearted consent of the British parliament and people. Now it all rests with the Patronage Secretary and on whether the bloodthirsty instru-ments of the guillotine and the closure can be manipulated . . . The Prime Minister and his Government have no mandate . . . more than 100 . . . members opposite (Conservatives) thought the subject of such paramount importance that they did not mention it in their election addresses.'

Foot was right about patronage and right about a mandate. The British people were never asked if they wished to join the EEC and give up sovereignty. Heath recommended a number of federalists for honours: Wistrich was made a CBE. When Britain formally joined the Common Market on 1st January 1973 Heath gave a triumphal banquet at Hampton Court Palace followed by an eleven day celebration round the country of music, plays and exhibitions, 'Fanfare for Europe'. It fell flat. But Monnet's aim of British membership had succeeded. Without British membership, he said, Euro-pean unity could not be created.[59]

Ireland followed Britain into the EEC with an 83 per cent vote in May 1972 for massive subsidies for Irish agriculture.

Ireland receives roughly five times its budget contribution back in subsidies. Without enthusiasm Denmark joined too. It had followed Britain's lead twice before and suffered de Gaulle's 'non' only because a substantial proportion of its trade was with Britain and it could not afford to see that disappear behind the Common External Tariff. In October 1972 63 per cent of the Danish people voted 'yes' to membership. Conversely the month before 53 per cent of Norwegians voted against after a campaign dominated by the loss of sovereignty and of fishing rights.

Harold Wilson had to resolve the problem caused by Roy Jenkins' splitting of the Labour Party. To win the 1974 General Election Wilson promised a referendum after renegotiating the terms. The renegotiation proved to be a frivolous exercise but for two and half years Britain's EEC membership was on hold.

The CIA, backing US Government policy, continued to be involved, though the full extent may never be known. In May 1975, the magazine 'Time Out'[60] published an unsigned article, the main source for which was disaffected CIA officers. They believed undue influence was being exerted by the US on a friendly ally: 'Cord Meyer Jr's main task as head of the (CIA's) operation here may be to ensure Britain's entry into the Common Market . . . Meyer and his predecessor as head of the CIA's International Division, Tom Braden, engaged in a major operation in the 1950s and 60s to secretly build up the groups which are now pushing Britain into Europe.'

On 5th June 1975 just over 60 per cent of the electorate voted on the question 'Do you think that the United Kingdom should stay in the European Community (the Common Market)?'. Two thirds voted to stay in and one third to come out. The Government's pamphlet to all voters emphasised that Britain's membership did not affect its sovereignty or its parliament; stressed the uncertainty if Britain voted to come out; and raised the fear of being outside the tariff wall.

The 'Britain in Europe' campaign backed the Government with Jenkins, its president and Heath a vice-president. Jenkins wrote, 'to come out would be . . . (a) self-inflicted injury. It would be a catastrophe. It would leave us weak and unregarded, both economically and politically.' He appeared to say that sovereignty would remain intact: 'We can work together and still stay British . . . The position of the Queen is not affected . . . English Common Law is not affected.'[61]

The 'No Campaign' rightly said 'The real aim of the market is, of course, to become one single country in which Britain would be reduced to a mere province'. To many voters that seemed so far fetched that it could not be true. It was true but the propaganda war had worked.

CHAPTER 7: TO A SUPERSTATE

Stagnation And The Action Committee

'Europeans' regard 1966 to 1985 as years of stagnation and demoralisation. Those are relative terms. From the very beginning there was a battle between the nation states and the fledgling superstate in Brussels. Yet below that discordant surface significant advances were made towards one state. De Gaulle's challenge had merely slowed the advance of the EEC on national governments, not stopped it in its tracks.

Was that appreciated outside the inner sanctums? For most, 'Europe' was only an issue for brief periods. The British in particular gravely misunderstood the forces which not only kept the EEC in being but were steadily strengthening it.

Jean Monnet's Action Committee for a United States of Europe was one of those forces holding Europe together. For twenty years, between 1955 and 1975 this committee subtly and gently guided the European agenda. Responsible to no country, it met only once or twice a year. Most of the action went on behind the scenes as Monnet wheeled and dealt full time. His close friend George Ball wrote, 'He redrew the economic map of Europe so extensively without ever holding elective office'[1]. Many would add the political map too. But he could not do that without outside help.

Monnet needed the constant support of his American friends. He would have achieved little if it had not been American policy to defeat EFTA; to put pressure on Britain to join the EEC; and ally closely with Germany. Monnet's Action Committee for a United States of Europe was in effect also an agency for American policy.

Members of the Action Committee reckoned it had three major successes.[2] First was to fight EFTA. Monnet thought the British challenge would otherwise have engulfed the EEC. Second was to establish European institutions. 'We are not integrating economies, we are integrating policies. We are not just sharing our furniture, we are jointly building a new and bigger house', wrote the first President of the Commission, Dr Hallstein of Germany.[3] The third success was to survive de Gaulle's challenges in the 1960s.

Survival was only part of the story. The advances were considerable: British membership was a major political coup for the federalists and, even before the Treaty of Rome was signed, the all embracing nature of the EEC began to change Britain's way of life. British membership gave the EEC the confidence to try to extend control from the economic to the political. Meanwhile the European Court of Justice quietly churned out judgements slowly engulfing all the nation states.

EMU Mark II And Political Union

When Britain applied to join the EEC for the third time Brussels had to face the likelihood that enlarging the Community might also dilute federalism. Viewed from Brussels the enlargement of the EEC created the need and the chance to move beyond the Treaty of Rome, to 'deepen' it, as federalists describe it.

Monnet was as concerned as ever to make sure that Britain, with her completely different approach to Government; her legal system based on common law, not Roman law; and her world wide trade, did not undermine the federalist principles of the EEC. All subsequent countries seeking to join the EEC have triggered further centralisation: all 'enlargements' have been accompanied by 'deepening'. For example the negotiations to 'deepen' the EU at the Fourth Inter-Governmental Conference of 1996 and 1997 are partly in preparation for enlargement to include countries from Eastern Europe.

During the three years when Britain went through the hurdles of joining, the EEC tried to make strides towards a political union. The first two stages were foreign policy co-operation, and – essential for union – monetary union. European Monetary Union (EMU) is a long standing aim of all federalists, cited time and again from 1919 onwards, and regarded as the key to political union. EMU was essential to Hitler's control of Europe: he was close to putting it into practice for the whole Continent when he lost the war.

Attempts to 'deepen' the EEC at the time of Britain's entry were substantially helped by the arrival of Willy Brandt as Chancellor of Germany in October 1969. Since the early 1930s Brandt had been a champion of a United States of Europe: his party, the SAP or Socialist Workers' Party, looked to the USSR as its natural ally and Brandt was a life long Soviet sympathiser. He was sent by his party to Oslo in 1931 to establish an SAP branch and stayed abroad until the end of the war.

From his war-time exile in Sweden, Brandt advocated a federation of Central and Eastern Europe to improve trade prospects, and then a 'united states of Europe' in which capitalism and imperialism have been destroyed, and all 'military, economic and other common tasks' were handed over to an international organisation.[4] Brandt's group (which included the future Austrian Chancellor Bruno Kreisky) was in close touch with other socialist groups especially Professor Laski's at the London School of Economics, the life long friend of Felix Frankfurter.

Brandt's Chancellorship marked the end of 'Little Europe', that cosy collection of Catholic countries, quietly backed by the Papacy, harking back to the mythical golden age of Charlemagne's Empire. That period, which reflected Adenauer's many years of ascendancy in Germany, was always an aberration when German history is viewed over a longer time frame. Germany was now reverting to her natural attitude of facing to the East. Under Brandt it went beyond that towards co-operation with the USSR.

Not surprisingly, France was anxious to offset Brandt's Ostpolitik and pro-Russian policies with British membership of the EEC. Monnet suggested to Brandt – and Brandt readily agreed – that 'the transformation of the Common Market into an economic and monetary union (EMU), the beginnings of political union, and negotiations with Britain are all possible.' So the December 1969 Hague Summit – the first meeting of the Heads of Government since de Gaulle's crisis over the Fouchet Plan six years before – launched both the process of enlargement and 'deepening' with EMU.

EMU was a big step beyond the Treaty of Rome. To add monetary union in 1957 had been a political impossibility: France was worried about opening up her markets even further and Chancellor Adenauer had already over-ridden his free trader colleague, Erhard. Monnet had asked Professor Robert Triffin and Pierre Uri to design a monetary system but the only concrete result was a reserve fund. Monnet was waiting for British entry in the early 1960s to be able to push for EMU. When de Gaulle vetoed British entry, the Action Programme for EMU had to be abandoned.

Pompidou, the French President who had just succeeded de Gaulle, saw EMU as a way of bolstering the parity of the franc within the CAP – all important to France. Equally France wanted the Community's agricultural policy to be underpinned in case the British should try to weaken it.

The EEC Commission's Werner Report of 1970 recommended a three stage move to a single currency by 1980. The Germans wanted majority voting within Ecofin – the guiding Council of Economics and Finance Ministers – but that was a step too far for the French Finance Minster, Giscard d'Estaing.

Stage one of EMU went ahead in 1971. Called the 'Snake' because the currencies were tied to each other within a 1.2 per cent band, it very shortly ran onto the rocks of currency upheavals as the Bretton Woods system of cross-parity rates against the dollar collapsed. It was relaunched within a year and this time included Britain, Ireland and Denmark, all of whom signed up to show their 'European' credentials ahead of joining the EEC. It collapsed again. The oil shocks of 1973 to 1974 put paid to serious thoughts of EMU for fifteen years, until the 1989 Delors Report.

Discreet moves to political union began in a small way with foreign policy: in October 1970 the Six agreed to hold regular meetings of Foreign Ministers and officials, called European Political Co-operation (EPC), to co-operate on foreign affairs.

In October 1972 at the Paris Summit (which included Britain for the first time, and before the British Parliament had agreed to the Treaty of Rome) the Heads of State agreed to set 'the major objective of transforming, before the end of the decade and with the fullest respect for the Treaties . . . the whole complex of the relations of members states into a

European Union.' Heath, Brandt and Pompidou were as one on the matter.[5]

British Membership Saves The EEC

With Georges Pompidou in the Elysée Palace, Edward Heath, the British Prime Minister, Roy Jenkins prepared to defy the Labour whip, the urging of Monnet, and the backing of the US, Britain's application to join the EEC was virtually a foregone conclusion. That is not how it looked from London at the time, but few in Britain realised the network which surrounded them.

Following in Britain's wake were Denmark and Ireland, her close trading partners. Norway already had an application on the table.

In Britain the debate was about joining a Common Market, a trading area. Much was made of the chance to negotiate the right terms, as it was too in the 1975 referendum. But the Treaty of Rome allows for no debate. Article 189 of the Treaty is central: regulations, directives and Court decisions – known as the acquis communautaire – are binding on member states, the point that was not lost on Lord Wilberforce and his fellow Law Lords.

Therefore when a country joins it is automatically committed to everything that has already been issued. There is very little room to negotiate. The main area is the amount of time allowed to make adjustments to existing Community practice. Other concessions, which may appear substantial, are certain to be minor and will be whittled away over time. If anyone cares to look at the experience of some German states under the Prussian Zollverein they would find exact parallels including the 'concessions' of opt-outs.

The only exception to this has been the creation of the Common Agricultural Policy (CAP) at France's insistence and to its benefit. But then the Franco-German axis has always been the centre-piece of the EEC. If that were to break, there would be no Community.

The importance of Britain's entry to the future of the EEC should not be under-estimated. There were the obvious benefits to Germany of making Britain a 'domestic' market for her goods and opening up the Commonwealth. The wishful thinking French believed Britain could help to withstand the worst of German control. Above all the injection of British money to the EEC saved the wasteful CAP, and with it French agriculture and thus the whole Community.

Britain now imported EEC rather than Commonwealth food and made a large contribution to the EEC Budget (over three quarters of which went to the CAP), so allowing the huge surpluses to continue – the wine lakes, butter mountains and excesses of every kind, all expensively stored. If Britain had not joined, the almost certain financial crisis might have torn the EEC apart. Allocating one per cent of all the Value Added Tax collected in the Community also helped to prolong the life of the unreformed CAP.

Britain Loses Her Fishing Rights

Because new members of the Community have to accept all directives, regulations and Court decisions made before they join, before British, Danish, Irish and Norwegian entry, countries rich in fish, the Six thought a fishing policy essential. It was rushed through in the autumn of 1970. A regulation decreed that all member states were to have equal access without discrimination to all Community waters.[6] What had been national waters were now to be Community waters.

Extensive negotiations when the four applied to join centred on transitional arrangements, which in the British case gave ten years before the full effect of the Common

Fisheries Policy took effect. The terms were not fully fixed before Britain joined – the British Parliament agreed to a blank cheque.

Even worse the British chief negotiator, Geoffrey Rippon, told the House of Commons in December 1971 that : 'It is clear that we retain full jurisdiction over the whole of our coastal waters up to twelve miles. Secondly, access to our coastal waters within six miles from our baseline is limited exclusively to British vessels. Next, in areas between six and twelve miles, where the baselines are not in themselves a sufficient safeguard or where the stocks are already fully exploited, the fishing will also be limited to British vessels and to those with existing rights to fish there for certain species of fish'.[7]

Rippon implied to the Commons that Britain could use her veto to renew the derogation after ten years. The House of Lords was explicitly told that was the case. After ten years, as the Government then knew, the veto would be gone and Britain would be outvoted – every other country has an interest in making sure that the former British waters are open to all.

A bad situation was made worse by the 1982 entry of Spain with her large fishing fleets into the EEC. 'British' waters were supplying sixty-five to seventy-five per cent of all EEC fish which now had to be opened as a 'common resource' to the Spanish. That meant cutting the fishing fleets and hit the British the hardest.

To reduce obvious conflict Brussels conceived the idea of allocating each nation a percentage share of certain fish species with the enticement that this share out would be permanent. Of course it could not be and has had to be adjusted twice since to allow for new members, each time reducing the size of the shares. It will be adjusted again. Nor could such a system be adequately policed. The Common

Fisheries Policy inevitably has led to violence at sea and substantial evasion of the rules. Subsidies are now mandatory for boats to be 'decommissioned'; those boats have physically to be broken up on the sea shore.[8]

Norway considered the proposed arrangements unacceptable and negotiated an open ended agreement. So keen was Edward Heath, the British Prime Minister, to join that he wrote to the Norwegian Prime Minister, Trygve Bratteli, pressurising him not to ask for a permanent arrangement which would, he said, be against EEC principles and to accept a six mile fisheries limit for part of Norway's southern coast.[9] If that had been tested in the European Court of Justice it would almost certainly have failed. At a referendum Norway voted against joining – fishing was the key issue and the Norwegians were realistic about what would happen to their fishing if they did join.

The Zollverein Strikes Again: Britain Goes Metric

Similarly the metric system, which was already used among the countries of the Six, but not in Britain or Ireland, was formally adopted before British entry and included changing Britain's currency from pounds, shillings and pence at a considerable cost and an increase in inflation. The key reason for the Six's sense of urgency had been identified by John Murray in his 1962 Memorandum for Hugh Gaitskell: 'Why should we give away our former colonial markets for which engineering products had always been specified in Imperial units, and, by metricating, open up the vast replacement and maintenance requirements to foreign competition, at the same time causing a massive retooling operation in our own factories?'[10]

It was the Prussian Zollverein all over again. An October 1971 directive[11] proposed the exclusive uses of metric units from the beginning of 1978. In signing the Treaty of Rome to take effect from 1st January 1973, Britain was therefore accepting that directive along with all the others. As with most other aspects of British entry the metric issue was fudged. A final 'decision' on Imperial units did not have to be reached until 1976.

When that date arrived some Imperial units were abolished in stages. Because most British could not accept the new standards, some were continued until another decision date in 1989. By that time the teaching of metric units in schools had had a sufficient effect. So most Imperial measures were abolished from the end of 1994.

The only Imperial measures allowed indefinitely are those for roads; pints of milk, beer and cider; acres for land registration only; and troy ounces for precious metals. But none are to be used by right, only by special dispensation from Brussels.[12] The issue was debated only once in the House of Commons, in April 1989, with eighty per cent of the House absent.[13]

Fishing and metrication are typical of the difficulty the British Government, in particular, has had in understanding the all-embracing compass of the Treaty of Rome and the European Court of Justice. The intention is to create, slowly, a new state absorbing the old nation states. Heath is one of the few in Britain who has fully understood from the beginning and agrees with the ultimate political aim.

VAT

Taxation is a sensitive area in which uniformity is slowly evolving. In 1967 the EEC agreed to adopt a value-added tax (VAT); therefore Britain adopted the VAT system ahead of entry. At first the rate and the goods to which VAT were applied varied greatly from country to country. Proposals to make VAT more uniform were made in 1985, 1987 and 1989 but made little headway. Since October 1992 the agreed standard rate of VAT has been the minimum of 15 per cent with some goods and services allowed a lower rate. Britain's zero rated goods and services have to be phased out by 1999. That includes books, newspapers, children's clothes, food and new houses. The British Government has already had to apply VAT to electricity and gas but has never admitted that it had no choice.

Heath Backs A Provisional European Government

Monnet and his Action Committee were unable to achieve the main item of 'deepening' – monetary union – but Monnet pressed for still more federalism. He wrote a draft proposing a Provisional European Government. In September 1973 he went to Chequers to discuss it with Heath. Monnet wanted to make a public statement but Heath said 'Let's just do it: that's enough and it's better'.[14] Heath changed the Provisional Government's title to 'Supreme Council' and suggested it meet every month instead of every three months. Brandt, Pompidou and the other heads of Government agreed.

Monnet explained that he wanted to move beyond the Treaty of Rome to push at the frontiers of national political power. But to do so 'would require a further delegation of sovereignty . . . gradually people would come to see how strong the machinery was . . . (it would) eventually earn its title.'[15]

Monnet was to be frustrated, first by the 1973 oil embargo, and then, temporarily in 1974, by changes of key heads of Government: Wilson replaced Heath in Britain, Schmidt replaced Brandt in Germany and, after Pompidou's death in 1974, d'Estaing became President of France. So it took until December 1974 before Monnet's idea of a Provisional

Government re-emerged as a European Council of Ministers to meet three times a year. That comprised the heads of Government and, importantly for the first time, the President of the Commission on equal terms.

The same meeting agreed another of Monnet's hard-fought-for aims, that of a directly elected European Assembly by 1978 to replace the existing national parliamentarians and so to by-pass all the national parliaments.[16]

Soon after those successes Monnet fell ill and his resignation in 1975 marked the end of the Action Committee for the United States of Europe. He died four years later in 1979 aged 91. One Committee member, Max Kohnstamm, remained at the centre of the network and revived it in 1982 but without much influence.

The European Court Of Justice

Throughout those years another institution worked quietly and by its judgements did far more than Monnet's Action Committee to create a United States of Europe. Almost certainly the European Court of Justice (ECJ) was the brainchild of the US Supreme Court Justice, Felix Frankfurter. He more than anyone understood how a Supreme Court could gently, and almost unseen, change a constitution. He himself regularly used his position as a US Supreme Court Justice to put his own political views into practice. Sir Patrick Neill QC has written that the ECJ has 'recognisable similarities to the American model'.[17]

Working undetected through Monnet, Frankfurter would have had no trouble in ensuring that the Court appeared in the Treaty of Rome and to have set its terms of reference, just like the European Coal and Steel Community, that state in embryo. Monnet's greatest strengths were his dogged persistence and outstanding presence, but intellectually he was not in Frankfurter's class.

In February 1965 Frankfurter died[18] after twenty-seven years as a Supreme Court Justice and forty-five years as a pre-eminent lawyer. He was active as a judge until late in 1962. An intellectual giant of immense energy his influence, most Americans would be surprised to learn, went far beyond his own shores. Possibly more than anyone else the United States of Europe is his creation.

One European judge has written of the 'magnitude of the contribution made by the ECJ to the integration of Europe'; that the EU has 'unprecedented law making powers'. The Commission has 'led the Court on the path towards further integration and increasing the Commission's power.' Just as Frankfurter anticipated 'the Court has sought to "constitutionalise" the Treaty, to fashion a constitutional framework for a quasi-federal structure in Europe'. He added, ominously, that being in Luxembourg has helped – 'out of sight, out of mind.'[19]

So the ECJ is far more than a Court – it creates legislation by what Sir Patrick Neill has described as 'strained interpretations of the (treaty) texts'. Sir Patrick summed up the ECJ, 'A Court with a mission is a menace. A supreme court with a mission is a tyranny.'

From that Court there is no appeal and equally from that legislature there is no appeal. The judges with their double role are unelected and unaccountable. They need have no judicial experience and most have not. The qualifications are the minimum required for its judiciary by each member country – in Britain that is ten years at the Bar. Most EU judges are academics and civil servants.

The Treaty of Rome was much more than a treaty or agreement between states. Walter Hallstein, the Commission's first President, wrote 'the Treaty does no more than lay down general aims and fix the framework of action'. It was unlike any other treaty: it had, he said, 'a new quality'.[20] It was 'an indissoluble union of European states' – the word 'irrevocable' is part of all Community treaties.

The judgements of the ECJ are all intended to further the primary purpose of the Treaty of Rome, 'to create an ever closer union' as the preamble states. It is therefore a political Court, not a Court to dispense justice as the British understand it. The Court's judgements are the most important parts of the acquis communautaire and for nearly four decades it has produced a substantial body of law, dwarfing the legal systems of the member states.

Acceptance of article 189 includes the central point of the Treaty of Rome: recognition of the primacy of Community law. Two other doctrines have grown out of that, 'direct effect' and 'pre-emption'.

All directives and judgements have to be transferred into the law of member states within prescribed time limits creating a new legal order. That is 'direct effect'. The critical case was that of Van Gend en Loos in 1962.[21] Directives and judgements have to take effect even if they conflict with existing national law and before that national law can be amended.

'Pre-emption' means that the Community has a decisive role in allocating power. Even if no Community measures have been taken, areas of Government can be deemed to be no longer in the control of national Governments. For example, because the Common Fisheries Policy existed, the European Court judged that fish conservation was no longer a national matter (May 1981).

In 1991 the Francovich judgement[22] took 'direct effect' one step further. The supremacy of European law was already long established, this ruling has given individuals the right to claim against their national governments for failure to implement directives, even when those directives are not deemed to have direct effect. It is another nail in the coffin of national governments.

Under the Frankovich judgement Britain has to compensate Spanish fishermen who are prevented from fishing Britain's fish quotas by the British 1988 Merchant Shipping Act.

Jenkins Leads Europe Into EMU Mark III

The oil crises of 1974 and 1979 shook world industry and recessions followed. Every country in the EEC became absorbed in its own affairs and 'Europe' really was in the doldrums. The brief spell of renewed drive towards European unity between 1970 and 1974, led by Heath, Pompidou, and Brandt began to look like an aberration.

Stagnation and lethargy reigned in Brussels. Monnet was gone and with him the close link with America. Many of the Americans from that unique network who had lobbied so hard from the war and even before had also either died or retired. Federalists wrote papers, lobbied and hoped but without leadership from Brussels, the United States or the biggest European states little could be achieved.

Curiously it was a Briton who came to the rescue. In 1976, it was Britain's turn to propose the next President of the Commission. The British Prime Minister, Harold Wilson, offered the job to Roy Jenkins, a committed federalist.

Jenkins had been a thorn in the side of the Labour Party for years; in 1962 he had quarrelled with Gaitskell over Europe and had left the Opposition Front Bench; in 1971 he had led sixty-eight fellow Labour MPs into the 'yes' lobby against a three-line whip and ensured that Heath took Britain into the EEC. He split the Labour Party and Wilson healed the wound with the device of the 1975 referendum on whether Britain should stay in or come out. Not surprisingly Wilson took the opportunity to send this rebel abroad to Brussels.

Heads of governments have often 'exiled' trouble makers to Brussels or sent those of little consequence to be Commissioners. Jenkins would have preferred to be leader of the Labour Party and when Wilson unexpectedly resigned, he stayed to fight. After losing to Jim Callaghan in 1976 he spent his first Christmas in Brussels. Jenkins gave a gravitas to the role of President and spent the next eight years trying to increase his power and that of the Commission. It was an uphill struggle.

Jenkins needed a cause. After taking soundings he rapidly alighted on the idea of relaunching the European Monetary Union, the key to political union. The first attempt at EMU was of course Hitler's. The second was in December 1969 as part of the package to 'deepen' the EEC and offset the possible weakening effect of British entry.

Throughout 1978 Jenkins pushed for a European Monetary System (EMS). It was not explicitly linked to monetary union and a single currency but that is what lay behind it. The EMS was established by a Resolution of the Council of Ministers and so did not form part of the Treaty of Rome but every country was automatically committed to it. The key part of EMS was the Exchange Rate Mechanism (ERM) – no timetable was set for countries to join. Jenkins said he had learnt to take the line of least resistance from Jean Monnet: ultimately that would win the day.

Jenkins had to convince both France and Germany. Luck was on his side. Helmut Schmidt of Germany was lukewarm to start with but a sharp fall in the dollar from $2.30 against the DM in October 1977 to $1.76 a year later seemed like a dollar rout and Schmidt was suddenly converted to the seeming security of a stable currency system. Each currency was allowed to fluctuate around agreed central rates with a top and bottom limit. If a currency hit its limits then Central Banks could intervene to bring them back into line. If that was not enough, interest rates could be adjusted and ultimately the currencies could be realigned. All the EEC countries, except Britain, joined the ERM when it started in March 1979.

It was the thin end of the political union wedge. This was a first step: the short life of the Snake in the early 1970s warned against a rapid introduction of a single currency and emphasised the need for a cautious, step by step approach. The ERM has also satisfied those Europeans who have long wanted to create a currency bloc shielding its members from the dollar and limiting dependence on the US. It is credited with reducing any temptation to devalue and to increase competitiveness.

Throughout most of Jenkins' Presidency the pull of the nation states was much stronger than any centralising force he could impose. Giscard d'Estaing, although a long term EEC supporter and a founder member of ELEC just after the war, played the traditional French line of keeping the Commission within strict limits. He had been anxious to keep Monnet's Provisional Government within the control of the nations by backing the creation of the Council of Ministers in 1974. But he could not stop Jenkins from attending the Summits – the first time an EEC President had done so. Jenkins wrote of the six months of the French Presidency in 1979, 'It was like living under the constant threat of an artillery bombardment.'[23]

By the late 1970s Brussels, with nine member states, had burgeoned into a complex bureaucracy far removed from the early days under Dr Hallstein. A Council of Ministers meant over two hundred people in one room; more than a hundred attended Political Co-operation meetings on foreign affairs.

With the veto widely used, or certainly threatened, items could languish on the agenda for years. Outside meetings civil servants lived up to the sobriquet of fleshpot living with sacrosanct lunch 'hours' in top restaurants and large expense accounts.

Mrs Thatcher Inherits The Tory Delusion

Mrs Thatcher shook Brussels out of its malaise but she did so from a position of ignorance. At the May 1979 British General Election which returned the Conservatives to power Europe was certainly not an issue. The revolution which Mrs Thatcher, the new Prime Minister, brought with her had been largely planned by a think tank, the Institute for Economic Affairs (IEA).

From its start in 1955 the IEA had explicitly focused on reversing the intellectual trend of the Fabians and tilting the political debate away from Government interference. Fabianism, said the IEA, had been at the cutting edge of politics since the beginning of the century. Yet Europe was a centrepiece of Fabian planning and over more than thirty years the IEA had only commissioned two papers on it, in 1962 and 1972.

If Conservative thinkers had realised that deeply hidden within the Fabian society there had been a small group who had pioneered the EEC expressly to create one socialist state encompassing all the European nation states, then they would have concluded that all their efforts to turn back the tide of socialism in Britain should first and foremost be concentrated on Brussels. As Edward Heath, advised by Lord Wilberforce, knew 'UK law was henceforth to be subordinated to European law': ultimately that meant a loss of all sovereignty.

The Conservative Party did not think or research deeply enough. It did not realise that British sovereignty was waning fast – sucked out by a conveyor belt of judgements from the European Court of Justice, decisions and regulations from the Commission. Richard Cockett commented in his review of British think tanks that 'The big black hole in the ideological re-think that consumed the Conservatives in the 1960s and the 1970s was Europe.'[24]

That hole was to negate many of the achievements of the Thatcher revolution and threaten the rest. An early example was the dramatic ending of fixed exchange rates in October 1979 which had so crippled British business under the Labour Government. Yet only six months earlier Britain had entered a commitment to join the Exchange Rate Mechanism which was still valid. No-one noticed the contradiction.

The Conservative Government thought it was sovereign in Britain. It was to take another decade or more before a few realised that it was not. Most still do not know.

Conservative politicians have debated, discussed and fought each 'European' issue on its merits, trying to take a pragmatic, reasonable and balanced view. Europe, all Government Ministers have declared, is a Europe of nation states. 'Europe' will not be allowed to interfere in sacrosanct areas of British life from defence to social issues. In any case it may never happen. If it is going to happen then Britain should help to shape it.

Those Ministers did not realise that they presided over a revolution in the way Britain is governed, a revolution pioneered by a few Conservative MPs in league with Marxists and introduced by a Conservative Government. A Europe of nation states has not been on offer since the 1948 Marshall Plan. The Conservatives should have learnt from de Gaulle's defeat at federalist hands.

At first under the new Conservative Government all seemed to be going well. Mrs Thatcher won her first battle with Europe over Britain's net contribution of over £1 billion. All agreed it was unfairly high. At the time only Britain and Germany gave more than they got back from Brussels in subsidies: the other seven countries were winners. A May 1980 deal after an eighteen hour session gave Britain a respite for two years with a £1.4 billion rebate. One Cabinet Minister, Nicholas Ridley, explained 'The leaders of all the other European states had been determined to frustrate her. They all benefited from Britain's forced largesse and they didn't want to pay any more money themselves. They thought a mixture of obduracy and hautiness would win the day.'[25]

Mrs Thatcher fought back with occasional fury but overwhelming tenacity until, at the June 1984 Fontainebleu Summit, the usual lengthy horse trading produced a rebate of 66 per cent of Britain's excess contribution, more than any of her advisers had expected. They would have given in long before. That earned Mrs Thatcher the respect of European leaders.

Spinelli: To Union Via Subsidiarity

Mrs Thatcher's first challenge to Europe in 1980 left the Community in a state of 'suspended crisis'. Building on his relaunch of monetary union, Jenkins intended to strengthen Political Co-operation.[26] That was foiled and instead 'Europe' looked as though it was in danger of drifting yet again.

Into the breach stepped Altiero Spinelli, then aged 73, and one of the few of the original 'European' planners still alive. Spinelli had been a Communist resister to Mussolini and paid the price of sixteen years in prison. He had then formed a new party, the MFE in Italy, to build 'Europe', had led an exiled group in Switzerland linked to all the resistance members round German occupied Europe and corresponded with the Fabian group in London and J. F. Dulles in the US.

Most of his overseas associates had long since died: J. F. Dulles in 1959, Professor Arnold Toynbee in 1975, and in Italy his old friends and colleagues Ernesto Rossi in 1967 and Professor Einaudi in 1961.

Developed in an underground conspiracy, Spinelli's view of Europe became the accepted way forward. He spent six years as a European Commissioner and then in 1976 was a member of the Italian Parliament for the Communist PCI party. At the same time he was a Member of the European Parliament where he was well known as a Communist though he described himself as an independent one.

For forty years Spinelli's influence on Europe had been eclipsed by Jean Monnet, both were men of powerful and conflicting egos. Monnet had had the key American links and the advantage of being a Frenchman and part of the critical Franco-German axis. Monnet had deliberately kept Spinelli out of the Action Committee for the United States of Europe. But behind the scenes Spinelli had been a constant critic of the slow pace of 'Europe' and nearly every European proposal has had Spinelli's hand in it, quite literally because Spinelli's amendments are scrawled on drafts over many years pushing for a superstate.

In early July 1980 when the initial furore over Mrs Thatcher's demand for 'our money back' had died down, Spinelli and eight others founded the Crocodile Club. They named it after the restaurant where they met in Strasbourg.

Spinelli and his Crocodile Movement aimed to make the European Parliament draft a new treaty for European Union – the next step beyond the Treaty of Rome. The Treaty was already twenty-five years old and some thought was outdated. A year later he persuaded the European Parliament to adopt his proposal, and naturally enough he was the rapporteur for the new project.

His proposals were based on an alliance between the Commission and the Parliament. Both wanted to increase their own power at the expense of the Council of Ministers and the nation states. They are natural allies. Spinelli wanted a Union which, as he said, 'will have the sole power to act by its own decisions and the end of inter-governmental co-operation'.[27]

Impatient with the long delay since 1945, Spinelli wanted to create one state in a single leap. The inter-governmental European Council would become part of the union; the European parliament would stop being consultative and became a formal legislature; majority voting would replace unanimity – even agreement on the new treaty would be by majority voting – so Britain for one could be outvoted and still find herself signed up to it. Spinelli was nothing if not direct.

The Commission would become the only executive body; the powers of the Court of Justice would be strengthened, the Union's control would be extended to foreign policy and defence. To all this Mrs Thatcher later said 'no! no! no!'

Spinelli's way of keeping the national governments quiet was to be the principle of subsidiarity. All decisions would be made at the lowest appropriate level of government. He said subsidiarity would help the 'transition to a higher level of union'.[28]

Yet Spinelli proposed subsidiarity only as a clever device, he never intended it to be a guiding principle of the European Union. Subsidiarity is part of the 1948 German constitution and German Basic Law states unambiguously in article 31 that 'Federal law shall override Land law'.[29] Therefore sovereignty lies with the Federal Government. It is the Federal Government which decides what issues shall be settled lower down by the Lander.

The Union was to be a step too far for the 1980s but the Maastricht Treaty (or the Treaty on European Union) was a watered down version and was effective from November 1993.

The nation states have all, to some extent, fallen for Spinelli's device. But the British Government has taken it to be an enshrining principle of the Maastricht Treaty. Spinelli meant it only as a means to an end. Subsidiarity is a political trick. The end is a single state.

At a seminar just before the Maastricht Treaty Agreement, European jurists, including the former president of the Court of Justice, affirmed that subsidiarity is 'political in essence', not judicial.[30] That is it is nothing to do with the Court. The Treaty says that subsidiarity only applies to areas which do not fall within the 'exclusive competence' of the Community.

Conveniently that excludes subsidiarity from the whole of the Single Market framework – just about the only aspect of 'Europe' in which Britain says it is interested.

In 1984 the European Parliament voted to recommend a version of Spinelli's Draft Treaty – to a superstate in one leap. Only two countries, Belgium and his own country of Italy, called for the treaty to be ratified. Spinelli was bitterly disappointed but that was not the end of it. His attempt inspired a new committee under the Irish Senator, James Dooge. Dooge's 1985 report called for 'a qualitative leap to a genuine political entity . . . i.e. a European Union.'[31]

Most of the Dooge Committee's proposals appeared either in the Single European Act or the Maastricht Treaty and they included much – but not yet all – of what Spinelli had been battling for. That progress was almost entirely due to Spinelli; the President of the Commission at the time, Gaston Thorn of Luxembourg, left little mark of his own.

The Single Market

Jacques Delors, the next Commission President, made at least as much progress as his fellow Frenchman, Jean Monnet, towards one state. Delors was another exile from national politics. Twice passed over as Prime Minister, he was a nuisance to Mitterand in France. Delors' two terms as President of the Commission from 1985 to 1994 were years of unprecedented centralisation. After moving away from the far left in French politics in 1979 he joined the Socialist Party. His route to politics was through the civil service and the trade union movement. Like Monnet he wanted no elected post and took some persuading by Mitterand to stand for the first European Parliamentary elections in 1979. After two years there he spent the next three as French Finance Minister. His vision was of a socialist centralist Europe.

Like Jenkins, Delors searched for a big idea to launch his Presidency from January 1985. He took the advice of Max Kohnstamm to turn the customs union of the Treaty of Rome into a single market and remove all the barriers to trade. Kohnstamm, once Monnet's chief assistant, warned him that to make it work a big increase in majority voting in the Council of Ministers would be needed.[32] This proved to be a momentous point.

Pressure had been building for some time to move 'Europe' forward. Spinelli was the strongest force, but the Foreign Ministers of Germany and Italy (Hans-Dietrich Genscher and Emilio Colombo) had together come up with a similar, if slightly weaker, scheme in 1981. The next year their plan was acknowledged by the member states in the non-binding Declaration of Stuttgart: 'to transform . . . relations between their states into a European Union'. It deliberately mimicked the first declaration of a drive to union at the 1972 Paris

Summit when Heath, Brandt and Pompidou led the other six and declared they would create a European Union by 1980.

This time Britain, Denmark and Greece feared the loss of the Luxembourg Compromise, the veto, and a corresponding increase in majority voting. Nor was there much enthusiasm in Paris and Bonn. The British Foreign Secretary remarked that Britain had not attached much importance to the Stuttgart Declaration at the time – it was not legally binding – but, he said, they should have done.

The third pressure came from Spain and Portugal who had applied to join the EEC. Enlargement again created the need to 'deepen', just as it had done in 1970 when Britain, Ireland, Denmark and Norway proposed to join the EEC. France in particular was reluctant to let in Spain and Portugal, both largely agricultural, which would challenge French farmers and reduce the EEC subsidies available.

To the British Conservative Government the Single Market seemed to spell, wrongly as it turned out, free trade and deregulation, issues which were at the heart of Conservative policy. Mrs Thatcher, now in her second term as Prime Minister, was looking for a positive issue for Europe which would turn it from any further attempt to be federal towards free trade. She and her Ministers, not understanding the issues, enthusiastically embraced Delors' Single Market.

In her autobiography Mrs Thatcher wrote that Britain pioneered the Single Market, 'to revive (the Treaty of Rome's) liberal, free trade, deregulatory purpose.' In a narrow sense she was right. A Briton, Lord Cockfield, newly appointed as Commissioner for trade matters, produced an ambitious White Paper, at Delors' request, detailing 300 legislative matters needed to create the Single Market.

The Single European Act went beyond a single market. Even the name of the Act encouraged a belief that it was about one market. It was, however, deliberately given that name to show that all the issues it contained were to be treated as one and not dismembered.

For the first time the Single European Act codified two important inter-governmental meetings. First, it recognised the European Council, the meeting of heads of government which had begun intermittently in the 1960s. From 1974, at Giscard d'Estaing's suggestion, the Summits were held regularly three times a year, later reduced to twice.

Second, it codified European Political Co-operation, which again had begun as inter-governmental only in 1970 to co-ordinate and discuss foreign policy and security. Now, although foreign policy still remained technically outside the ambit of the Community, it was to be given Treaty status and for the first time the Commission was to be 'fully associated' with it. The member states agreed to 'ensure that common principles and objectives are gradually developed and defined' and thus have a common foreign policy.[33] The President was to initiate action, co-ordinate and represent members states with a Secretariat in Brussels with diplomatic status.[34] After five years this would be reviewed. London thought this a good and harmless idea: it did not involve coercion.[35]

Again it was the thin end of the political wedge. Mrs Thatcher and her Government failed to recognise it. She wrote 'At Brussels (January 1985) I also launched an initiative on deregulation designed to provide impetus to the Community's development as a free trade and free enterprise area. It was intended to fit in with our own economic policy . . .'[36] ,

Mrs Thatcher's view was far from the truth. The Single European Act was Delors' initiative, widely welcomed by federalists, and it responded to the pressure from Spinelli, from the Genscher-Colombo Plan and to the need to centralise further given the Spanish and Portuguese applications to join, to 'deepen' before 'widening'.

Nor did Mrs Thatcher understand that what she called a free trade area was a customs union, a protectionist bloc, designed to achieve political union just as the Zollverein had done in Germany in the nineteenth century and Hitler had repeated. Hitler's planners had expressly said they wished to rid Europe of the British free trade influence. Britain was moving steadily away from international free trade and into a protectionist trading bloc.

Denis Healey predicted that the protectionism of the Single Market would force North America and Japan to answer back in kind which would lead to trade wars.[37] NAFTA has proved him partly right and the EU may yet cause the world to divide into protectionist blocs.

Yet it is typical of the way the Community is seen from London where few understand the driving force behind 'Europe' and think only in British terms of free trade and practical results. Mrs Thatcher bemoaned the fact that Lord Cockfield rapidly went 'native' in Brussels and 'tended to disregard the larger questions of politics – constitutional sovereignty, national sentiment and the promptings of liberty.'[38]

Lord Cockfield, on the other hand, wrote of the Single Market: 'Europe stands at the cross roads . . . We can now either resolve to complete the integration of the economies of Europe . . . or . . . allow Europe to develop into no more than a free trade area.'[39]

As the federalists have always said, first create economic union, then political union. Equally as Heath understood in 1967: 'the primary reason for our negotiation was political: the negotiation itself was mainly concerned with economic matters. And this will be so with any future negotiation.'

Mrs Thatcher did not then understand. Nor did any of her Ministers.

'Deepening' Again Ends The Veto

The additions of Spain and Portugal to the Community reinforced the general view that majority voting would have to be increased substantially. Against the wishes of Britain, Denmark and Greece the pressure built for the Luxembourg Compromise to end. The French President, François Mitterand, began to shift France's long held position and declared that there should be a move back to the Treaties. At the June 1985 Milan Summit, with Britain, Denmark and Greece protesting that there was no need to amend the treaties, the Community voted to summon an Inter-Governmental Conference to revise the Treaties. That conference was held at Luxembourg at the beginning of December 1985.

Those who believed the national veto would survive the Single European Act (SEA) were to be surprised. As late as 1994 Geoffrey Howe, formerly British Foreign Secretary, thought the Luxembourg Compromise was not affected.[40] Once the SEA came into force in July 1987 the Luxembourg Compromise or national veto ended. Furthermore, majority voting replaced unanimity in sixteen areas on top of the twenty-five of the Treaty of Rome. Centralisation was increasing at the expense of the nation states. Neither the Commission nor the European Court of Justice had ever recognised the Luxembourg Compromise. That may be a lesson for any other compromises made in the national interest outside the Treaties – they will not long survive.

So the Single European Act was not the tidying up exercise some had thought. It increased the centralising power of Brussels substantially. Nonetheless the massive public relations campaign in Europe only 'sold' the Single Market.

1992, the year when the market was to come into effect, was so heavily 'sold' that many people expected a glorious revolution to occur. When 1992 came and went it was something of a let down.

Lord Cockfield had done a good technocratic job to simplify frontier formalities. That extended to harmonising public health, product safety and consumer protection and setting a minimum rate for most Value Added Tax at 15 per cent. Tax, a sensitive area, is slowly being pulled inside the Community net with each new treaty.

In Britain, after a six day debate in April 1986, the Single European Act went through the House of Commons under a guillotine motion as an amendment to the European Communities Act. Peers said 'it went through the House of Lords on the nod'. The Government sold it as a triumph for free trade. Much later many MPs thought that if time had been allowed for debate it would never have passed.

Lord Denning, that passionate defender of English Common Law, argued that 'sovereignty is being eroded and that we are coming under another sovereignty – that of Europe . . .' just as he had when Britain first joined, 'the Treaty is like an incoming tide. It flows into the estuaries and up the rivers. It cannot be held back.'[41] Though never in favour of the EEC[42] Lord Denning's attitude has always been that if you cannot stop the tide then you have to make the best of it.

Too late Mrs Thatcher realised what she had done. She had told the House of Commons after the IGC, 'I am constantly saying that I wish that they would talk less about European and political union . . . they mean a good deal less than some people over here think they mean.' In her autobiography she added, 'Looking back I was wrong to think that. But I still believe it was right to sign the Single European Act, because we wanted a Single Market.'

And too late Mrs Thatcher realised that 'A Franco-German bloc with its own agenda had re-emerged to set the direction of the Community. The European Commission . . . was now led by a tough, talented European federalist . . . And the Foreign Office was almost imperceptibly moving to compromise with these new European friends.'[43] That was not surprising because she had signed a treaty including harmonising foreign policy. That was a high price to pay for a misunderstood Single Market.

take back your bratwürst

CHAPTER 8: REBELLION

The Challenge Of The Bruges Speech

Jacques Delors, the Commission's President, told a session of the European Parliament in July 1988 that within ten years 'eighty per cent of our economic legislation, perhaps even fiscal and social as well' would be enacted by an embryonic European Government. On 8th September Delors told the British Trades Union Conference: 'collective bargaining should henceforward take place at European level.' Geoffrey Howe, Britain's Foreign Secretary, mused in the midst of planning meetings for EMU, 'I often found myself wondering why the European agenda seemed to be unfolding at such breakneck speed.'[1]

One reason was the impetus which had been building

throughout the 1980s driven by Spinelli's Crocodile Movement and his draft Treaty on European Union; the Genscher-Colombo plan of 1981; and the 'deepening' of the Single European Act with its Single Market by '1992' and European Monetary Union. Success bred success, and unlike the earlier push towards Union by Brandt, Pompidou and Heath in 1970, it was not destroyed by oil shocks and recession.

The public relations campaign for '1992' created such a bandwagon and drew in so many businessmen that federalists started to believe their own marketing. The two most important national leaders, Kohl of Germany and Mitterand of France, were secure at home after being re-elected in early 1988. Surely the charge towards one superstate was unstoppable.

Then, on 20th September 1988, Mrs Thatcher challenged the United States of Europe at the College of Europe in Bruges. She may not have realised the irony of the place: the College was the result of Fabian (PEP) war-time planning to provide 'Europe's' future administrators. Hers was the first serious challenge to 'Europe' since de Gaulle.

Like de Gaulle, Mrs Thatcher spoke of a Europe of nation states, a family of nations, and explicitly rejected federalism. 'We have not successfully rolled back the frontiers of the state in Britain, only to see them reimposed at a European level, with a European super-state exercising a new dominance from Brussels.' Like Churchill she said, 'We must never forget that east of the Iron Curtain peoples who once enjoyed a full share of European culture, freedom and identity have been cut off from their roots.'[2]

Mrs Thatcher, by then a world leader of immense stature, had understood enough of 'Europe' to shake the Commission and all federalists. Federalists reacted immediately with fury and planned for her demise.[3] They remembered the wasted years caused by de Gaulle, the Fouchet Plan and the Empty

Chair. Then 'Europe' was young and vulnerable. Tactics had to suit that vulnerability. Now 'Europe' was strong with a United States of Europe just round the corner. The reaction could afford to be severe. It could also afford to wait.

In a little over two years Mrs Thatcher was to pay the price for the courage of her Bruges Speech. The issue which led to her downfall was EMU.

EMU had been included in the Single European Act, albeit only in the usual preliminary, vague co-operative terms. Then Jacques Delors, looking for a way forward, used the Stock Market Crash of October 1987 as an excuse to restart the EMU process. 'If the ECU today shared the role of a reserve currency with the dollar and the yen, we would have been able to avoid . . . even stock market crises.' He claimed the Single Market would not work without a single currency and implicit in that was the abolition of national currencies.[4]

Delors manoeuvred until he had set up a committee of twelve Central Bank Governors with himself as chairman. They met between the month of Mrs Thatcher's Bruges speech in September 1988 and April 1989. It was to be the mechanism by which an unholy alliance of two British Cabinet Ministers and Brussels got rid of Mrs Thatcher.

Mrs Thatcher had no doubts. Backed by her adviser, Alan (later Sir Alan) Walters, she was against a single currency and increasingly against Britain's joining the Exchange Rate Mechanism, even though Britain was already committed to it in principal following Roy Jenkins' 1977 initiative when President of the Commission. 'When the time is right' stalled Mrs Thatcher.

She was challenged by two of her most senior Cabinet colleagues. Geoffrey Howe, her first Chancellor of the Exchequer, had been in favour of both the ERM and EMU. He did not agree that one currency meant the end of sovereignty and saw monetary union only as a way to provide currency stability. To boost his position in 1982 Howe had appointed a sympathetic Governor of the Bank of England, Robin Leigh Pemberton (later Lord Kingsdown).

In 1983 Nigel Lawson succeeded Howe; Howe went to the Foreign Office. Lawson too campaigned strongly for early entry to the ERM though, unlike Howe, he did not favour a single currency. In March 1987, frustrated by what he saw as Mrs Thatcher's intransigence, Lawson unofficially began to make sterling shadow the DM. It was the ERM by the back door. By then Lawson had moved onto a larger stage than Britain and was beguiled by his ability to wheel and deal with the other Finance Ministers of the Group of Seven – even to lead. It was a heady business stabilising exchange rates with massive interventions and holding the US dollar against the yen and the DM.[5]

According to Howe and Lawson the two enemies of Britain's entry to the ERM were Alan Walters (with his 'remote control of Margaret's thinking' as Howe put it) and the timing. When Britain did join the ERM in October 1990 it was, they said, five years too late and the relative positions of the currencies were wrong. The bogeyman, Alan Walters, who had been Mrs Thatcher's personal economic adviser from 1981 to 1984 and returned again in May 1989, was strongly against fixed exchange rate systems.

Howe also diverged from Cabinet policy after Mrs Thatcher's challenge to 'Europe' at Bruges. He was highly ambitious and may well have seen himself as the next Prime Minister with a conciliatory European policy in sharp contrast to the 'obstinacy' of Mrs Thatcher.

The press started to report on a Cabinet split and the Government's public credibility began to erode. With two of her most senior Cabinet Ministers playing their own line, Mrs Thatcher began to look isolated. It was the beginning of the end.

'Europe' Brings Down Mrs Thatcher

In April 1989 the Delors Committee reported. It asserted, but admitted it was unable to prove, that EMU 'could' bring economic benefits to participating countries. Currencies were to be irrevocably fixed in a three stage process with a tight timetable culminating in 1999. National governments would never again be masters of their own economies. They would no longer control their own competitive position and, if hard times hit, they would not be able to alleviate the distress of unemployment. More sovereignty was to be surrendered.

The scene was set for the June 1989 Madrid Summit when the Community accepted the Delors Report, signed by all twelve Central Bank Governors. Britain's Sir Robin Leigh-Pemberton feebly said he did not want to be the only one to say no. Mrs Thatcher was outvoted. With Howe and Lawson threatening to resign, she came up with a formula for the conditions under which Britain would join the ERM.

The Summit's main issue was EMU: Britain's position on the ERM, which most had joined ten years before, was merely a side-show but was intended to be a deadly one for Mrs Thatcher. Everyone else was sweeping on to bigger issues which made Britain look even more isolated.

All the member states agreed to begin stage one of EMU on 1st July 1990, removing exchange controls between eight countries with the rest to follow. The biggest inducement for the Central Bank Governors was to be the 'independence' of all the Central Banks from their national governments as a precursor to full monetary union. That was irresistible. Later, of course, they would lose that 'independence' and become mere agencies of the European Central Bank.

For the German Bundesbank, always independent and the very symbol of Germany's recovery after the Second World

War, EMU would only be acceptable if the new Central Bank mimicked the Bundesbank. The Bundesbank set tough terms within the Delors Committee believing that no other country would accept them, and so frustrate the EMU project which it saw as a threat to its survival. To its surprise the other countries accepted all its terms because they (notably France) wished to rid themselves of something they viewed as even worse, the 'grip of the DM.'[6]

The Madrid Summit led inexorably to two further Inter-Governmental Conferences held in parallel, one on monetary union and the other on political union, to amend the treaties yet again. As this conveyor belt towards union rolled on, a conveyor belt Britain did not want to be on, Mrs Thatcher was ever more isolated.

At home Lawson and Howe were now openly against Mrs Thatcher. In July 1989 Mrs Thatcher had moved Howe against his will from the Foreign Office though he remained in the Cabinet. He was replaced by Douglas Hurd from the Home Office who had been a protégé of Edward Heath. For many years he was a member of ELEC, the economists' group which did so much to further the creation of the ECSC in alliance with the US and was set up expressly to create political union via the economic back door. Nigel Lawson resigned as Chancellor of the Exchequer in October 1989, saying petulantly that either Alan Walters must go or he would.

The Irish Prime Minister, host to the other Prime Ministers of the member states at the April 1990 Dublin Summit, knew even then that Mrs Thatcher would almost certainly not be British Prime Minister for much longer.[7] Delors and his associates at the Commission were intensifying the campaign against her.

Many outside the British Government called for Britain to join the ERM and ultimately a single currency. The Governor of the Bank of England had signed the Delors report in favour of monetary union; the CBI was pushing hard for it saying British businessmen wanted it; so was the 'The Economist', its echo was taken up by other leading papers, especially the 'Financial Times'.

From Brussels, Delors hectored daily, so did Britain's Senior Commissioner, Leon Brittan. In October with the new Chancellor, John Major, dropping hints about Britain's membership, the pressure from the federalists became irresistible and Britain joined the Exchange Rate Mechanism.

On 1st November Howe resigned from the Cabinet and made a virulent and damaging attack on Mrs Thatcher in his resignation speech in the House of Commons. Three weeks later Mrs Thatcher was forced out of office. Above all it was the European issue which finished her Commons' career and both Howe and Lawson, unintentionally, acted as executioners for Delors and the many federalists who saw her as a block to union. Deliberately they had kept moving the agenda forward at that 'breakneck speed' noted by Howe so that Mrs Thatcher, trying to save the nation state, was increasingly isolated and doomed. They created the circumstances for Mrs Thatcher's demise and then had only to wait for the events they had unleashed to have their inevitable effect. The closest they came to direct involvement was to be prominent in the chorus disapproving of Mrs Thatcher. It may act as a cautionary tale for any future defenders of the nation state.

Maastricht And The First Pillar

Europe, freed of Mrs Thatcher, went on to the next stage. The two parallel inter-governmental conferences, which began in December 1990, led to the Treaty on European Union or the Maastricht Treaty to amend the Treaty of Rome. It was agreed at the Dutch town of Maastricht in December 1991. Inevitably it was a compromise and Spinelli would have been disappointed. Again it moved 'Europe' much farther forward. For the first time the Treaty of Rome was to include the establishment of a European Union, that is a political union, and citizenship of that union. Cleverly the treaty only mentioned rights, notably voting rights, for citizens and failed to mention any duties. Some worried about a blank cheque.

Maastricht created three so-called pillars: the European Community, Foreign Policies, and Home Affairs. The central pillar was the old European Economic Community, now called the European Community, which was almost entirely subject to qualified majority voting. The new angle was EMU and the Germans were its main champions. As Chancellor Kohl said in a 1991 speech, 'Political and economic monetary union are inseparably linked. The one is the unconditional complement of the other.'[8] Writing in the 'Financial Times' in 1993 Kohl reiterated, 'we can preserve all our economic achievements only if we secure them politically. An economic union can only survive if it is based on a political union.'[9]

The first of the three stages of EMU had already begun. The second stage, a Monetary Institute to oversee EMU began in January 1994 and, almost inevitably, it was in Frankfurt. The Bundesbank set stiff convergence criteria for countries to join a single currency (the ECU) hoping of course that they could not be met. The new European Central Bank, (also to be based in Frankfurt) is likely to be the most powerful central bank in the world. Only the ECB will have the right to set money supply, issue money, hold and manage official foreign reserves and require credit institutions to hold minimum reserves with the ECB. Now the Bundesbank is calling for central EU control over tax and public expenditure.

Deliberately, the Central Bank will be unaccountable to any elected or unelected organisation. Its full time executive board of six bankers will hold office for eight years and can only be sacked by the European Court of Justice, but what standard they have to maintain is not specified. Its main object will be to 'maintain price stability', but that too is not quantified.[10]

An essential twin to EMU is strengthening the regions. In the Delors Report regional policy featured simply as grants for research, training and infrastructure. Just as Britain's poorer regions are helped by grants and subsidies so the same would have to be true of Europe. Regional grants have always led to tension on the part of both the givers and the receivers. That tension on the grand scale of Europe could lead to disintegration. One report calculated that nearly ten per cent of the Community budget would be needed to offset the effects on the poorer regions.[11] That would increase the British contribution alone by seven or eight fold. A second fund, the Cohesion Fund, is intended to subsidise regions of countries participating in EMU to offset the considerable unemployment EMU will cause.

Emphasising the regions has another deliberate effect – to reduce the authority of the nation states. That is already happening: regions of Britain, like the West Midlands, have direct representation in Brussels. Over time that will weaken the national government just as creating a direct link between the citizens of Europe and Brussels is intended to do. The regional policy has been institutionalised under Maastricht with a Committee of the Regions.

Another part of that policy is to encourage the break-up of Britain: for example, Brussels funds the development of the Welsh language through educational grants and through support of television programmes. There are suspicions that some campaigners are being encouraged to lobby for Welsh and Scottish national assembles.

Two More Pillars

The other two pillars of the Maastricht Treaty are inter-governmental: Foreign Policy (also covering defence and security) and Home Affairs. That follows the well established pattern of starting with co-operation and then switching to majority voting, the subtle way to win compliance for total union.

As promised in the Single European Act, foreign policy co-operation was reviewed and substantially strengthened by such articles as member states 'shall refrain from any action which is not in the interests of the union' and 'ensure their national policies conform to the common position.'

So divorced had Brussels become from the need to be sensitive to the nation states that even before the new treaty had been ratified a Commissioner was appointed to oversee foreign policy. Shortly afterwards a new department of two hundred and fifty excluding experts and foreign diplomats was set up. In 1994 the Commission set up the Unified External Service to run the Commission's 116 delegations round the world, all of which have diplomatic status. Their main function, so far, is to manage trade policy on behalf of the member states. But the diplomats are already suggesting foreign policy options as provided for under Maastricht.

Under Maastricht there will 'eventually' be a common defence policy under the Western European Union (WEU). The WEU was set up by a 1948 treaty lasting for fifty years, that is until 1998, when it will almost certainly be renewed in a different form. 'Eventually' sounds like a long time but a start has already been made with the Eurocorps intended, so the leaders of both France and Germany say, to be the stepping stone to a European defence force. Fifty thousand men, mainly French and Germans, are under arms and more countries are beginning to contribute. Britain is strongly opposed to present proposals to a phased integration of the EU and the WEU.

The nine member states which are existing members of the WEU agreed to co-operate in planning and logistics, with the possibility of creating a European armaments' agency and a European Security and Defence Academy. The aim is for a renewed WEU to replace NATO and remove the Americans from Europe. That will satisfy a long standing goal of some French and German politicians.

Education, culture and history, public health, consumer protection, trans-European networks, and industrial policy were added: their importance has still to be appreciated.

National Rebellions: Denmark and France

The Maastricht Treaty was negotiated in secret and resulted in a series of complicated amendments to existing treaties. To most people, politicians included, it is unreadable and unintelligible. Between the Maastricht Agreement in December 1991 and November 1993 when it came into force, misgivings grew as its impact was deciphered.

Those misgivings were compounded by German reunification in October 1990. To sustain international confidence in the DM, the Bundesbank kept German interest rates high. The other members of the ERM similarly raised interest rates so that their currencies stayed within the permitted narrow band against the DM. A currency crisis followed and on 16th September 1992 both the Italian lira and sterling left the ERM amidst political uproar. Germany was widely attacked for putting its own interests first regardless of the cost to others. It was a warning of things to come.

In June 1992, in the midst of this economic upheaval, the Danish Parliament failed to pass the Maastricht Treaty; then the country narrowly voted 'no' in a referendum by 50.7 per cent to 49.3 per cent. Brussels was surprised. The campaign was bitter: the Danes accused German politicians of interfering. Even though the Treaty specified that all twelve countries had to ratify and the Danes had not, the other eleven decided to ignore that requirement and press on to ratification.

Denmark secured two opt-outs from the Maastricht Treaty: from stage three of EMU and from 'decisions and actions of the Union which have defence implications.' At a second referendum in May 1993, the 'yes' camp won with 56.8 per cent in favour. This time some Danes said they had been frightened into voting 'yes' at a time of high unemployment by the threat of economic isolation.

The small size of Denmark has enabled the influence of European money to campaign for a 'yes' vote to be more transparent than it might be in a larger country. In the second referendum over six times more money was spent by the 'yes' campaign in a flood of propaganda. Half the country was against Maastricht and yet 46 out of the 48 newspapers pushed the 'yes' campaign. Only the Communist paper, read by about two hundred people, pressed the 'no' case. Of the eight Danish political parties only one was against.

Two months before the referendum the Danish Ministry of Finance released a report which stated that 'the consequences of a Danish NO-vote will be that Denmark will have to leave the EU. The result of that will be that Denmark will lose around 150,000 work places until 1997.' That would have amounted to an increase of fifty per cent in unemployment.

That was not true: had Denmark voted 'no' it would not

have had to leave the EU and the unemployment claims were later shown to be spurious. The intention was to create fear.

There were strong suspicions that leading industrialists, who had voted 'no' the first time, were under pressure to switch to a 'yes' vote. F. L. Smidth and Co, one of Denmark's largest international companies, stated in its internal newspaper with a circulation of 14,000 that a 'no' vote would mean that 'we would have to reduce our activities in Denmark and transfer even more of the necessary future growth abroad.' All the Danish banks, the Council of Agriculture, the Council of Industry (the employers' organisation) all put on pressure to vote 'yes'.

The European Movement in Denmark, which is not an elected organisation, received money from Brussels and from the Danish Government. Other sources of funds were the European Parliament and other Community organisations. No such monies were available for the No Campaign. Published accounts give no indication of how much money was spent. Nor is it known for sure what pressures may have been exerted on businessmen and journalists though stories of pressure and threats to individuals' livelihoods from Brussels abound.

Because of the tough economic and political climate, President Mitterand resolved to have a referendum in France to reinforce his position. Again the campaign was bitter and not helped by Black Wednesday, when, only four days before the referendum day, the lira and sterling left the ERM. The French voted in favour of Maastricht by just 51.05 per cent. Strong rumours circulated that votes from the French overseas territories had tipped the balance and had been pressurised by Paris.

British Reluctance

Britain caused Brussels by far the biggest problem. In the April 1992 General Election John Major's government was returned but with a much smaller majority than that won by Mrs Thatcher. So those few opposed to the Treaty had more power in the House of Commons. Britain, like Denmark, had secured two opt-outs, one from stage three of EMU – that is the single currency and the European Central Bank – and the other from the Social Chapter. No-one in British politics remembered the lessons of the German states in the last century when Prussia gave worthless opt-outs.

The Social Chapter for a social Europe was Delors' second great crusade after the Single Market. It was intended to form part of the Treaty but because of British intervention is now a protocol at the end. It gives the Community the opportunity to cover every aspect of employment including trade union rights. Many large European firms welcomed it because it would impose the high, and uncompetitive, social costs of Germany on low cost countries. They were thinking of Britain.

Britain has an opt-out from stage three of EMU but not from stages one and two. Therefore Britain has to conform to exchange rate convergence and rejoin the ERM. Brussels will increasingly put pressure on Britain to do so and given past experience will probably succeed. Despite Britain's opt-out from the Social Chapter the Commission has found a way around. The forty-eight hour week has been imposed under two other articles in the treaty of Rome: article 118a on health and safety at work and article 100a on single market measures. That has shocked many in Britain. It will add massive costs to British industry especially through the requirement for elaborate paperwork.[12]

The opposition to Maastricht in Britain surprised the

British Government. The Single European Act had gone through within a week and doubtlessly the Government Whips thought the same thing would happen again. Almost certainly deliberately, the Government did not publish the proposed Treaty until after the April 1992 General Election although it was available for publication well before in Her Majesty's Stationery Office. With little public information no wonder 'Europe' was not an election issue. The Government promised to produce a readable consolidated treaty. It has not done so; such a treaty was only available from the European Commission after Maastricht was ratified.

One Conservative MP, William Cash, tabled over four hundred amendments to the proposed Bill in the Autumn of 1992. Still the Government took no notice, expecting those amendments to fall quickly. But Cash set up a small outside research group to provide briefs to keep MPs on their feet speaking to those amendments. Instead of the fast passage of the Single European Act, the Maastricht Bill took fourteen months to go through both Houses of Parliament in a blaze of publicity, accusation and counter-accusation.

At first John Major's Government responded to press coverage by saying the rebels, the so-called Fresh Start Group of about twenty-five Conservative MPs, were wasting valuable Parliamentary time which could be better spent on other matters more important to the nation. As the months went past the Government had to take the issue more seriously.

The House of Lords, with amendments tabled again and the 'rebels' briefed by the same outside group, held only one division. That was on the issue of a referendum. Many peers were only slightly aware of the issues and the 'rebels', including Lady Thatcher, lost the vote by 445 to 176. Lawson and Howe voted with the Government. Some peers said they felt that it was not their place to upset the equilibrium as they saw it.

When the Bill had to be returned to the Commons because of a Lords' amendment to the Social Protocol, the Government nearly fell on a confidence motion. Nearly all the Conservative rebels voted with the Government because its future was at stake. Had they had stuck to their principles the Bill would have been defeated. One Labour MP said later that if the rebels had pursued the issue sufficient Labour MPs would have joined the rebels to defeat it. The Labour Party is at least as divided as the Conservative Party: sixty-eight Labour MPs voted against Maastricht on the third reading.

When Roy Jenkins returned to Britain after two terms as President of the Commission he and three others (the Gang of Four) left the Labour Party to start the pro-European SDP (Social Democrat Party). The key issue was Europe over which Jenkins had resigned twice from the Labour Front Bench and split the Party when Heath took Britain into the EEC. The Labour Party of the early 1980s, led by Michael Foot, was against 'Europe' and only began to switch when it looked as though political capital could be made out of issues like the Social Chapter. Under Tony Blair, whose over-riding interest is the pursuit of power, the party's policy is cautiously pro 'European'.

German Hesitation

A less publicised revolt took place in Germany. Dr Manfred Brunner, a Munich lawyer, and a former Chief of Cabinet to Germany's senior commissioner (1989 to 1992), sued the German Government for breach of the constitution. He wrote 'The Maastricht Treaty must be buried.'[13] The central issue was the transfer of sovereign powers. At Karlsruhe in October 1993 the Federal Constitutional Court ruled that the pillars of the Union were essentially inter-governmental, an association of states, so it did not offend article 23 of

German Basic Law. Nor were the democratic guarantees in the Basic Law compromised. At that point in the argument the federalists stopped, their case won.

The Court also concluded that the European Union must not become a federal state; that the word 'irrevocable' in the Treaty of Rome cannot apply, nothing is inevitable and nothing is irreversible. A state can always leave the Union; the European Court must not enlarge the competencies of the Community any further; the EMU convergence criteria must not be changed; and for Germans the German Court is a higher Court than the European Court. As and when it suits the German Government can Germany put a stop to the centralisation of 'Europe' and Germany can withdraw.

Since then Dr Brunner's group has been sidelined by the Kohl government and has little influence in Germany.

Nordic And Swiss Doubts

Further enlargement has encountered problems. Sweden, Finland and Norway all applied to join – Norway for the second time – and the campaigns ahead of the referenda were tightly fought. Sweden said 'yes' by 52 per cent, Finland by 57 per cent as it turned from its close relations with the old USSR towards its neighbour Germany. Norway again said no with 52.5 per cent against. So in January 1995 only Sweden and Finland joined the EU.

Soon afterwards many in Sweden began to have second thoughts and according to more recent polls a majority would like to withdraw. The Swedish people had not realised beforehand the impact Brussels legislation would have on Swedish life as 'European' rules were applied. One of the first areas to be hit was sugar beet production: rules for planting and cultivation which were suited for more southern climes were arbitrarily applied to Sweden.

The 1992 Swiss referendum on joining the half way stage of the European Economic Area was dominated by fears of abandoning neutrality (also a big issue in Sweden and Finland) and doubts as to the trade benefits. In contrast, Austria, closely linked to the German economy, had a trouble free accession to the Community in 1995.

Maastricht has awakened such reservations round Europe that in most countries there are either dedicated political parties, as in France, or groups within parties, working to reduce or eliminate Brussels' power.

In May 1994 Claude Cheysson, the former French Foreign Minister, told 'Le Figaro' that the Europe of Maastricht could not have been constructed except in the absence of democracy. The present problems, he complained, are caused by the fact that a democratic debate was allowed to take place during the referendum campaign in France.[14]

Nearly There

Especially after the Single European Act, let alone Maastricht, Europe's power is now considerable. As Jacques Delors has said, 'the European institutions are little known, the issues rarely explicit'. But those institutions have been considerably strengthened by Delors' two terms as President of the Commission, especially his second four years. Now the Commission, headed by Jacques Santer of Luxembourg, is more politicised with the development of a Presidential system of Government.

Brussels' influence has increased insidiously. In the 1950s there was much talk of 'engrenage', which meant in this context enmeshing all the civil servants of Europe together so that large numbers did not have to be employed in Brussels. The term faded under de Gaulle's challenge but the policy of deliberately delegating work to the national civil services continues so that they in effect become agencies of Brussels. It follows the German example of relations between the Bund and the Lander. Federalists say that joint committees of European and national civil servants in Brussels has the advantage of educating the latter to think in a 'European' way.

Today there are 21,000 civil servants in Brussels. That figure is often used as an illustration of how little can be the influence of Brussels on national life with so few civil servants. Christopher Booker and Dr Richard North have written extensively of Brussels' influence on every aspect of British business even though that business is administered by British civil servants.[15] That is exactly what the federalist planners' intended from the first. That is 'engrenage' in practice.

One result is that in Britain where the Civil Service has always been responsive to public opinion, the Ministries most affected so far by Brussels legislation (Agriculture and Fisheries, the Foreign Office, and the Department of Trade and Industry and to a lesser degree the Home Office) now behave more like their Continental colleagues who exercise power in an authoritarian way. Lord Denning was right, 'the Treaty . . . flows into the estuaries and up the rivers. It cannot be held back.' With daily judgements from the Court, a more powerful Commission, a Brussels' civil service increasingly linked to national ones, Lord Denning's remark seems ever more apposite.

As the 1993 Hansard Society report stated, about sixty per cent of the legislation going through the British Parliament was then from Brussels. Parliament is a rubber stamp. The national veto has almost been eliminated, national legal supremacy has ended, so ' . . . Parliament has little, if any impact upon the process of European law making. Where successful changes are introduced from the UK, these are usually done by various interested sectors and bodies . . . this must have serious implications for the traditional view of parliament as a legislative body.'

Christopher Booker constantly highlights in his column in 'The Sunday Telegraph' how Britain now receives so much of its legislation in the form of statutory instruments issued by the British civil service, largely at Brussels' behest which have no need to go before Parliament. They are running at the rate of 3,000 a year. So Booker estimates that ninety-five per cent of British laws are made by civil servants issuing decrees. This is a toppling of democracy in Britain yet scarcely anyone has noticed.

Federalists are quite open about saying there are four outstanding issues to be resolved to achieve the superstate.[16] First is a closer association between the European Parliament and the Commission – Parliament should be able to initiate legislation. Second, the Commission has to be made responsible to Parliament. Third, foreign policy has to be brought into majority voting within the Community institutions and co-operation ended; defence has to move in the same direction but at a slower speed (memories of the ill fated EDC – the European Defence Community of the 1950s – remain strong). Fourth, European Monetary Union has to succeed.

Of the four issues EMU is the most advanced already being part of the treaties. After a period of debate, monetary union is now on target for the introduction of a single currency by 1st January 1999 on terms set by the Bundesbank with the full backing of the German Government. With monetary union, as Chancellor Kohl pointed out, will go political union. Britain is havering over EMU: it will wait and see, it may never happen and the terms are not known. That is an old story. Britain is not as robust as Denmark which has said a definite 'no' to EMU though it is under constant pressure to give up its opt-outs. In time Britain will be forced to join

EMU and will have to abandon its control of the British economy.

There may be short term doubts as political parties in Germany jostle for favour ahead of the general election. EMU is not popular with the German electorate especially with those who remember the 1920s when a wheelbarrow of notes was needed to buy a loaf of bread. On the other hand, as Germans acknowledge, they are used to changes of currency.

Once the German election is out of the way the road to EMU will be resumed with a propaganda campaign for a 1999 start which is supported by the main German parties. Almost certainly not all EU countries will be 'in' the first group to join and those which do will have indulged in creative accounting, or fudging, to achieve the convergence criteria. Italy has imposed a one-off 'Euro-tax' to narrow its budget deficit. France has raided the pension fund of the partially-privatised France Telecom. Belgium has encouraged state bodies to invest in government bonds. Germany will probably manoeuvre to ensure that countries like Italy, Greece and Spain will not be part of the first group and may also have to fudge their accounts.

Britain has objected to a German proposed Stability Pact which will impose the convergence conditions on all EU countries whether they are 'in' or out' thus dictating their economic policy.

From The Atlantic To The Urals

The ratchet is turning again towards a centralised Europe at the fourth inter-governmental conference which began in March 1996 in Turin. The key issues are foreign policy, defence and home affairs. This 'deepening' is in part to cope with a future enlargement when Eastern European countries may join and the number of member states could be as high as twenty-five.

Thirteen applications are on the table or imminent, nearly all from Eastern Europe (the others are Cyprus, Malta and Turkey). Four more, Albania, Macedonia, Moldova and the Ukraine which are members of the staging post to the EU, the Council of Europe, may apply to join. Russia which is also a member of the Council of Europe, will remain a controversial candidate. Iceland, Norway, Switzerland and Liechtenstein have not applied (Iceland) or reapplied.

There could yet be a Europe from the Atlantic to the Urals, as Sir Winston Churchill and General de Gaulle proposed, but with a structure which both would find alien. Neither man thought Britain should be a part of it.

The federalists have commented, 'It would be unworthy of a British government to hamper the unification of eastern and western Europe. Yet this would be the result if the UK were to refuse at the IGC to deepen the European Union.'[17]

Amsterdam And Beyond

Because of the national reaction to Maastricht from most European countries and the greater prize of European Monetary Union still to come, the Amsterdam Treaty looks like a fine tuning rather than a great leap forward. Looks can be deceptive.

Meanwhile rebellion is building all round the EU against the monolithic, centralist state which is daily becoming more evident. Groups in each country opposing centralised power have linked up to make common cause and, similarly, parliamentary groups from each country are allied to each other. Debate and determination are growing. They have much to fight.

Among Amsterdam's key points covering a broad spectrum

are that member states which violate basic freedoms will face the suspension of their voting rights in the Council of Ministers; the 'third pillar' of justice and home affairs will be brought into the treaties to join the economy; the European Parliament will be significantly strengthened and will be virtually co-equal with the Council of Ministers; the European Court of Justice will have more powers, and those states which wish to move together without waiting for others may do so by majority voting but only in limited policy areas. The EU will have a legal personality.

The EU has moved a stage closer to one foreign and security policy by agreeing that a secretary-general rather than a high ranking politician should represent the EU's foreign policy. Unanimity will still be required for policy decisions while joint actions can be agreed by qualified majority voting but not to any decisions with military or defence implications.

The agreement made between five countries initially in 1985 to work towards a frontier free zone, known as the Schengen Agreement, will be incorporated into EU Law in the Amsterdam Treaty. Britain has an opt-out from a 'Europe' without internal frontiers but one which may not withstand an onslaught from the European Court of justice. A frontier free continent has wide implications especially for policing.

A rudimentary Europol already exists and the Germans have been forcefully arguing for it to be the executive arm of the European Court of Justice. Britain has argued against and especially against extending the ECJ's role into criminal law. The excuse for creating Europol is increasing drug trafficking and terrorism, though no mention is ever made of Interpol's established role or of successful co-operation between nation states. At present Europol is run by a German with a computer in the Hague on a co-operative but limited basis with the national police forces. He wishes to create files on European citizens. Steadily Europol's powers are likely to increase.

Co-operation between police forces, customs and other specialised law enforcement agencies will be strengthened under Amsterdam including training and secondments. Europol will be able to ask national police forces to conduct specific investigations and establish a research base on cross border crime.

Amsterdam will institutionalise the 1986 Joint Declaration on Racism and Xenophobia. Federalists regard EU enlargement, especially to the east and home to many ethnic minorities, to be the chance to 'redress the balance against the essentially illiberal doctrine of the "self-determination" of states.' It is a moot point whether or not this proposed extension to Article 3 of the Treaty of Rome will be used to combat 'nationalists' who campaign for the continued existence of the nation states. There is nothing to stop it.

Because the Amsterdam treaty failed to reach agreement on changing the weighting of votes in the Council of Ministers a further intergovernmental conference may be convened after the German elections in the autumn of 1998. It will be essential before the next enlargement of the EU planned for 2002. The European Commission has published a wide ranging 'Agenda 2000' to push the EU forward.

Still to come the EU may become a signatory to the European Court of Human Rights (ECHR) in the next treaty (this Court began in the aftermath of the Hague Congress of 1948). If that proves to be politically impossible the EU's Court of Justice will extend its jurisdiction to cover the rights of both European citizens and foreigners on a case by case basis.

The longer term aim is to bring the ECHR within the EU on the grounds that 'the European citizen needs to know how he or she is governed, by whom and from where.'

Politically it is still too early to introduce a Bill of Rights and a European Constitution, though both are planned. The European Constitution has been on hold since the last draft in 1993.[18] Meanwhile, Britain is incorporating the ECHR into UK law – a back-door way of extending Brussels' powers over British subjects.

Chancellor Kohl has advocated the use of proportional representation throughout Europe and suggested that Britain, with a first-past-the-post system, could be given a transitional period to adjust. Federalists would like to see genuine European parties and a uniform electoral procedure with lists of candidates by party so that electors can vote for the list as happens in Germany. That would weaken the association between the candidate and the area which he is representing. It is contentious enough to have to wait for a treaty beyond Amsterdam.

Equally 'new and sophisticated methods of campaigning' will be needed to elect the President of the Commission or President of Europe. That too will wait for a future treaty.

The Committee of the Regions, which so far has had a limited role, is to be strengthened. Members are likely to be chosen from the regions or local authorities. That would be another measure weakening the role of the national governments or the 'old centralised states' as federalists call them. Britain's division into regional assemblies and a parliament in Scotland will fit into the strengthened Committee of the Regions.

Once EMU stage three has been achieved in 1999 (the euro will have replaced national currencies by 2002) there will be a further excuse to give 'Europe' an international personality and increase the EU's role in foreign affairs from trade to all aspects of the economy.

Education has yet to receive a higher profile: the federalists' aim of European-wide curricula is still some way off. In the

1980s cultural projects to create 'a people's Europe' were started, for example the Erasmus and Socrates' programmes of university exchanges, and education about Europe in schools to create a sense of European citizenship. Prussia did the same thing in the mid-nineteenth century using culture to promote one identity.

Immediately after the fourth IGC the EU budget has to be renegotiated. The central issue will be the reform of the Common Agricultural Policy which despite the extension of the role of the EU still takes over half of EU spending.

The contentious issue of fraud, which has never been seriously tackled will be on the agenda. Cautious estimates are that ten to twenty per cent of the EU budget is used fraudulently. For a long time the Commission would only acknowledge a figure of one per cent. When spot checks have been carried out on trains and vehicles transporting EU goods across frontiers fifty per cent have been found to be fraudulent.[19]

Britain's rebate, for which Mrs Thatcher fought when Prime Minister, is almost certain to be cut, if not abolished, in these negotiations.

The sensitive area of the 'second pillar' of defence will be left until last although the WEU will be gradually integrated into the EU and under Amsterdam the WEU will foster closer relations.

The Challengers

Federalists think they have won control of Europe. They have increasingly come into the open to explain how they have achieved it and are more strident in demanding centralisation beyond the economic. They are being challenged.

The first challenger for the prize of Brussels' power is Germany.

The second challenge is from the nation states of Europe whose people are more and more aware of the flow of power to Brussels. Those strains may break the socialist superstate. No longer can the EU be disguised as a free trade area. In the early days that had fooled most people. Brussels is still some way from taking all power away from the nation states. The nation states still have the power to withdraw, if they do not do so soon they will only be able to achieve independence by force.

Three countries are the most likely to break the edifice. Germany could take the view that its interests lie to the East and not with 'Europe'. France might wake up to the domination of Germany. Britain, all along the most unwilling to give up its freedom, could pull out. Mrs Thatcher, when negotiating for 'our money back' at Fontainebleu, had a short Bill drafted to repeal the European Communities Act.[20] That is all it would take.

In Denmark eleven politicians have challenged the Government in the High Court. They say Denmark's accession to Maastricht has been unconstitutional. The Danish constitution states that devolving sovereignty to any body other than parliament is unconstitutional. If the High Court agrees Denmark could be forced to withdraw from the EU. That would not break the EU but it could create the critical atmosphere in which a major country challenges the authority of the EU.

German Control

Having come so close to dominating and controlling Western Europe, and at a substantial cost to the German tax payer, Germany is unlikely to give it up and will want a return on its money. In September 1994 the ruling CDU/CSU coalition published a paper, 'Reflections on European Policy' with proposals to the Bundestag. It has the backing of Chancellor Kohl and calls for a complete programme of political union, which Chancellor Kohl calls a 'United States of Europe'.

The main proposals were for a European Constitution for a federal state; reform of the Community institutions on the German model;[21] the end of the national veto; a formal group of five nations (Germany, France and the Benelux three) to proceed to monetary union; a European army; enlargement to the east by the year 2000, and before that 'widening' more 'deepening'. Finally, the Commission should become the Government of Europe.

The paper called for Germany to be 'integrated' into Europe with the Central European countries based on the fear that '(European) Union . . . will become . . . a loose knit grouping of states' because of what the Germans call 'regressive nationalism'.

The paper threatened that 'If European integration were not to progress, Germany might be called upon, or be tempted by its own security constraints, to try to effect the stabilisation of Eastern Europe on its own and in the traditional manner. However this would far exceed its capacities and, at the same time, erode the cohesion of the European Union especially since everywhere memories are still very much alive that historically German policy towards the East concentrated on closer co-operation with Russia at the expense of countries in between.'[22]

Reading the German original confirms that 'in the traditional manner' means by armed force.

Kohl's policy of European domination is directly descended from the Prussian civil servants of the nineteenth century, from Bismarck, Kaiser Wilhelm and Hitler. First Prussia controlled the German states and principalities economically via the Zollverein, then Bismarck unified them politically and through three wars Germany became one of the holders of the European balance of power. Under Kaiser Wilhelm Germany took on the British Empire to displace it as a world power. Finally Hitler again controlled mainland Europe, which he called 'the United States of Europe', and like Bismarck did a deal with Russia.

After Germany's defeat Nazi planners exiled in Madrid produced a three part scheme for Germany which was nearly identical to Chancellor Adenauer's policies. First, Germany would rise again as a sovereign state and a partner in a unifying Europe, financed initially by US dollars. Then Germany would again become a great power in the world and dominant in Europe. The third phase was to be close co-operation with Russia to isolate the US.[23]

Germany has achieved the first two. As the largest economy Germany is by far the biggest contributor to the Community budget. Germany wields the greatest power. By constantly insisting that Germany must be tied into Europe or there might be war, a refrain repeated since the early 1950s, Germany has steadily increased its domination of the Community. Chancellor Kohl has frequently ended his demands for policies with the threat that if they are not achieved then there will be war but never pointing his finger at Germany as the instigator of war.

Germany is forcing the pace on EMU on its own terms. Germany and the Bundesbank will never give up the DM and when the semantics of the currency are finally decided, it will be the DM in all but name. Social policy, enacted from Brussels, is descended from List, Rathenau and the Nazi war planners.

The Eastern Empire

Since the fall of the Berlin Wall in 1989 and re-unification in 1990, Germany's economic and political interests have increasingly followed their traditional path to the East. The DM is the most widely used currency in the former Yugo-slavia and in Eastern Europe. German businessmen dominate both.

In November 1990, when they signed a Treaty on Good-Neighbourliness, Partnership and Co-operation, Germany and the USSR also agreed to divide Central Europe between them.[24] Kohl and Gorbachev signed a near repeat of the Molotov-Ribbentrop Pact of 1938. They did not intend it to be published but it was leaked onto the streets of Prague fifteen months before one of its key conditions was carried out.

The Russians agreed to the division of Czechoslovakia into two. Then within twelve to fifteen years the Czech and Moravian regions would be incorporated into Germany. In return the Germans agreed to compensate the USSR for any costs incurred. Hungary is to be restored to its pre-1920 borders with Transylvania becoming part of Romania. The Ukraine, Lithuania, Latvia and Estonia would remain within the USSR's sphere.

Poland, regarded as an empty space by the Nazis and now occupying former German land, is not mentioned at all. Churchill may yet be proved right when he wrote 'One day the Germans would want their territory back, and the Poles would not be able to stop them.'[25] Poland would cease to exist.

In the 1990 Treaty the USSR agreed to the division of Yugoslavia and that Croatia and Slovenia (states once part of Nazi Germany) would enter Germany's economic sphere. Most commentators agree that the start of the war in Yugo-slavia can be dated to Germany's official recognition of Croatia and Slovenia. At the time rumours circulated widely in political circles that Britain's opt-out on EMU was in exchange for its rapid diplomatic recognition of those countries. The British Foreign Office denied them.

The USSR has always had a single minded view of a bloc on its doorstep: it must be stopped. It has always feared encirclement. Today the EU, led by Germany, is seeking to include former Soviet satellite countries. NATO is also planning to enlarge to the east. President Clinton has called for 'an undivided democratic Europe' which would involve an 'expanded NATO by 1999'.[26]

George Kennan, the acknowledged American expert on the USSR, wrote in February 1997 ' . . . expanding NATO would be the most fateful error of American policy in the entire post-cold war era.' He said that it would inflame nationalists and drive Russian foreign policy in directions entirely adverse to Western wishes. Russians, he wrote in the New York Times, 'would see their prestige (always uppermost in the Russian mind) and their security interests as adversely affected.'[27]

When he was a member of the State Department in 1946 Kennan was alone in the US in drawing attention to the threat that the USSR was posing to the West. He rightly predicted that in the long term the Soviet Empire contained within it the seeds of its own decay. He also chaired the committee which recommended the Marshall Plan.

Empire building by Germany leading the EU eastward as it tried to do under Hitler is almost certain to lead to friction with Russia and a renewal of some kind of Cold War.

The French Dichotomy

France may yet conclude that the main purpose of European union from its point of view – tying down Germany – has failed. Harold Wilson, the British Prime Minister, related a discussion with General de Gaulle in 1967. Wilson asked de

Gaulle "Did he not fear that after de Gaulle France would be relegated to a second class status against the power of a strong Germany?" De Gaulle replied "Les Allemands seront toujours les Allemands." He had no doubt what would happen but he would not be there to prevent it . . .'

France could still wake up to the threat to its sovereignty. Once again it is losing to its German neighbour but this time, unlike the previous three occasions, Germany will achieve its aim without armies.

France has paid a high economic price for its membership of the ERM and linking the French Franc to the DM. Unemployment has long been in double figures and French industry is labouring under the ruinous real interest rates needed to sustain the 'franc fort'. Now the political price may be too much. Delors was typical of many French politicians when he said that 'France will grow in stature by means of Europe, as Europe, a group of middle ranking nations, asserts itself as a first-ranking power'.[28] That has long been the Parisian justification. Half France voted against Maastricht. As the power of Germany increases more may join the 'no' vote though Vichy France illustrated the dichotomy that is France.

For France to abandon the central plank of its economic and foreign policy may take a cataclysm. Unlike Germany and Britain France believes, rightly or wrongly, that it has no choice. Germany has a huge hinterland to the East and Britain has the open sea and a world dominated by Anglo-Saxon culture and language. For the French elite to admit that after all 'Europe' was a blind alley, and that henceforth France would become 'Atlanticist', would need a searing intellectual and emotional revolution. That could come from a popular revolt, as in 1968, or from the massive psychological shock that British withdrawal would cause.

The Second Battle Of Britain

Britain is the most likely country to withdraw. As more and more areas of British national life are affected so the pressure to pull out of Europe may become irresistible.

Trade is usually cited as the main reason Britain must stay in with over half of British visible exports going to the Community. But when invisibles are included, only two-fifths of British exports go to the Community, while over three-quarters of its foreign direct investment and portfolio investment are with the rest of the world. It would make more sense for Britain to join with the US, its biggest trading partner.[29]

Britain is still talking the language of 'partnership', of 'free markets' and of proposals which may never happen. Yet over twenty-five years ago Britain agreed to a new constitution, the Treaty of Rome. After a thousand years Britain changed its way of government. No-one yet dares call the Treaty a constitution, it is too sensitive. Yet American constitutional lawyers point out that the Treaty of Rome is just like the US Constitution which is constantly amended. A European Bill of Rights is planned, again just like the US, but in the short term the European Court of Human Rights will be a proxy. The European Court of Justice is both a court and a legislature and has been working for forty years to extend the power of the constitution.

Britain has a 'window' through which to withdraw and escape from the socialist superstate. It will not be there for much longer.

If Britain continues, however reluctantly, to agree to Brussels' proposals which increasingly bear the German imprint, then within a few years it will be a province of Germany just as it would have been if the German armed forces had succeeded in defeating the British in the Second World War.

We are now engaged in the second Battle of Britain.

NOTES

INTRODUCTION

[1] 'Britain in Europe' 1998. Published to mark the UK's Presidency of the EU

[2] Ibid.

[3] See Federal Trust Papers No 6: 'Justice and Fair Play. The Intergovernmental Conference of the European Union 1996' page 19

[4] The Common External Tariff (CET) – the tariff wall surrounding the EU

[5] Torquil Dick-Erikson 'A Threat to our Legal System' in The European Journal, April 1997

[6] 'Britain in Europe' op.cit

[7] Implementation of Maastricht required the ratification of all twelve states – when Denmark stalled the EU changed the rules

[8] The Rt. Hon Michael Howard QC MP 'A Europe of Nations' in 'The Legal Agenda for a Free Europe' published by the European Research Group

[9] 'Britain in Europe. The European Community and Your Future' the Foreign and Commonwealth Office November 1992

[10] When Bismarck's army defeated the French at Sedan

[11] Report of the Hansard Society's Commission on the Legislative Process 1993

[12] Anthony Nutting 'Europe Will Not Wait A Warning and a Way Out' 1960

[13] The French and Danish Governments were the only ones not in exile in London during the war. Neutral Denmark accepted Germany's terms of non-interference in their internal affairs, despite physical occupation. Acceptance turned to ever increasing resistance by the Danish people who among other acts of heroism saved nearly every Jew in their country. According to Ole Lippmann, a leader of Danish SOE and latterly Chief Allied Representative on the Danish Freedom Council, many Danes wanted 'a Norwegian situation' – open war. With no popular support, in August 1943 the Government resigned. Lippmann wrote 'Danish Nazi Governments after five years of German occupation and pressure never became

of any importance or recruited any Danes of any standing.' The Danes organised a brilliant three week operation to smuggle 6,500 Danish Jews to Sweden on fishing boats under the noses of the Germans

CHAPTER 1: A GERMAN EUROPE

[1] Dean Acheson 'Present At the Creation' 1970
[2] Albert Speer 'Inside the Third Reich' 1970
[3] Stuart Airlie 'Charlemagne' in the 'The Historian' Summer 1992
[4] Other than Romania
[5] For an analysis of Prussia's role see W O Henderson 'The Genesis of the Common Market' 1962 and his 'Fredrich List, economist and visionary' 1983
[6] H von Treitschke quoted in W O Henderson op.cit.
[7] Ibid.
[8] Ibid.
[9] The metric system abolished local distance measures such as the meile, the fuss, the klafter and the ruthe.
[10] Bismarck 1815-1898, chief architect of the German empire, dismissed in 1890.
[11] See Bruce Waller 'Bismarck' Historical Association Studies
[12] Richard Coudenhove-Kalergi 'An Ideal Conquers the World' 1953
[13] Ibid.
[14] A H Fried 'Pan Amerika' 1917
[15] Coudenhove-Kalergi op.cit.
[16] Winston S Churchill 'The Second World War' 1989 edition
[17] Arthur Salter 'The United States of Europe' 1933
[18] Coudenhove-Kalergi op.cit.
[19] Mackinder was the advocate of geopolitics, an expression he coined. The 'new geography' linked geography and manpower. He was the first professor of geography at Oxford, and the Principal of the London School of Economics, recently founded by the Webbs, and moved in Fabian circles. He backed the Fabian idea of the League of Nations, international law and an ultimate World Empire.
[20] Halford J. Mackinder 'The scope and methods of geography and the geographical pivot of history' 1904

[21] Harry Kessler 'W Rathenau' 1928

[22] W F Bruck

[23] G Stolper 'German Economy 1870-1940' 1940

[24] At the beginning of the war Daitz headed the Gesellschaft fur Europaische Wirtschaftsplanung und Grossraumwirtschaft. He organised the economic integration of the occupied territories and in 1940 proposed a Reich Commission for the Greater European economic sphere.

[25] Allen Dulles 'Germany's Underground'

[26] William L Schirer 'The Rise and Fall of the Third Reich' 1960

[27] Ibid.

[28] Thomas Reveille 'Spoils Of Europe' Free Europe Pamphlet 1942

[29] Leo Amery 'My Political Life' vol. 3 1953-55

[30] The then President was Peter Bennett; the Director General, Guy Locock

[31] 'The Times' 17.3.1939

[32] Ibid.

[33] Ibid.

[34] Adolf Hitler 'Mein Kampf' 1925, 1926

[35] Allan Nevins 'This is England Today' 1941

[36] Reveille op.cit.

[37] Walter Lipgens ed. 'Documents on the History of European Integration: Vol. 1, Continental Plans For European Union 1939-1945' (pp 56 – 70) 1985 published by Walter de Gruyter, Berlin for the European University Institute (EUI) Florence. The EC Commission fully financed the English edition via a grant administered by Max Kohnstamn, President of the EUI

[38] Shirer op.cit.

[39] Lipgens op.cit.

[40] Reveille op.cit.

[41] Lipgens op.cit. pp 58, 59

[42] The Madrid Geo-Political Centre 1950 quoted in T H Tetens 'Germany Plots with the Kremlin' 1953

[43] Lipgens op.cit. p 94, 28.11.1941. Said to the Finnish Foreign Minister

[44] Lipgens op.cit.

[45] F.R. Willis 'France, Germany, and the New Europe'

[46] Albert Speer 'Inside The Third Reich' 1970

[47] 'The Association of Berlin Business People and Industrialists with the Berlin School of Economics: Wirtschaftsgemeinschaft'
[48] Lipgens op.cit. p 96
[49] Henri Frenay 'La Nuit Finira'
[50] Lipgens op.cit. p 102
[51] Lipgens op.cit. p 106
[52] Mary Fulbrook 'A Concise History of Germany' 1990
[53] David Marsh 'The Bundesbank: The Bank That Rules Europe' 1992
[54] Tetens op.cit.
[55] Prof. Adam Zoltowski 'Germany, Russia and Central Europe' Free Europe Pamphlet No 4 March 1942

CHAPTER 2: THE SOCIALIST VISION

[1] Leo Amery 'My Political Life' vol. 1 1953-55
[2] Quoted in Robert K Massie 'Dreadnought. Britain, Germany and the Coming of the Great War' p. 157
[3] Robert Ensor 'England 1870-1914' 1992
[4] There are parallels with the deep split in the Conservative Party under John Major over membership of the European Union.
[5] The Commonwealth Federation Act was passed in 1900
[6] Quoted in Amery op.cit.
[7] Dictionary of National Biography
[8] By Arnold Toynbee in 'Acquaintances'
[9] To a Chatham House audience in London
[10] M J C Vile 'The Structure of American Federalism' 1961
[11] Amery op.cit.
[12] F S Oliver 'Alexander Hamilton. A Study in American Union' 1931 edition
[13] Quotation from Amery op.cit. There are so called federations outside the former British Empire but each is centralised. Yugoslavia's 1946 and 1953 constitutions were federal but based on the 1936 constitution of the USSR. Yugoslavia has collapsed in war. German federation has been a success, but is highly centralised, and not without its German critics. German Basic Law states unambiguously in article 31 that 'Federal law shall override Land law'; therefore sovereignty lies with the Federal Government.
[14] The attempt to federate Malaya and Singapore failed.

[15] Arthur Salter was in the British Civil Service, then the League of Nations, then Oxford as Professor of Political Theory and a Fellow of All Souls. He was an MP from 1937-1953 and a Cabinet Minister in the first post-war Conservative Government

[16] Sir Walter Layton 1884-1966, editor of the Economist 1921-1938, owner and executive head of the 'News Chronicle'; director of National Federation off Iron and Steel Manufacturers; uring the Second World War in Ministries of Supply and Production; 1952-55 Deputy Leader of Liberal Party in House of Lords; Vice-President Council of Europe, Strasbourg

[17] Quoted in C E Carrington 'Chatham House and its Neighbours' 1959

[18] Heath was speaking at a banquet held in November 1970 to celebrate the 50th birthday of Chatham House.

[19] Arnold Toynbee 'Acquaintances' 1967

[20] Chatham House soon spawned the Institute for Pacific Relations.

[21] Carrington op.cit.

[22] Townsend Hooper 'The Devil and John Foster Dulles'; Richard Gould-Adams 'The Time of Power'

[23] Ed. John Poman 'Joseph Retinger, Memoirs of An Eminence Grise' 1972

[24] Goold-Adams op.cit.

[25] Henry A Kissinger 'Diplomacy' 1994

[26] Between 1930 and 1939

[27] Chatham House was the co-ordinator for the British delegates to the Annual Conference of Institutions for the Scientific Study of International Relations

[28] Toynbee in 'International Affairs' vol. X

[29] Arnold Toynbee 'Lectures on the the Industrial Revolution of Eighteenth Century England' 1884

[30] Rose L Martin 'Fabian Freeway: High Road to Socialism in the U.S.A' 1968

[31] Toynbee 'Acquaintances' op.cit.

[32] See F. A. Iremonger 'William Temple, Archbishop of Canterbury'

[33] The Fabians took their name from the Roman general Quintus Fabius Maximus, the Delayer, who defended Rome against Hannibal by elusive tactics avoiding pitched battles

[34] G D H Cole 'Fabian Socialism' 1943

[35] Margaret Cole 'The Story of Fabian Socialism' 1961

[36] In the 1906 House of Commons the Fabians had 29 Liberal seats and 42 Liberal seats in 1911. After the switch to the Labour Party in 1919, from which the Liberal Party never recovered, 10 Fabians sat in the 1922 parliament. 47 won seats for Labour in the 1929 election with 19 government posts. In the 1930s, the numbers fell, but with the Labour landslide victory in 1945, over half the Labour MPs were Fabians, 229 including 10 Cabinet Ministers, 35 Under Secretaries, 11 Parliamentary Private Secretaries. As one Fabian happily remarked, 'It looks just like an enormous Fabian School.'

[37] R W G Mackay

[38] Fabians on the Council in 1940 and 1941 included Sir William Beveridge, Master of University College; historian, Henry Brailsford; the headmaster, William Curry; lawyer, Dr Ivor Jennings; Professor Joad of Birkbeck College, London University (famous as a BBC panellist in the 'Brains Trust'); lawyer R W G Mackay; Labour MP, John Parker, the 1943 general secretary of the Fabians; Barbara Wootton, chairman of Federal Union Executive and National Committees, later a Professor, a Baroness and a deputy speaker in the House of Lords; and Kanni Zilliacus, later a Labour MP.

[39] Viscount Astor owned the 'The Observer' newspaper and a country house, Cliveden, a week-end retreat half way between Oxford and London.

[40] See Richard Mayne and John Pinder 'Federal Union: The Pioneers' 1990 and Lipgens 'Documents on the History of European Integration op.cit. vol. 2 Plans for European Union in Great Britain and in Exile 1939-1945'

[41] William Curry 1900-1962, scholar Trinity College Cambridge and physicist. Schoolmaster. Also taught at Bedales and Oak Lane County School Philadelphia. Headmaster at 29. At Dartington 1931-57

[42] Then run by Philip Noel-Baker MP

[43] Formally constituted in March 1940

[44] E.g. 'The Idea of a United States of Europe' by Dr Ivor Jennings published in 1938. Jennings was a constitutional lawyer and later a Vice Chancellor of Cambridge University.

[45] Norman Angell 1872-1967. Labour MP 1929-31, knighted 1931

[46] Henry Brailsford 1873-1958, London University Lecturer. Joined

Independent Labour Party in 1907. Prolific author on the League of Nations and related subjects. Quotation from 'The Federal Idea'.
[47] Lionel Robbins: Professor of Economics, LSE, for over thirty years to 1961. In the 1930s renowned academically for the seminars he gave with fellow economist, von Hayek. Quotation from 'The Economic Causes of War'
[48] Lipgens op.cit. vol. 2 p. 35
[49] Lipgens op.cit. vol. 2 p. 108
[50] Ibid. p. 102
[51] Harold Wilson 1916-95 Labour MP 1945, President of the Board of Trade 1947-51, Leader of the Opposition 1963-64 and 1970-74, Prime Minister 1964-70 and 1974-76
[52] Lipgens op.cit. vol. 2 p. 118
[53] Lionel Curtis 'Decision' 1941
[54] J B Priestley 1894-1984 novelist, playwright and broadcaster
[55] Lipgens op.cit. vol. 2 p. 65
[56] Manchester Guardian 9.11.1939 reporting Attlee
[57] Monnet 'Memoirs' 1978
[58] For a detailed study especially of the final days of the project see Max Beloff 'The Anglo-French Union Project of June 1940' funded by the Rockefeller Foundation in M P Renouvin 'Etudes d'Histoire des Relations Internationales' 1966
[59] Toynbee 'Acquaintances' op.cit.
[60] Richard Mayne and John Pinder 'Federal Union: The Pioneers' 1990
[61] Quoted in Monnet 'Memoirs' from Monick's 'Pour mémoire'
[62] Winston S Churchill 'The Second World War'
[63] Ibid.
[64] When the French fleet failed to respond to the British ultimatum, on 3rd July at Oran in Algeria the British largely destroyed it
[65] Churchill op.cit.
[66] William H McNeil 'Arnold J Toynbee A Life' 1989

CHAPTER 3: UNDERGROUND

[1] Spinelli was sentenced to 10 years in prison and then 6 more on the confino islands of Ponza and Ventotene
[2] Mazzini 1805-1872 Italian patriot for a united Italy. Published journal, 'Young Italy'. Exiled to London in 1837, returned as dic-

tator of the short lived Roman Republic in 1848, fore-runner of Italian union, which was put down by French forces.

[3] Rossi 1897-1967 Founder and moving spirit of GL. In Italian Government as Minister for Reconstruction in 1945

[4] Luigi Einaudi 'La Societa delle Nazione e un ideale possibilie? Corrierre delle Serra 5.1.1918

[5] Giovanni Agnelli and Attilo Cabiati 'Federazione Europea o Lega delle Nazione?' Turin 1918

[6] One of two brothers, fellow students of Rossi, he was assassinated in France in 1937

[7] Ed. C Grove Haines 'European Integration' 1957

[8] Eugenio Colorni (head of the Socialist Party until his arrest in 1938), Enrico Giussani, Dino Roberto and Giorgio Braccialarghe.

[9] Lipgens op.cit. vol. 1 p. 471

[10] Ibid. p. 484

[11] Ibid. p. 489

[12] Ibid. p. 493

[13] For a description of this period see Charles Delzell 'Mussolini's Enemies – The Italian Anti-Fascist Resistance' 1961

[14] Lipgens op.cit. p. 514

[15] First edited by Colorni, then Rollier see Charles Delzell 'European Federalist Movement in Italy First Phase 1918-47' in 'The Journal of Modern History' XXXII 1960

[16] Giussani and Usellini

[17] Henri Frenay 'La Nuit Finira' op.cit.

[18] Uwe Kitzinger 'Challenge of the Common Market' 1961

[19] Monte had gone into exile at 19, studied in London and worked for the BBC.

[20] Lipgens op.cit. p. 674-682

[21] Ibid.

[22] Set up by exiled socialists after April 1942, the British Labour Party tried but failed to control it

[23] 'Geography' vol. XXX 1945

[24] Lipgens op.cit. p. 689

[25] Delzell 'European Federalist Movement in Italy First Phase 1918–47' in 'The Journal of Modern History' XXXII 1960

[26] Ibid.

[27] 29.7.1947 Lipgens vol. 3 p. 167

[28] Lipgens vol. 1 op.cit. p. 264

[29] Ibid. p. 277

[30] Lipgens op.cit. p. 273

[31] Frenay op.cit.

[32] Lipgens op.cit. vol. 4 p. 9

[33] Lipgens op.cit. vol. 1 p. 289

[34] The Preamble of the Constitution of the Fourth Republic said 'On conditions of reciprocity, France will accept the limitations of sovereignty necessary to the organisation and defence of peace.' Italy's Article 11 of the 1947 constitution read similarly.

[35] Lipgens op.cit. vol. 1 p. 347

[36] Monnet 'Memoirs' op.cit.

[37] Lipgens op.cit. vol. 1 p 1083

[38] See William Shirer op.cit.

[39] In a memorandum 'The Overall Situation'

[40] Lipgens op.cit. vol. 1 p. 397

[41] Dulles 'German Underground' op.cit.

[42] Lipgens op.cit. vol. 1 p. 436

[43] Ibid. p. 381

[44] Shirer op.cit.

[45] A development of the ecumenical movement for world- wide Christian unity which formally began in 1910. The Lambeth Conference series began in 1867. Conferences are held every ten years.

[46] According to Visser 't Hooft 'Memoirs' 1973

[47] 'Life and Work' and 'Faith and Order'

[48] Paton was secretary of the International Missionary Council

[49] Visser 't Hooft op.cit.

[50] Others were Max Huber from Switzerland, Charles Rist from France, O H van der Gablentz from Germany, F M van Asbeck from the Netherlands

[51] Lipgens op.cit. vol. 2 p. 699

[52] The Pope had called for the right to life and independence of all nations; an end to the arms race; the creation or building of international institutions; recognition of the needs of ethnic minorities; and justice as proclaimed in the Sermon on the Mount.

[53] Lipgens op.cit. vol. 2 p. 718

[54] The American Commission For a Just and Durable Peace led by its President, the Rev. Dr Henry Van Dusen. See McNeil 'Toynbee. A Life'

[55] 'Some Considerations Concerning the Post War Settlement' 12.3.1941
[56] Lipgens op.cit. vol. 2 p 713
[57] Ibid. p. 732
[58] Later to be Britain's permanent representative to the UN Security Council.
[59] Diaries of Alexander Cadogan OM 1938-45 ed. David Dilks p 462
[60] And the Carnegie Endowment for International Peace.
[61] 17.3.1947
[62] Ligens op.cit. vol. 2 p. 740
[63] Ibid p. 747
[64] Later Ward-Jackson
[65] de Brouchère and Camille Huymans. Belgium had been part of the Kingdom of the Netherlands. It broke away in 1830 and before that had variously been under the control of Spain, Austria and revolutionary France.
[66] J H Huizinga 'Mr Europe. A Political Biography'
[67] Ibid.
[68] Lipgens op.cit. vol. 2 p. 438
[69] The proposed Benelux Customs Union, or Zollverein, was not strictly an agreement between three states. It was between the Netherlands and the pre-war Belgian-Luxembourg economic union. When they reached economic union it became a three state treaty.
[70] For an analysis of this period see James Meade 'Negotiations for Benelux'
[71] Lipgens op.cit. vol. 2 p. 435
[72] Ibid. p. 455
[73] Ed. M.R.D. Foot 'Holland At War Against Hitler; Anglo-Dutch Relations 1940-45' 1990

CHAPTER 4: THE AMERICAN TRIGGER

[1] Pascaline Winand 'Eisenhower, Kennedy and the United States of Europe' 1993
[2] Martin 'Fabian Freeway' op.cit.
[3] Joseph P. Lash 'From the Diaries of Felix Frankfurter' 1975
[4] Martin 'Fabian Freeway' op.cit.
[5] Ibid.

[6] As published in Federal Trusts' literature

[7] Norway, Belgium, Luxembourg, the Netherlands, Greece, Yugoslavia, Czechoslovakia and Poland

[8] Joseph Retinger 'Memoirs of an "Eminence Grise"' ed. J Pomian 1972

[9] Retinger op.cit.

[10] Walter Lipgens 'A History of European Integration 1945-47'

[11] Charles Bohlen 'Foreign Relations of the United States, The Conference at Cairo and Teheran 1943' 1961

[12] Winston Churchill 'The Second World War' Ch. XXII

[13] Ibid.

[14] Quoted in 'American-Soviet Relations' Peter G Boyle from FO 371/44539/AN3373 4.11.45

[15] George Kennan 'Memoirs' vol. 1

[16] Ibid.

[17] The USSR rejected membership of the IMF and the World Bank

[18] In the November 1946 elections the Communists won 171 seats in the National Assembly, nearly 40 per cent of the total and controlled the trade unions

[19] Kennan op.cit.

[20] Johnson was later president of the Carnegie Endowment for International Peace

[21] Kennan op.cit.

[22] Kennan 'Memoirs' vol. 2

[23] Tomlinson was a minor Treasury official from Idaho. He died young in his early 30s

[24] Eric Roll 'Crowded Hours' 1985

[25] Kennan 'Memoirs' vol. 2

[26] Michael J Hogan 'The Marshall Plan – America Britain and the Reconstruction of Europe 1947-52' 1987

[27] 5. 4. 1946

[28] 5. 4. 1947 and 1. 5.1947

[29] Harriman had held a number of Ambassadorships including that to Britain and had spent part of the war in London organising war supplies.

[30] Martin 'Fabian Freeway' op.cit.

[31] Two of these were also members of the BAC, CED or NPA. The other CFR members were Frank Altschul (also of the NPA); Herbert

Feis; Herbert Lehman; Frederick McKee; Hugh Moore; and Herbert B Swope.

[32] In January 1946 Dulles had put forward rebuilding Europe on federal lines to the National Publishers Association in New York, backed by Governor Thomas E Dewey and Senator Vandenberg. Two months later he orchestrated resolutions for a United States of Europe in Congress

[33] Lipgens op.cit. vol. 4 p. 193

[34] Also Sir Edward Beddington-Behrens, a City businessman and former permanent secretary of the League of Nations; and Sir Arthur Salter who had worked with Jean Monnet in both World Wars and served with Layton in the League of Nations

[35] Including Francois Ponçet, Michel Debré, André Voisin and André Noel

[36] Retinger 'Memoirs of an Eminence Grise' op.cit.

[37] See Retinger, Lipgens vol. 4 p.188 and Richard J Aldrich 'OSS, CIA and European Unity: The American Committee on United Europe, 1948-1960' in 'International History Review' 1995

[38] From 1917 to 1920 Leffingwell had been Assistant Secretary in the US Treasury

[39] Wiseman had spent the latter stages of the First World War in Washington as head of the British Secret Intelligence Service (MI6)

[40] According to Joseph Retinger

[41] Lipgens op.cit. vol. vol. 4 p. 202

[42] Lipgens op.cit. vol. 3 p. 634, from an essay 'Power Politics and the Labour Party' in 'New Fabian Essays' ed. R H Crossman 1952

[43] C R Attlee 'As It Happened' 1954

[44] The Je Maintiendrai resistance group

[45] Also on the UEM committee were Bob Boothby, David Maxwell Fyfe (Viscount Kilmuir), Lady Violet Bonham Carter, and Lady Rhys Williams.

[46] François de Menthon of the French resistance group Combat was chairman; RWG Mackay drafted a constitution

[47] In October 1948 the UEM formally changed its name to the European Movement with four honorary Presidents, Churchill, Spaak, Blum, and de Gaspari. Each country had a national committee and exiles from Eastern Europe and Spain represented their home countries

[48] Brugmans, Silva, Dautry and Serruys were on the committee

[49] Lipgens op.cit. vol. 4 p. 328-333

[50] Lipgens op.cit. vol. 4 p. 16

[51] The other MPs were David Heathcoat-Amory, Norman Bower, Simon Wingfield Digby, A Dodds-Parker, F J Erroll, J C Maude, Hugh Molson, David Renton, and Peter Roberts.

[52] Sir Edward Beddington-Behrens 'Look Back, Look Forward' 1963

[53] E.g. Speech to October 1948 Conservative Party Conference Lipgens op.cit. vol. 3 document 214

[54] Mayne and Pinder 'Federal Union. The Pioneers' 1990

[55] Bevin said: (It is time for) 'the free nations of Europe (to) draw together. These nations have a great deal in common – their wartime sacrifices, their hatred of injustice and oppression, their parliamentary democracy . . . I believe the time is ripe for a consolidation of Western Europe . . . I mean to begin talks with those countries (Benelux) in close accord with our French allies . . . we are now thinking of Western Europe as a unit including Germany when she becomes a democracy.'

[56] Dean Acheson 'Present At the Creation' op.cit.

[57] Richard Mayne 'The Recovery of Europe: From Devastation To Unity' 1970

[58] Jacques Attali 'Man Of Influence' 1986

[59] Lipgens op.cit. vol. 4 pp 333-347

[60] Ibid. p. 338

[61] The MSEUE (Mouvement Socialiste pour les Etats-Unis d'Europe) and the NEI (Nouvelles Equipes Internationales

[62] Peter Novick 'Resistance Versus Vichy' 1968

[63] René Massigli 'Comedie des Erreurs 1943-56' 1978

[64] Quoted by Mayhew PUS at the FO in Michael Charlton 'The Price of Victory' 1983

[65] Mayne and Pinder op.cit.

CHAPTER 5: CREATION

[1] Robert Lovett

[2] Sir Edmund Hall-Patch quoted in Michael J Hogan 'The Marshall Plan' op.cit.

[3] Ibid.

[4] Footnote marked on p 149

[5] Hogan op.cit.

[6] The Committee for a Free and United Europe

[7] For a full analysis of the ACUE see Aldrich 'OSS, CIA and European Unity' op.cit.

[8] 1941 US Co-ordinator of Information; 1942, Director Office of Strategic Services (OSS)

[9] Quoted in Aldrich op.cit.

[10] In 'Europe Integration' ed. C Grove Haines 1957

[11] Lipgens op.cit. vol. 2 p. 722

[12] Lipgens op.cit. vol. 3 p. 732 13.10.1949

[13] Lipgens op.cit. vol. 4 p. 413 Sep. 1949

[14] Lipgens op.cit. vol. 4 doc. 97 from Denis Healey's confidential report on the Assembly for the Labour Party International Committee

[15] Aldrich op.cit.

[16] Ibid.

[17] Kennan 'Memoirs' vol. 2

[18] Quoted in Michael J Hogan 'The Marshall Plan. America, Britain and the Reconstruction of Europe 1947-1952' 1987

[19] François Duchêne 'Jean Monnet, The First Statesman of Interdependence' 1995

[20] Monnet 'Memoirs' op.cit.

[21] See Bruce Allen 'The Brandeis/Frankfurter Connection. The Recent Political Activities of Two Supreme Court Justices' 1982 and Joseph P Lash 'From the Diaries of Felix Frankfurter'

[22] Allen op.cit.

[23] Ibid.

[24] Duchêne op.cit.

[25] Monnet op.cit.

[26] America and Britain recognised French annexation of the Saar four months later as the price of French recognition of Bizonia – their former separate zones in Germany.

[27] Monnet 'Memoirs'

[28] Ibid.

[29] Pascal Fontaine 'Jean Monnet, A Grand Design for Europe' 1988. Fontaine was Monnet's assistant between 1973 and 1977

[30] 25.4.49 at Westminster

[31] Eric Roll 'Crowded Hours' 1985

[32] On 7.3.1950. Smith was with the American International News Service

[33] Frank R Willis 'France, Germany and the New Europe 1945-67' 1965

[34] Charles Wrighton 'Adenauer – Democratic Dictator' 1963

[35] Winand op.cit.

[36] Wrighton op.cit.

[37] Hansard vol. 476 col. 36

[38] Monnet op.cit.

[39] Ibid.

[40] Duchêne op.cit.

[41] Lipgens op.cit. vol. 3 p. 743

[42] Denis Healey 'Time of My Life' 1989

[43] 26th and 27th June 1950

[44] 20.6.1950

[45] Quoted in Willis op.cit.

[46] Quoted in Duchêne op.cit.

[47] Articles 65 and 66 of the ECSC

[48] By the end of 1950 the ECA switched its funds from economic to military use and then lost its own battle for funds in Washington. The ECA was closed at the end of 1951.

[49] Quoted in Willis op.cit.

[50] Quoted in Mayne and Pinder 'Federal Union. The Pioneers'

[51] Quoted in Willis op.cit.

[52] 3.12.1949 Richard Mayne 'The Recovery of Europe' 1970

[53] Winand op.cit.

[54] Speech of July 1951

[55] Wrighton op.cit.

[56] The EDC passed all its legislative stages between July 1952 and March 1953.

[57] Essay in ed. c Grove Haines 'European Integration'

[58] Aldrich op.cit.

[59] See Retinger and Wrighton op.cit.

[60] Aldrich op.cit

[61] Winand op.cit.

[62] Monnet op.cit.

[63] Duchene op.cit.

[64] A Republican but a supporter of internationalism, and of corporative neo-capitalism. E.g. was against Erhard's free trade policies

[65] Evident after Adenauer's visit to Washington in 1956

[66] Quoted in Paul-Henri Spaak 'Combats Inachevés' 1969

[67] Quoted in Willis op.cit.

[68] Ibid.

[69] Quoted in Spaak op.cit.

[70] Lord Strabolgi in Hansard 11. 7.1939 vol. 114 no 84

[71] From 'Holland At War Against Hitler' ed. Prof. M.R.D. Foot op.cit.

[72] From Aldrich op.cit.

[73] Monnet op.cit. Letter dated 13. 10.1955

[74] Duchêne op.cit.

[75] The Radical Edgar Faure was the new French Prime Minister, and the Foreign Minister Pinay

[76] Hansard 7.6.1993 vol. 546 no 148/579

[77] The delegates were: Ambassador Ophuls of Germany, Baron Snoy of Belgium, Felix Gaillard of France, Ludivico Benevenuti of Italy, Lambert Schaus of Luxembourg, Prof. Verryn Stuart of the Netherlands

[78] Willis op.cit.

[79] Cited in Duchene op.cit.

[80] Quoted in Willis from 'Le Monde' of 20. 3. 1957

[81] Spaak op.cit.

[82] Quoted in Willis op.cit. from the Joint Declaration of the Fifth Session in Paris 16/17. 10. 1958

[83] On the minor occasion of the registration of all vineyards

[84] Gilbert Perol 'De Gaulle's Vision of Europe' in 'The European Journal' March 1994

[85] Ibid.

CHAPTER 6: THE BRITISH 'U' TURN

[1] Comment by Lord Rodgers (formerly William Rodgers MP, one time General Secretary of the Fabian Society)

[2] Harold Macmillan 'The Middle Way' 1938

[3] The New Deal was conceived by a Fabian member, Stuart Chase. He acknowledged the influence of the Webbs and John Maynard Keynes.

[4] Monnet 'Memoirs'

[5] Ernest Wistrich 'The Federalist Struggle in Britain' published in The Federalist No 3 of Dec. 1984

[6] Quoted in Beddington-Behrens 'Look Back – Look Forward'

[7] Harold Macmillan 'Tides of Fortune 1945-55' 1969

[8] C.(52)56[CAB 129/50]

[9] The Seven agreed to reduce tariffs on industrial goods by 20% on 1. 7. 1960 and to abolish all quotas and tariffs on industrial goods within ten years. There was no outer tariff wall and no harmonisation of tax and social legislation.

[10] Winand op.cit.

[11] General Agreement on Trade and Tariffs

[12] EEC quotas were to be abolished by 31.12.1961; the first stage of customs reductions was to be increased from 30% to 50% by making tariff cuts of 20% on 1.7.1960 and 31.12.1961. The second approximation of national tariffs to the CET were to be made on 1. 7. 1960 and not 1.1.1962

[13] Quoted in Lionel Bell's 'The Throw That Failed. Britain's Application to Join the Common Market' 1961 page 5

[14] Quoted in Lecouture 'De Gaulle' 1970

[15] In October 1959

[16] Hansard 7. 6.1993 vol. 546 no 148/579

[17] Lord Gladwyn 'The European Idea' 1966

[18] Quoted in Bell op.cit.

[19] John Campbell 'Edward Heath' 1993

[20] Interviews with MPs

[21] Harold Macmillan 'Pointing the Way 1959-61' 1972

[22] 'The Diaries of Cynthia Jebb' Ed. Miles Jebb 1995

[23] Willis op.cit.

[24] For a full assessment of Britain's first application to join the EEC see Lionel Bell's excellent analysis op.cit.

[25] Winand op.cit.

[26] ibid.

[27] Letter from Hugh Gaitskell to John Murray, a member of the committee, quoted in 'The European Journal' April 1995

[28] Mayne and Pinder 'Federal Union' op.cit. Federal Union had three national chairmen, David Barton, Norman Hart and John Pinder, then of the Economist Intelligence Unit. Others who occasionally took part included Derek Ezra (later Lord), Maurice Foley (later a Labour Minister), John Wakeham (later Conservative

Leader of the House of Commons) and Shirley Williams, then Labour, and later a founder of the Social Democrats. During the 1950s about 100 MPs supported world government and giving the UN federal powers. In June 1958 Duncan Sandys, then Conservative Secretary of State for Defence, proposed in the Commons a world security authority and international police force. Another Conservative MP, Sir Edward Boyle, set up a Parliamentary Committee on teaching non-chauvinist history. Lord Hailsham argued for a World Authority and was President of the Parliamentary Group for World Government. World governmental organisations had the same kind of intellectual currency in the 1950s as the League of Nations had had in the 1920s.

[29] Lord (Sir Lionel) Robbins was director of the Economist Intelligence Unit. He chaired 'The Financial Times' 1961 – 1970

[30] Aldrich op.cit.

[31] Ibid.

[32] Mayne 'The Recovery of Europe' op.cit.

[33] Winand op.cit.

[34] Quoted in Winand from Schlesinger's 'A Thousand Days'

[35] Winand op.cit.

[36] Ibid.

[37] Harold Wilson 'The Relevance of British Socialism' 1964

[38] See George Brown 'My Way' and Peter Patterson 'George Brown'

[39] See Roy Jenkins 'The Next Steps' Introductory address to Federal Union Study Conference on 'A New European Policy for Britain' 11.6.1960

[40] Gladwyn 'De Gaulle's Europe or Why the General Says No' 1969

[41] Norway applied to join the EEC in 1962 and 1967

[42] Command 4289

[43] Command 4715

[44] Lord Wilberforce confirmed to the author that that included Lords Diplock and Simon

[45] Hansard vol. 546 no 148 574/5. Debate on the Maastricht Bill, June 1993

[46] 10.4.1962 Speech to the Ministerial Council of the WEU. HMSO

[47] 'Old World New Horizons' Harvard Lectures March 1967

[48] Edward Heath. 'European unity over the next ten years from Community to Union.' The Inaugural Lothian Memorial Lecture of 3.11.87 published in 'International Affairs' Spring 1988 p. 199

[49] Interviews with MPs

[50] Campbell op.cit.

[51] See Ernest Wistrich 'The Federalist Struggle in Britain' The Federalist No. 3 Dec. 1984

[52] Andrew Shonfield 'Europe's Journey to an Unknown Destination' Reith Lecture Nov. 1972

[53] Hansard 21.10.71

[54] Editors since then: Donald Tyerman to 1956-65; Alistair Burnett 1965-74: Andrew Knight 1974-86; Rupert Pennant-Rea 1986-93; Bill Emmott 1993-

[55] Quoted in Sir Richard Body's 'Europe of Many Circles' 1990

[56] See Hansard vol. 823 nos. 202 – 206

[57] Interview with Sir Teddy Taylor

[58] 'The Poisoned Chalice' a Barraclough Carey Production in association with Crux Productions

[59] Monnet 'Memoirs' op.cit.

[60] 'Time Out' April 1975

[61] Mayne and Pinder 'Federal Union' op.cit.

CHAPTER 7: TO A SUPERSTATE

[1] In 'Jean Monnet. The Path to European Unity' edited Douglas Brinkley and Clifford Hackett. 1991

[2] Pascal 'The Action Committee for the United States of Europe' Jean Monnet Centenary Symposium 1988. See also Action Committee for the United States of Europe. Statements and documents 1955-67.' Published by Chatham House and PEP

[3] Dr. Hallstein 'United Europe' 1962

[4] In 'The War Aims of the Great Powers and the New Europe' in 1940 published in Lipgens op.cit. vol. 2 p. 568

[5] Monnet 'Memoirs' op.cit.

[6] Council regulation no 2141/70

[7] Hansard 13.12.1971

[8] See John Ashworth's pamphlet 'The Common Fisheries Policy' published by *eurofacts* 1997

[9] Published in 'Skipper Owner' January 1972 and Aftenposten 7th December 1971

[10] Quoted in John Murray's article 'The Dream That Turned to Ashes' in the European Journal of April 1995

[11] Dir. 71/354/EEC

[12] The relevant directives are 76/770/EEC; 80/181/EEC; 89/617/EEC

[13] From 31.12.1977 furlongs, nautical miles, cubic yards, bushels, drams and knots were abolished and from 31.12.1979 so were yards, square inches yards and miles, cubic inches and feet, hundred weights tons, therms, horsepower and Fahrenheit

[14] Monnet op. cit

[15] Ibid.

[16] The first direct elections were held in 1979

[17] Sir Patrick Neill QC 'The European Court of Justice, A Case Study in Judicial Activism'

[18] Frankfurter died aged 82

[19] G Frederico Mancini 'The Making of a Constitution for Europe' in ed. Robert Keohane and Stanley Hoffmann; 'The New European Community' 1991

[20] In 'Problems of British entry into the EEC' published by the RIIA and PEP

[21] Case 26/62 Van Genden Loos v. Nederlandse Administratie der Belastingen (Netherlands Inland Revenue Administration (1963) ECR 1

[22] Joined Cases C-6/90 and C-9/90 Andrea Francovich and Others v. Italian Republic (1991) ECR I-5357

[23] Jenkins 'European Diary' op. cit

[24] Richard Cockett 'Thinking The Unthinkable' 1995

[25] Nicholas Ridley 'My Style of Government' 1991

[26] Roy Jenkins 'European Diary' 1989

[27] See Altiero Spinelli 'Towards the European Union' Florence 13.6.1983 The Sixth Jean Monnet lecture

[28] Ibid.

[29] 'Politics and Government in Federal Republic of Germany: Basic Documents' 1984

[30] Brigadier Anthony Cowgill's The Maastricht Treaty in Perspective' 1992

[31] Penguin Companion to European Union' 1995 Timothy Bainbridge with Antony Teasdale

[32] Charles Grant 'Delors. Inside the House That Jacques Built' 1994

[33] SEA article 30.2(c)

[34] SEA article 30.10 (g) and 11

[35] Ridley op.cit.
[36] Margaret Thatcher 'The Downing Street Years' 1993
[37] Denis Healey 'The Time of My Life'
[38] Thatcher op.cit.
[39] Cockfied White Paper
[40] Geoffrey Howe 'Conflict of Loyalty' 1994
[41] Quoted in Iris Freeman 'Lord Denning' 1993
[42] Letter to author from Lord Denning
[43] Hansard 26.7.86 vol. 1055

CHAPTER 8: REBELLION

[1] Geoffrey Howe 'A Conflict of Loyalty' 1994
[2] Thatcher op.cit. and Ridley op.cit.
[3] See Bernard Connolly 'The Rotten Heart of Europe, The Dirty War for Europe's Money' 1995
[4] Charles Grant 'Delors. Inside The House That Jacques Built' 1994 and Jacques Delors 'Our Europe' 1988
[5] Louvre Accord in Paris, March 1987
[6] Marsh 'The Bundesbank' op.cit.
[7] Private information passed to the author
[8] Speech in France 3.12.91
[9] 'Financial Times' 4.1.93
[10] See Ian Milne 'Maastricht: The Case Against Economic and Monetary Union' 1993
[11] MacDougall Report March 1977
[12] See Martin Howe 'Maastricht and "Social Europe", An Escape or an entrapment?' 1993
[13] See Dr Manfred Brunner 'Functional Realities of Trade, Sovereignty and Democracy' in ed. Stephen Hill 'Visions of Europe' 1993
[14] Quoted by Sir James Goldsmith in a speech at Bournemouth 11.10.94 and reprinted by The European Foundation
[15] Christopher Booker and Richard North 'The Mad Officials' 1994, 'The Castle of Lies' 1996 and Christopher Booker's weekly column in 'The Sunday Telegraph'
[16] See Professor John Pinder 'European Community, The Building of a Union Updated Following the Maastricht Treaty' 1991
[17] Federal Trust Paper Number 5 'Enlarging the Union' 1996

[18] See Working Document and Draft report on the Constitution of the European Union' 1993 Published by Nelson and Pollard
[19] According to Professor Klaus Tiedemann of Freiburg
[20] Enoch Powell, speech to the Bruges Group June 1994
[21] MacDougall Report March 1977
[22] Translated from the German by the British Management Data Foundation
[23] Tetens op.cit.
[24] Available on the streets of Prague at the time and published in Christopher Story's 'International Currency Review' volume 22 number 1
[25] Churchill 'The Second World War' op.cit.
[26] January 1997 State of the Union Address
[27] Kennan's article in The New York Times quoted in the Times 7.2.1997
[28] Delors op.cit.
[29] See ed. Patrick Minford 'The Cost of Europe' 1992; Brian Hindley and Martin Howe 'Better Off Out?' 1996; Rodney Leach 'Monetary Union: A Perilous Gamble' 1997; Brian Burkitt 'There Is An Alternative' 1996

INDEX